Democratizing Deliberation

A Political Theory Anthology

Derek W. M. Barker, Noëlle McAfee, and David W. McIvor, Editors

Kettering Foundation Press

Democratizing Deliberation: A Political Theory Anthology is published by Kettering Foundation Press. The interpretations and conclusions contained in this book represent the views of the authors. They do not necessarily reflect the views of the Charles F. Kettering Foundation, its directors, or its officers.

For information about permission to reproduce selections from this book, write to:

    Permissions
    Kettering Foundation Press
    200 Commons Road
    Dayton, Ohio 45459

This book is printed on acid-free paper.

First edition, 2012

Manufactured in the United States of America
    ISBN 978-0-923993-41-2

Library of Congress Control Number: 2012931765

CONTENTS

ACKNOWLEDGMENTS

We are grateful to the authors for their generous contributions to this volume. Not only did they allow us to use their work, they were also collegial and efficient in working with us throughout the editorial and permissions processes. David Mathews originally suggested this project, and, as is evident in his foreword, provoked our conceptual thinking about common criticisms and misunderstandings of deliberation. Special thanks are due to the Deliberative Theory Working Group, including Harry Boyte, Mark Button, Albert Dzur, Carmen Greab, Roudy Hildreth, Ekaterina Lukianova, Michael Neblo, Melvin Rogers, and Se-Hyoung Yi; and Kettering Foundation colleagues, including John Dedrick, Alice Diebel, and Debi Witte, who participated as ad hoc members. The group met on several occasions to provide feedback on our selections for the manuscript and review our introductory essay. David Alexander granted us permission, on behalf of the late Iris Marion Young, to include her work. Finally, we thank Kettering Foundation staff Val Breidenbach and Sarah Dahm for administrative support.

FOREWORD

Democracy has many meanings, and debating its meaning is one of the characteristics of a democracy. It should not be surprising, then, that there are also different interpretations of public deliberation and its role in democracy. At the Kettering Foundation, we have never felt that there is one true definition of either term—only that we need to be as clear as possible about what we mean when we use these words. That necessity led us to look at how political theorists have defined deliberation, because we draw on that rich body of work. In this foreword, I will describe how Kettering has come to see deliberation as a key democratic practice and an entry point into democratic politics writ large.

The story of Kettering's use of deliberation begins with a distinction that former Kettering board member Daniel Yankelovich made in his analysis of public opinion. He found a qualitative difference between the initial, ever-shifting reactions people have to politicians and policies and the more stable, reflective judgments people often make when it comes time to vote or pass a law. This distinction led Kettering to collaborate with Public Agenda, a nonprofit organization founded by Yankelovich and Cyrus Vance, in preparing briefing books for citizens on major policy issues facing the country (Social Security financing, for example). The purpose of these books was, and continues to be, to help people move from first and often hasty reactions to more thoughtful, shared judgments.

The books, now called National Issues Forums (NIF) issue books, have been used since 1981 by civic, religious, and educational institutions—and even some prisons—in all 50 states. There are variations of these books being used from the Middle East and Africa to Latin America and the Pacific

Basin. Participants in deliberative forums based on these books often notice something different about these conversations. But initially, we didn't have a word to describe what was happening; we only knew that forums are neither discussions nor debates.

The search for a term to describe what was going on eventually led us to settle on *deliberation* or, more precisely, *public deliberation*. The word appealed to us because it has a history. In Latin, *libera* refers to a pound (*libra*) or the act of balancing or weighing, as on a scale (*libro*). These roots call to mind thoughtfully considering a matter, in consultation with others, in order to make a balanced decision.[1] Carefully weighing in the process of determining the worth of something also suggests the exercise of our faculty for judgment. Personally, I like Thucydides' account of Pericles' funeral oration, which describes the talk (*logo*) used before people act in order to teach themselves (*prodidacthenai*, a word that lacks any English equivalent) how to act.[2] In addition, we drew on Isocrates' discussion of the particular kind of reasoning he advocated in the *Antidosis* and on Aristotle's concepts of moral reasoning and *phronesis*, or practical wisdom.[3] Yet, *deliberation* had the advantage of being familiar to English speakers, and Latin won out over Greek equivalents.

Our foundation has learned a great deal about public deliberation from NIF and similar forums. For instance, participants aren't always content to deal with national issues and policy choices. Many people have gone on to use deliberative framings and decision making to foster collective action on the problems that they encounter in their local communities. Most everyone has recognized that something in the community is not as he or she wants it to be; yet people may not agree about what the problem is or what should be done about it. And the disagreements are normative; people differ not so much over the facts as over what the facts mean. They struggle with determining the right thing to do. When the issues are controversial, like how to prevent the spread of AIDS or whether to permit a clinic that offers abortions, this is particularly evident. The deliberation we see is as Aristotle described it, an attempt at moral reasoning.

Moral reasoning has proven particularly relevant to our colleagues in the Middle East. Modern democracy—or more precisely, representative

government—depends heavily on rational decision making. Reason and
logic work fine when factual matters and tangible interests are in contention
but not when values derived from identity and religious convictions are involved. One of our associates, Randa Slim, explains this when writing about
the Middle East:

> The prevalent form of democracy people have come to know so far has
> been representative democracy. What the West has most cared about
> is the holding of elections, people going to the voting booths.
> Though these acts of citizen participation are an essential first step
> in a society transforming itself into a democratic state, they are rarely
> by themselves sufficient to usher in an era of sustainable stability. . . .
>
> In divided societies, the challenge for any political intervention aimed
> at promoting sustainable democratic change is to move the individual
> from the confines of his or her self (often defined by the
> tribe or ethnic identity) to the wider realm of a citizen actor.[4]

These experiences, both domestic and international, led us at the foundation to expand our understanding of deliberation. We see deliberation as
decision making on normative or morally charged issues that require the
exercise of judgment rather than reason alone. This decision making proves
to be difficult because things that people hold dear or consider valuable are
in tension with one another, and the tensions can't be eliminated because
they grow out of shared concerns. Watching hundreds of forums over some
30 years, we have found citizens grappling with political imperatives—the
need to be free, to be secure, to be treated fairly. Yet in making decisions on
what to do in specific situations, these imperatives pull people in different
directions. For example, actions that would make citizens more secure might
impose limits on their personal freedom. We have called these imperatives
simply "the things people value," although they seem more basic and common than values. Because the tensions can't be resolved by eliminating one
or more of the imperatives, they have to be worked through to the point
that people find some balance and can move ahead, even if they aren't in full

agreement. We have found that these tensions lie behind many problems that appear to be technical yet can't be solved unless the tensions are recognized and addressed.

We have also come to see deliberative decision making as part of acting, not as something separate or distinct. We have called this integrated activity "deliberative politics." It begins in deciding on a name or description of a problem that resonates with the things people consider valuable. It continues in creating a framework for decision making that puts all the major options for action people want to consider on the table—along with the tensions inherent in each option. As people weigh these options, they think about the resources they will need and the allies that will be critical. They imagine how they might organize their efforts. And, most of all, people seem to be learning as they go along—learning what the problems really are as they take in the experiences of others, learning what trade-offs have to be made, and learning which actions are and are not likely to gain support. Deliberation seems much as Pericles described it, the talk people use to teach themselves as they prepare to act. As a means of learning, deliberation has its own way of knowing, by using experience as interpreted by the things people hold dear, and its own kind of knowledge, practical wisdom. It employs the human faculty for judgment (a faculty that neuroscientists have mapped in the brain).

Most important of all, for democracy understood as people having the power to shape their future, deliberation makes citizens political actors in their own right with the ability to produce public goods themselves or co-produce them with governments and other institutions.

The dilemma that Kettering has encountered is that the more precise we have become in describing what we see as deliberation, the more we have given the misimpression that we have in mind some special, esoteric technique that can only be mastered by highly trained experts. (There may be some types of deliberation that require considerable expertise, and even the deliberation used in the National Issues Forums is demanding and requires preparation.) To correct the misimpression that NIF deliberation is a technique for experts, we are now exploring the deliberative elements in everyday conversations. Regardless of how our understanding of deliberation compares with that of political theorists, many themes in this volume resonate with our experience. One thing is certain: political theory has multiple concepts of deliberation available to illuminate our experience and deepen our research.

David Mathews
Kettering Foundation

NOTES

1. Charlton T. Lewis and Charles Short, eds., *A Latin Dictionary: Founded on Andrews' Edition of Freund's Latin Dictionary* (1980, repr., Oxford: Clarendon Press, 1879).

2. Thucydides, *The Landmark Thucydides: A Comprehensive Guide to the Peloponnesian War*, ed. Robert B. Strassler, trans. Richard Crawley (New York: Touchstone, 1998), 2.40.2; for the Greek see Thucydides, *Historiae in two volumes* (Oxford: Oxford University Press, 1942), (accessed September 21, 2001) http://www.perseus.tufts.edu/hopper/text?doc=Perseus%3Atext%3A1999.01.0199%3Abook%3D2%3Achapter%3D40%3Asection%3D2.

3. Isocrates, "Antidosis," in *Isocrates,* trans. George Norlin, vol. 2 (1929; reprint, New York: G.P. Putnam's Sons, 2000), 179-365 and Aristotle, *The Ethics of Aristotle: The Nicomachean Ethics*, trans. J. A. K. Thomson (London: Penguin Books, 1953).

4. Randa Slim, "Facing the Challenges of Emerging Democracies," *Kettering Review* (Winter 2007): 29.

Introduction:
Democratizing Deliberation

by Derek W. M. Barker, Noëlle McAfee, David W. McIvor

In the mid-20th century most people had come to think of democracy as the biannual trip to the ballot box punctuated by occasional protests and letters to the editor and supplemented with membership in a special-interest group. During the latter part of the century this conception of democracy started wearing thin, especially with Watergate's breach of public confidence in the political system.[1] A quiet revolution within democratic theory and practice began to take place as scholarly attention turned to civil society and the importance of public deliberation about matters of common concern. By the 1990s, political theorists in academia and practitioners of community forums around the world were using the language of deliberative democracy to describe their new focus.

Even with this transformation, the theory and practice of deliberative democracy did not always converge. Instead, first-generation deliberative theorists hypothesized a rather narrow conception of deliberation as rational discourse that could guarantee the legitimacy of democratic procedures and decisions, putting theory at odds with the rich but messy world of deliberation in practice. Deliberative democracy in turn became stereotyped as impractical and divorced from action. But during the past decade another generation of thinkers and practitioners has started developing ideas about deliberative democracy that are open to more forms of political talk, practical on a wider scale, and better connected with collective action. In so doing, theory and practice have together arrived at more robust forms of deliberation than had been proposed in the original generation of deliberative theory. This latest turn is the subject of this collection of essays.

The authors whose work is collected in this volume have each contributed to deliberative theory in their own ways. Combined, however, they represent a trend within deliberative theory towards a "democratized" conception of deliberation. If, as John Dryzek has argued, the 1990s saw a "deliberative turn" in democratic theory, the essays included in this volume reflect a "democratic turn" within deliberative theory.[2] In addition to attending to the core norms of deliberative democracy, "democratized" deliberation emphasizes how deliberation might play a central role in creating a culture of civic action, confidence, and collective self-rule. In this view, deliberation is not a narrow procedure for adjudicating conflict, but a crucial practice for facilitating civic life. The theorists in this book provide a new way to understand deliberation, as an attempt to rename political problems as subject to real choices and actions by citizens, rather than having "given" solutions dictated by expertise, ideology, or special interest.

This democratization of deliberative theory addresses a series of related challenges to deliberative theory and practice. The concept of deliberation that still dominates political theory today is a rational discourse ideal of consensus reached through free and uncoerced public discussion. This concept of deliberation provides a compelling alternative to narrow conceptions of democracy as majority rule, voting for representatives, or a balance of power among competing groups. However, the rational discourse ideal has raised problems of its own. In various ways, critics and even proponents of deliberative democracy have challenged this concept of deliberation as too narrow to be truly democratic. Moreover, the model has been seen as too demanding to actually engage citizens in practice. As a result, deliberation has been said to be purely communicative and divorced from action; to privilege elites; to ignore conflict; and to apply only to small-scale, controlled settings. While the scholarship in this book retains many of the core features of deliberative theory—particularly the fundamental aim of restoring confidence in collective decisions and the central role of public discourse in a democracy—it has moved toward a broader understanding of deliberation as a set of practices open to different forms of communication and applicable in a wider range of public spaces and practices. In so doing, this work shows that most criticisms of deliberative democracy in fact apply only to a particular concept of deliberation. As a result, this collection reframes deliberative democracy in a way that is more sensitive to deep conflicts, nonrational forms of communication, and aspirations for increased civic agency.

Due to these advances, the theoretical scholarship in this volume also has the potential to both influence and draw upon a new generation of deliberative practitioners. One of the most exciting aspects of deliberative theory is its dynamic relationship with a network of practitioners that has been engaging citizens in deliberative politics for more than 25 years. These efforts include organizations such as National Issues Forums, Everyday Democracy, America*Speaks*, the Deliberative Democracy Consortium, and the National Coalition for Dialogue and Deliberation.[3] Many of the practitioners of deliberative politics have been influenced by deliberative theory, and deliberative theory in turn has drawn upon these practical experiences. In many respects the practice of deliberation was ahead of deliberative theory. As David Mathews argues in the Foreword to this volume, practitioners all along have aimed at neither perfect discourse nor rational argumentation, but rather at the pragmatic goal of clarifying tensions and reaching decisions on difficult issues. Practitioners of deliberative politics are perhaps in the best position to testify to the broader and more democratic concept of deliberation that informs this body of work, having encouraged and witnessed firsthand, for instance, the powerful role in deliberative contexts of emotion, storytelling, and other varieties of communication.

Nevertheless, the articles collected here also challenge practitioners to take more seriously the notion of democratizing deliberation. Democratizing deliberation asks practitioners to look beyond what Martín Carcasson calls "first-order" goals, such as producing deliberation within forums and informing citizens about specific issues. A broader concept of deliberation must also push toward intermediate goals, such as public action, and, most important, toward ultimate aspirations to strengthen democracy as a whole.[4] At first glance, these goals seem consistent. However, focus on the immediate task of producing deliberation can invite the common criticism that deliberation is "all talk and no action." The use of specific techniques for producing deliberation can signal that democracy requires advanced skills that are, ironically, beyond the capabilities of most citizens. The articles in this volume encourage practitioners to think critically about the extent to which they have internalized a narrow concept of deliberation, using deliberation as a technique to produce a certain type of discourse, or manufacture a consensus within a discrete forum. Democratizing deliberation encourages a broader view of deliberation as an exercise in civic agency, an effort to make visible to citizens the choices they have available to them in politics, and to cultivate these citizens' capacities to make a difference in the lives of their communities. Democratizing deliberation does not reject or trivialize the first-order work of convening forums, but rather seeks to inform that work with more robust conceptions of deliberation that treat citizens as capacious civic actors.

The literature on deliberative theory is now vast as well as highly specialized. However, the democratization of deliberation has implications far beyond academic debates within political theory and philosophy. This volume is intended for audiences interested in the frontiers of deliberative theory and practice. With this audience in mind, we have gathered together works that best reflect the democratizing of deliberation. To introduce these pieces, we begin with a genealogy of deliberative democracy that provides an introduction to the field, and, more important, the challenges it currently faces. We then highlight the ways in which the contributions together respond to many of these challenges and push deliberative theory in more robustly democratic directions.

A Genealogy of Deliberative Democracy

Over the past three decades, deliberative approaches to democracy have achieved a certain gravity in both academic circles and broader public discourse. These various approaches have coalesced into a paradigm that is now perhaps the dominant—if not the hegemonic—orientation within democratic theory. Yet the consolidation of deliberative democracy as a paradigm of political thought has served to obscure its plural origins and its ongoing tensions and controversies. In this respect, deliberative theory is not only an identifiable orientation to democratic life that has, as some have argued, "come of age,"[5] it is also—perhaps appropriately—an ongoing and oftentimes fractious conversation about how democratic life can and should be organized. This section will trace a genealogy that marks out key political conditions that prompted the deliberative turn and crucial moments in its development and contestation. As we argue, deliberative theory both usefully addressed a variety of maladies within democratic societies yet simultaneously created new challenges and obstacles for democratic theorists and practitioners. As a result, deliberative theory must continue to broaden its focus and engage with the pressing challenges that democratic citizens face today.

In the latter half of the 20th century, political events and philosophical trends in the United States converged to challenge and ultimately overturn the dominant understandings of democracy within the academy and the larger public. With historical roots in the theory of the *Federalist Papers*, prevailing theories of democracy at the time identified democracy with contested elections and institutional checks and balances for maintaining equilibrium among competing interest groups.[6] Growing social complexity and intensifying political and social cleavages seemed to threaten the identity of a people, or *demos*, that could govern itself. Dominant paradigms within social theory, such as "pluralism" and "social choice," were valuable because they seemed to account for the ways in which a highly fragmented system could remain relatively stable without a thick sense of a common good.[7] These theories rested on a sharp distinction between the "liberties of the ancients," understood in terms of collective self-rule and public action, and the "liberties of the moderns," rights of noninterference, leading to a minimalist conception of citizenship.[8] Jane Mansbridge described the dominant system as "adversarial democracy," in which organized groups compete against one another for advantage, but formal channels of governance function by limiting and fragmenting their power.[9]

Yet pluralist and social choice theories of democracy—and the assumptions about civic life on which they were based—soon came under heavy fire from a variety of angles. The 1960s and 1970s witnessed a steep decline in trust towards democratic institutions and public officials, resulting in a largely disaffected and alienated citizenry. Citizens felt that they had been sidelined by large institutional actors and were denied a voice in the decisions that shaped their lives.[10] Dominant theories of democracy could not account for this dissatisfaction nor provide any enticing avenues for civic redress. They also could not account for long-term trends, such as growing public concern over both the hyperpolarization of electoral politics and the increasing power of special interests.

Concurrent with the collapse of public trust in the institutions of democratic governance, political theory experienced a revival of interest in participatory politics and a local autonomy. This revival gained impetus from a variety of sources, ranging from the Civil Rights Movement to the free speech movement to the community control movement, each of which emphasized the rights and obligations of citizens to have a role in shaping the organizations and institutions that governed their lives.[11] These demands for a more robust participatory politics dovetailed in many ways with the renewal of civic republican traditions that emphasized local control and an active citizen body.[12] For instance, Jane Mansbridge argued that citizens could find common norms and interests through practices of "unitary democracy," albeit in specific circumstances limited by the dominant forces of the adversarial system described above.[13] Both civic republican and participatory critics, moreover, were deeply critical of what they saw as the narrow instrumentalism underlying dominant conceptions of citizenship within social choice and pluralist theories of democracy. Within each tradition, citizens were seen not as narrowly rational actors who pursued their own discrete agendas but as agents whose preferences and beliefs were susceptible to social influences and mutable through democratic procedures. Democracy on these terms was not reducible to the clash of pre-political interests but rather was seen as the process of forming, reforming, and transforming preferences and opinions through civil dialogue and widespread public participation.

As the consensus around the dominant paradigm of democratic theory unraveled, the foundations of deliberative democracy were set in political theorists' efforts to reconstruct theories of democratic legitimacy. As noted above, the collapse in public confidence and growing complexity and increased pluralism challenged the foundations of democratic institutions and processes of political decision making within advanced industrial democracies. These trends threatened the idea of political legitimacy founded on the autonomous decisions of the collected citizenry. In his highly influential *A Theory of Justice*, the American political philosopher John Rawls constructed a grand theory of liberal justice on the basis of a decision procedure that could be seen as legitimate in spite of social and class stratification.[14] Relatedly, in response to a perceived crisis of democratic legitimacy, Jürgen Habermas, a leading voice in European philosophy, developed his theory of communicative action, the view that democratic decisions are legitimate only if citizens could come to consensus through free, uncoerced dialogue.[15]

Combined together, the trends in democratic society and political theory reflected a deep dissatisfaction with the dominant practices of democratic politics and corresponding paradigms of democratic theory. The conception and practice of democracy as an adversarial contest for resources had increased the influence of special interests and frozen out or alienated ordinary citizens. The elite-dominated clash of factions and the growing influence of unresponsive administrative bodies were incompatible with mounting demands for participatory politics and local control. Moreover, the narrative of citizens as combatants with preformed and inflexible preferences was incompatible with the still-robust democratic faith in a citizen body concerned with the common good and for a political life that displayed the virtues of civic friendship and social solidarity. In sum, the conditions were ripe within democratic theory and practice for a paradigm shift.

This shift occurred under the banner of deliberation. In 1980, Joseph Bessette is widely attributed with coining the term *deliberative democracy*, using it to recognize the failures of democratic institutions to reflect the interests and desires of citizens.[16] Bessette's term quickly gained adherents, who began to challenge the reduction of democracy to interest-group politics and the electoral system. As political theorists continued to work out concepts of democratic legitimacy, the term became an increasingly popular alternative paradigm for thinking about politics. Democracy understood as a deliberative process among citizens represented a promising response to the collocation of civic distrust and discontentment, emergent demands for public participation and local control, and worries over legitimacy in complex and pluralistic societies. The subsequent shift within democratic theory was both rapid and thorough. Within 20 years after Bessette coined the term, John Dryzek confidently remarked that, at least among theorists, "the essence of democracy itself is now widely taken to be deliberation, as opposed to voting, interest aggregation, constitutional rights, or even self-government."[17]

Deliberative theory maintains that legitimate decisions must be essentially *deliberative*. They cannot result from the mere aggregation of preferences or heuristics, such as tradition or voting. In other words, the realization of political autonomy is "talk-centric" rather than "voting-centric"; it depends upon the public deliberations of the collective body politic.[18] This deliberative work, moreover, is characterized not by antagonistic negotiation, but rather what Jürgen Habermas calls the "unforced force of the better argument."[19] This idea promised an alternative to both the dominant pluralist paradigm, which could not account for the loss of confidence in the contemporary system, and its communitarian rivals, which had failed to propose an alternative appropriate to complex pluralistic societies.[20] The new theory supplied an aspirational view of politics as mutual persuasion beyond the clash of interests described in pluralist theories. Yet the theory did so by locating legitimacy in democratic procedures rather than any kind of thick underlying unity favored by communitarians. Deliberative democracy seemed to incorporate the best features of interest-group pluralism and communitarianism while correcting their deficiencies.

This broad understanding of deliberation, however, took on more specific meanings as leading philosophers further developed the theory. This process began in part through Habermas' early work on "universal pragmatics."[21] Habermas argued that certain norms were immanent to human speech, and that the search for consensus was an inescapable presupposition of communication. The presupposition of an orientation towards consensus within ordinary communicative action was seen by Habermas as a guide for social action in a variety of contexts—including democratic politics. These idealizing presuppositions gave democratic theorists a strong (if not impossibly strong) standard for evaluating democratic procedures. Perhaps because of such criticisms, Habermas shifted terminology in developing what he called "discourse ethics."[22] According to what Habermas called the "discourse principle," decisions were legitimate if they could be accepted by all affected through the course of a reasonable discourse. Yet even in the wake of this move, democratic discourse seemed overconstrained by idealized requirements that did not resemble any known political procedures.

In his later work, Habermas developed his theory with an eye towards these challenges. In particular he sought to reconcile the normative claims of deliberative theory with the cultural, administrative, and economic realities of advanced industrial democracies.[23] On this new account, deliberation did not consist of the direct public authorization of legislation but of an ongoing process of public will-formation taking place through a de-centered discursive network. During this time, however, the concept of ideal deliberation articulated earlier by Habermas continued to exert a deep influence within the literature on deliberative democracy.

Deliberative democracy received an important endorsement from John Rawls, considered at the time to be the leading political philosopher in the United States. Rawls' early work contained quasi-deliberative elements, such as his famous "original position," an imaginative process in which participants could recognize the fair terms of social cooperation and the demands of justice. Rawls argued that policies could be justified if and only if we could imagine agreeing to them regardless of the contingent features of our social and historical background, such as class, race, or gender inequalities. The original position, however, was not a deliberative space so much as it was a method of philosophical discovery. Rawls called it a "device of representation" and a "means of public reflection and self-clarification" rather than a public process of deliberation.[24] However, like Habermas' ideal speech situation, Rawls' emphasis on impartiality and rationality were deeply influential for deliberative theorists.

Late in his career, Rawls, like Habermas, shifted his emphasis as he took on the challenges to advanced industrial democracies represented by increasing religious, cultural, and moral pluralism. In response to these pressures, Rawls attempted to articulate a more practical conception of his theory, meaning that the theory was not "metaphysical" but "political": rooted in existing constitutional tenets and traditions of interpretation, rather than being based solely on abstract moral norms.[25] Coinciding with his political turn, Rawls introduced the idea of "public reason" to account for how citizens and public actors who are motivated by different moral and religious traditions can nevertheless come to agreement on the basic terms of social cooperation.[26] Public reason, on this reading, carries within itself the norms of reciprocity and inclusion. Reciprocity requires citizens to offer reasons that all might reasonably accept, and inclusion necessitates that democratic procedures must be open to all citizens.[27] Later, Rawls explicitly identified his ideal of a "well-ordered constitutional democracy" with the term *deliberative democracy*.[28]

Due largely to the influence of Habermas and Rawls, the dominant concept of deliberation that emerged in political theory in the 1980s and 1990s was the ideal of rational discourse governed by norms of reciprocity, inclusion, and (in some versions) the search for consensus. The ideal of rational discourse seemed to provide a clear alternative to power politics and partisan polarization, and the Rawlsian norm of public reason gained precedence. Deliberative theorists, such as Amy Gutmann and Dennis Thompson, for instance, regarded the "reason-giving requirement" inherent in Rawls' concept of public reason as central to all accounts of deliberative democracy. Deliberative democracy, on their reading, insists above all else that citizens have an obligation to justify their views to their fellow citizens, using reasons that "should be accepted by all free and equal persons."[29] Similarly, Joshua Cohen introduced the ideal of "rationally motivated consensus," and Seyla Benhabib endorsed rationality as an essential element of deliberation.[30]

What had originally been conceptualized broadly as decision making over contentious issues in opposition to power politics was reconceived in narrower terms as rational discussion according to strict procedures.[31]

As soon became apparent, however, the growing dominance of this concept of deliberation created new challenges for democratic theory, just as it had resolved old ones. In various ways, the rationalistic view of deliberation has been criticized for undermining other key democratic goals of inclusion and active citizenship, while failing to address practical questions of how citizens can shape their common life together. The critiques that have emerged in response to the reason-centered concepts of deliberation now provide the intellectual context of the current generation of deliberative theory, including the contributions in this book.

First, political theorists often argue that the deliberative ideal could not make room for different identities or forms of expression. Even theorists sympathetic to the deliberative ideal, such as Iris Marion Young and Lynn Sanders, now recognize that the goal of rational consensus seemed to inherently privilege elite voices and conservative outcomes, against minorities and "activist" politics.[32] Similarly, theorists of "agonistic" democracy, for whom difference is a necessary and desirable feature of democracy, worry that deliberation aiming at consensus would repress conflict.[33] Sympathetic critics, such as James Bohman, argue that deliberative theory has forsaken its roots within critical theory and is too accommodating to the structural forces that continued to stifle the possibility of democratic life.[34] Proponents of the rational discourse view of deliberation reinforce these criticisms by locating deliberation primarily within elite institutions. Rawls, for example, associates the ideal of public reason with "judges, legislators, chief executives, as well as candidates for public offices."[35] With deliberation defined as rational consensus and located within elite institutions, deliberative democracy opens itself to the critique that it privileges some voices and silences others.

Second, deliberation is seen as purely communicative and divorced from action, a central value in democratic theory. Agonistic critics fault proponents of hyperrational deliberation for repressing not only difference, but also the passion often found in democratic movements. As Chantal Mouffe argues, "The prime task of democratic politics is not to eliminate passions nor to relegate them to the private sphere in order to render rational consensus possible, but to mobilize those passions towards the promotion of democratic designs."[36] Agonistic political theory celebrates Hannah Arendt's theory of action as the "political activity par excellence," in contrast to Habermas' discourse theory of the "public sphere," where civic action is seemingly reduced to the organized influence of formal institutions.[37] Even theorists deeply committed to the deliberative ideal acknowledge that the practical challenge of linking up deliberation and action remained unresolved.[38] Outside of political theory, studies of deliberation in practice similarly struggle to show the impact of forums on larger forms of collective action.[39]

Finally, theorists argue that even if the deliberative ideal is desirable, it is too impractical to make a difference on a large scale. The abstract nature of deliberative theory suggests that the inquiry is still oriented by "ideal theory," which began from normative presuppositions rather than political realities.[40] Critics see deliberation as a superficial form of political interaction that ignores the realities of power and interest in favor of an "academic seminar" model of politics.[41] Some argue that citizens are simply incapable of deliberation, especially in the context of human beings' structural and psychological tendencies to avoid conflict and diversity.[42] Still others are skeptical that a large-scale mass public could be capable of deliberation.[43] Despite evidence of deliberation from a generation of experiments in convening small-scale, face-to-face forums, critics remain unconvinced that these efforts were making a difference in the systemic problems that the theory purported to resolve. Moreover, practitioners have difficulty reconciling the messiness of deliberation with the lofty ideal of consensus reached through rational discourse, leading them to struggle to conceive of success in broader terms. Perhaps most important, the practicality challenge is intertwined with the democratic critiques of deliberative theory, for if deliberation is in practice beyond the experience or capabilities of most citizens, then elite decision making would seem to be the default location for political power in any practical effort to achieve deliberative principles on a large scale.

These criticisms add up to the pressing question, how democratic is deliberation? While we acknowledge that many of these criticisms have merit, our genealogy shows that they assume a particular view of deliberation that is neither intrinsic to, nor representative of, deliberative theory as such. Rather, the scholarship we have gathered in this volume makes the case for a broad and democratic concept of deliberation that resists many of these common criticisms. In the next section, we identify a few common ways these articles have broadened the concept of deliberation and pushed it in a more democratic direction.

The Democratic Turn in Deliberative Theory

This collection includes seven pieces written since 1999. Individually these pieces respond to various issues within deliberative theory and practice, but combined they reflect what we refer to as a "democratic turn" within this literature. As noted above, the first generation of deliberative theory drew a sharp line between reason and rhetoric, thinking that deliberation had to be protected from the undemocratic forces of partiality, emotion, inequality, rhetoric, and coercion. But the critics of this approach saw the sharp line to be an impediment to democracy, privileging elite voices at the expense of alternative modes of speech. So one of the first trends in democratizing deliberation has been to broaden the understanding of deliberative reason and discourse, to welcome more forms of expression by making room for affect, emotion, storytelling, and particular perspectives. Instead of narrow "reason-giving" that can be universally understood, deliberation can occur—and often does occur—through the offering of particular stories and perspectives that help shed light on how problems are perceived by people different from oneself. In her "Three Models of Democratic Deliberation," Noëlle McAfee argues that in addition to the market-style model of deliberation aimed at clarifying preferences and the rational model of coming to consensus, there is a third "integrative" model of deliberative democracy that weaves together partial perspectives. Not only does this model have more explanatory and productive force than the first two, she argues, it welcomes particular perspectives, stories, affect, and difference. In his piece, "Rhetoric and Public Reasoning," Bernard Yack draws on Aristotle's account of deliberation to show that, while there is certainly a place for impartial reason, it is not in a political deliberation, that is, a deliberation aimed at deciding what to do. Impartial reason should rule in a court of law, when the question is about what happened in the past. "But deliberation about future action is a completely different matter," Yack writes. "Decisions about future action … draw on an inseparable mix of desire and intellect, emotion and reason. In other words, it requires a live reason propelled by desire out into the world rather than the dead, emotion-less reason that best serves legal judgment." Likewise, in her contribution to this volume, Jane Mansbridge argues that in "both legislative bodies and the rest of the deliberative system, the concept of 'public reason' should be enlarged to encompass a 'considered' mixture of emotion and reason rather than pure rationality." In "Difference Democracy," John Dryzek elaborates on the value of storytelling, rhetoric, and other forms of communication that might be included in a broader concept of deliberation. According to Dryzek, a more expansive deliberative theory can address the core goal of noncoercive decision making without privileging elites or repressing conflict.

Instead of focusing on reaching consensus, the thinkers in this volume recognize that often disagreement is an unavoidable aspect of the process of working through difficult choices. Even without universal agreement, deliberation can serve a number of important democratic functions. Rather than rush to consensus, deliberations can first ensure that all the relevant perspectives are brought to the table. Based on her experience as an observer of National Issues Forums, Noëlle McAfee sees deliberation in pragmatic terms, as achieving tentative agreements for specific purposes of decision making and action, without necessarily resulting in any thick or permanent consensus. As John Dryzek observes, deliberation cannot aim at consensus, because difference is itself a precondition for deliberation. In her essay, "Everyday Talk in the Deliberative System," Jane Mansbridge argues that deliberation can help to clarify the issues at stake in political conflicts, allowing each side to better understand the concerns of the other even while acknowledging the reality of disagreement. Even if some disagree with the ultimate decision, citizens can have confidence through deliberation that their voice has been heard and the process has been fair.

By broadening the criteria for deliberative processes and outcomes, the thinkers in this volume have, in turn, allowed for new theories of how deliberation might be practical on a larger scale and in a wider variety of contexts. McAfee's essay begins this move by bringing deliberative theory into conversation with John Dewey and the tradition of American pragmatism. She argues that deliberation should be assessed not according to abstract moral standards but for its utility in solving public problems. To those who say that deliberative democracy is impractical on a large scale, some, like Iris Marion Young, point to the necessity of widespread public deliberations in complex modern societies. In the essay, "De-centering Deliberative Democracy," Young draws on Habermas' observation that it is in informal public spheres that public problems are identified and brought to the attention of formal spheres of government. Young develops a concept of de-centered democratic deliberation in which discrete forums and larger political processes, and state institutions and informal social spaces, are all "linked" and aligned together. Similarly, for Jane Mansbridge, with a more relaxed standard for deliberative dialogue, scholars and practitioners can recognize the value and importance of everyday talk about matters of common concern. For example, the "highly informal, unconscious, and aggregative processes" of everyday talk in the public sphere can help identify problems and possible courses of action.

As for the worry that deliberation is only about communication and is divorced from action, many of the pieces in this book develop an idea of deliberative democracy as a practical, problem-solving, and world-building activity. As David Mathews suggests in his Foreword, deliberation has been seen in this way, at least at an implicit level, within the world of deliberative practice from its beginning. As deliberative practice continues to develop, the pieces in this section explicitly reconceive deliberation as pragmatic and action-oriented. In "Sustaining Public Engagement," Elena Fagotto and Archon Fung explore the value that comes from having deliberative practices embedded in communities to solve local problems and complement the work of formal institutions. This work also sees deliberation and democratic politics as aiming not just to direct the actions of governments but also to develop ideas and collective will for public action. Instead of seeing deliberation as about agreeing on policies, this work sees deliberation as a public activity deciding what kind of political communities we want to be. Finally, Harry Boyte's essay, "Constructive Politics as Public Work," provides perhaps the most radical reconstruction of deliberative theory in terms of civic agency and public work. Boyte sees deliberation as a way of "unfreezing" politics, exposing new opportunities for citizens to engage in moral judgment and act collectively on issues typically thought to be matters of scientific planning and top-down administration.[44] Here Boyte explicitly challenges Habermas' reduction of deliberation to rational discourse and instead adopts a more expansive view of deliberation similar to others proposed in this volume. In this way, Boyte sees deliberation not as divorced from action, but as itself an expression of agency in a technocratic world, part of a common enterprise along with community organizing and global traditions of public work. From Boyte's perspective, this politics of agency represents the true promise of deliberation.

The thinkers in this volume present a more complex picture of deliberative theory than is commonly recognized—both by its proponents as well as its critics. Rather than dichotomous oppositions between reason and emotion, consensus and difference, freedom and power, thought and action, and theory and practice, these essays present a view of deliberation that is sensitive to the complexity of democratic politics in large-scale pluralistic societies. We believe these developments reflect a state of maturity within deliberative theory, but this body of work also raises new questions and challenges. Beyond outcomes that can be observed in organized forums, how might practical experiments in deliberation affect the sphere of informal talk in everyday life? Beyond impacts on discrete policy issues, does deliberation produce a more active and engaged citizenry? Beyond deliberation in small face-to-face settings, how can the professions and institutions of large-scale centralized systems align or link their routines with a deliberative citizenry? This volume raises these and other questions as deliberative theory and practice continue to evolve.

NOTES

[1.] *Distrust, Discontent, Anger, and Partisan Rancor: The People and Their Government* (Washington, DC: Pew Research Center for the People and the Press, 2010).

[2.] John Dryzek, *Deliberative Democracy and Beyond: Liberals, Critics, and Contestations* (Oxford, UK: Oxford University Press, 2000).

[3.] Mark Button and Kevin Mattson, "Deliberative Democracy in Practice: Challenges and Prospects for Civic Deliberation," *Polity* 31:4 (1999); John Gastil and Peter Levine, *The Deliberative Democracy Handbook: Strategies for Effective Civic Engagement in the Twenty-First Century* (San Francisco, CA: Jossey-Bass, 2005); Scott London, *Doing Democracy: How a Network of Grassroots Organizations Is Strengthening Community, Building Capacity, and Shaping a New Kind of Civic Education* (Dayton, OH: Kettering Foundation, 2010).

[4.] Martín Carcasson, *Beginning with the End in Mind: A Call for Goal-Driven Deliberative Practice* (New York: Public Agenda, 2009).

[5.] James Bohman, "Survey Article: The Coming of Age of Deliberative Democracy," *The Journal of Political Philosophy* 6:4 (1998).

[6.] James Madison, Alexander Hamilton, and John Jay, *The Federalist Papers*, ed. Isaac Kramnick (New York: Penguin, 1987 [1787-1788]).

[7.] Robert A. Dahl, *A Preface to Democratic Theory* (Chicago, IL: University of Chicago Press, 1956); David B. Truman, *The Governmental Process: Political Interests and Public Opinion*, 2nd ed. (Berkeley, CA: Institute of Intergovernmental Studies, 1971; reprint, 1993); Kenneth Arrow, *Social Choice and Individual Values* (New Haven, CT: Yale University Press, 1970).

8. Jürgen Habermas, "Three Models of Democracy," in *Democracy and Difference: Contesting the Boundaries of the Political*, ed. Seyla Benhabib (Princeton, NJ: Princeton University Press, 1996); Joshua Cohen, "Democracy and Liberty," in *Deliberative Democracy*, ed. Jon Elster (Cambridge: Cambridge University Press, 1998).

9. Jane J. Mansbridge, *Beyond Adversary Democracy* (Chicago: University of Chicago Press, 1983).

10. Richard C. Harwood, *Citizens and Politics: A View from Main Street America* (Dayton, OH: Kettering Foundation, 1991); David Mathews, *Politics for People* (Urbana, IL: University of Illinois Press, 1999).

11. Benjamin Barber, *Strong Democracy: Participatory Politics for a New Age* (Berkeley, CA: University of California Press, 1984); Carole Pateman, *Participation and Democratic Theory* (Cambridge, UK: Cambridge University Press, 1970); Thomas A. Spragens, *Getting the Left Right: The Transformation, Decline, and Reformation of American Liberalism* (Lawrence, KS: University Press of Kansas, 2009).

12. Robert Putnam, *Bowling Alone: The Collapse and Revival of American Community* (New York: Simon & Schuster, 2000); Michael J. Sandel, *Democracy's Discontent: America in Search of a Public Philosophy* (Cambridge, MA: Belknap Press, 1996).

13. Mansbridge, *Beyond Adversary Democracy*.

14. John Rawls, *A Theory of Justice* (Cambridge, MA: Harvard University Press, 1971). Of course, the legitimacy of this decision process (which Rawls called the "original position") was guaranteed precisely because it was abstracted from the economic and social stratifications of advanced industrial democracies. See below.

15. Jürgen Habermas, *Legitimation Crisis*, trans. Thomas McCarthy (Boston: Beacon Press, 1975); Jürgen Habermas, *The Theory of Communicative Action, Volume 2: Lifeworld and System: A Critique of Functionalist Reason* (Boston: Beacon Press, 1985).

16. Joseph Bessette, "Deliberative Democracy: The Majority Principle in Republican Government," in *How Democratic Is the Constitution*, ed. Robert A. Goldwin (Washington, DC: American Enterprise Institute Press, 1980).

17. Dryzek, *Deliberative Democracy and Beyond*, 1.

18. Simone Chambers, "Deliberative Democratic Theory," *Annual Review of Political Science* 6 (2003).

19. Jürgen Habermas, *Moral Consciousness and Communicative Action*, trans. Christian Lenhardt and Shierry Weber Nicholsen (Cambridge, MA: Massachusetts Institute of Technology, 1990).

20. Jürgen Habermas, "Three Models of Democracy"; Jon Elster, "The Market and the Forum: Three Varieties of Political Theory," in *Foundations of Social Choice Theory*, eds. Jon Elster and Aanund Hyland (Cambridge: Cambridge University Press, 1986), 103-132.

21. Jürgen Habermas, *Communication and the Evolution of Society* (London: Heineman Educational Books, Ltd., 1979 [1976]).

22. Habermas, *Moral Consciousness and Communicative Action*.

23. Jürgen Habermas, *Between Facts and Norms: Contributions to a Discourse Theory of Law and Democracy* (Cambridge, MA: MIT Press, 1996 [1990]).

24. Rawls, *A Theory of Justice*, 17-22; John Rawls, *Political Liberalism* (New York: Columbia University Press, 1993, 1996), 24.

25. John Rawls, "Justice as Fairness: Political Not Metaphysical," *Philosophy and Public Affairs* 14:3 (1985); Rawls, *Political Liberalism*.

26. Ibid.

27. For differences in how Habermas and Rawls (and their various successors and contemporaries) each understand public reason—including both its content and its location, see Evan Charney, "Political Liberalism, Deliberative Democracy, and the Public Sphere," *American Political Science Review* 92:1 (1998): 97-110.

28. John Rawls, *The Law of Peoples with "The Idea of Public Reason Revisited"* (Cambridge, MA: Harvard University Press, 1999), 138-140.

29. Amy Gutmann and Dennis Thompson, *Democracy and Disagreement* (Cambridge, MA: Belknap Press, 1996), 3.

30. Seyla Benhabib, "Toward a Deliberative Model of Democratic Legitimacy," in *Democracy and Difference: Contesting the Boundaries of the Political,* ed. Seyla Benhabib (Princeton, NJ: Princeton University Press, 1996); Joshua Cohen, "Deliberation and Democratic Legitimacy," in *Deliberative Democracy*, eds. James Bohman and William Rehg (Cambridge, MA: MIT Press, 1999).

31. Michael Neblo, "Impassioned Democracy: The Role of Emotion in Deliberative Theory" (paper presented at the Southern Political Science Association Annual Meeting, New Orleans, LA, 2005).

32. Lynn Sanders, "Against Deliberation," *Political Theory* 25:3 (1997): 347-376; Iris Marion Young, "Activist Challenges to Deliberative Democracy," *Political Theory* 29:5 (2001): 670-690. See also Nancy Fraser, "Rethinking the Public Sphere: A Contribution to the Critique of Actually Existing Society," in *Habermas and the Public Sphere*, ed. Craig Calhoun (Cambridge, MA: MIT Press, 1992).

33. Chantal Mouffe, "Deliberative Democracy or Agonistic Pluralism," *Social Research* 66:3 (1999): 745-758.

34. James Bohman, "Survey Article"; James Bohman, "Review: Complexity, Pluralism and the Constitutional State: On Habermas' *Faktizitat* and *Geltung*," *Law and Society Review* 28:4 (1994): 897-930.

35. Rawls, *The Law of Peoples*, 135.

36. Mouffe, "Deliberative Democracy or Agonistic Pluralism," 754-755.

37. Hannah Arendt, *The Human Condition* (Chicago: University of Chicago Press, 1958), 9; Dana R. Villa, "Postmodernism and the Public Sphere," *American Political Science Review* 86:3 (1992): 712-721.

38. Amy Gutmann and Dennis Thompson, *Why Deliberative Democracy?* (Princeton, NJ: Princeton University Press, 2004), 59-63.

39. David M. Ryfe, "Does Deliberative Democracy Work?" *Annual Review of Political Science* 8 (2005): 49-71.

40. Raymond Guess, *Philosophy and Real Politics* (Princeton, NJ: Princeton University Press, 2008).

41. Ian Shapiro, "Enough of Deliberation: Politics Is about Interests and Power," in *Deliberative Politics: Essays on Democracy and Disagreement*, ed. Stephen Macedo (New York, NY: Oxford University Press, 1999).

42. Diana C. Mutz, *Hearing the Other Side: Deliberative Versus Participatory Democracy* (Cambridge: Cambridge University Press, 2006).

43. Simone Chambers, "Rhetoric and the Public Sphere: Has Deliberative Democracy Abandoned Mass Democracy?" *Political Theory* 37:3 (2009): 323-350.

44. On public work as "unfreezing" politics, see Harry Boyte, *Civic Agency and the Cult of the Expert* (Dayton, OH: Kettering Foundation, 2009).

Public Reason and Beyond: Broadening Concepts of Deliberation

Three Models of Democratic Deliberation[1]

by Noëlle McAfee

This paper comes out of my experience working at the intersection of three models of deliberative democracy: (1) the preference-based model held by many deliberative theorists in the social sciences; (2) the rational proceduralist model suggested by John Rawls' political philosophy and Jürgen Habermas' discourse ethics; and (3) what I will call an integrative model that has been overlooked in the literature but can be seen at work in most actual deliberative forums composed of members of a polity deliberating on that polity's direction. The latter includes the National Issues Forums (NIF), a network of civic organizations that run deliberative forums consonant with a quasi-Deweyan approach to public deliberation. My aim in this paper is to see the extent to which any or all of these models can be mapped onto actual deliberative forums, including deliberative polls, the method developed by James Fishkin.[2] These three models are not mutually exclusive. A deliberator might see herself engaged in more than one sort at a time (perhaps testing out, as in the second sort, whether a justification for a policy is acceptable to all, while at the same time hoping to find some integration even where participants cannot reach accord, as in model three). Any combination could work, in practice, even though some of the methods may, again in practice, work at cross purposes. For example, focusing largely on the normative aims of the second model might lead one to minimize the empirical facts of people's actual, strategic aims, of which the third model is highly aware. I want to draw out the theoretical differences between these approaches and show how these differences matter in practice.

My own intersection among these three approaches is rather makeshift: I happened to begin working with Fishkin on a deliberative poll we called the National Issues Convention (NIC) while I was a graduate student at the University of Texas (writing a dissertation, in part, on Jürgen Habermas). I was never Fishkin's student, rather our collaboration began because of my association with the Kettering Foundation, which is a major force behind the NIF.[3] Fishkin became allied with NIF and the Kettering Foundation because of their shared interests in deliberation and because Kettering offered support with finding trained moderators and putting together issue briefing books. All the while, most of the deliberative theory swirling in the air drew on the resurgence of political philosophy brought on both by Rawls' work and by Habermas' notion of reasoning, that in moral, ethical, and political discourse participants should try to offer justifications for their favored policies that would be agreeable to all others affected by a policy.

My particular affiliations aside, the intersection of deliberative thought in the interstices of deliberative polling, normative political theory, and actual deliberative practice is a more general phenomenon. All draw on the key term *deliberation*, and observers expect a commonality because of this shared term. But this intersection is not an altogether seamless one. Many of those who take part in deliberative experiments have rather different ideas of what *deliberation* means; still, the term often gets used as if everyone agrees, though they do not. The differences are not merely semantic; they are rooted in very different conceptions of politics. Because it operates at the intersection of these differences, deliberative polling, specifically the two National Issues Conventions held in the United States, offers a useful case study of how these approaches converge and diverge. In these pages I describe the three models I see at work and offer some preliminary ideas of how they make their way into deliberative polling. My goal here is not to offer an encyclopedic account of these models but rather enough details to flesh out the key differences in their orientations and goals.

The Preference-Based Model

The first model I consider comes out of the social sciences, primarily via political scientists' adoption of the language and theoretical structures of economics.[4] From the point of view of classical economics, human beings are *homoeconomicus,* beings who see the social world as a market in which they try to maximize their own preferences. Political science takes this notion and makes it democratic by saying that a democracy would be rule by the people in a way that helps them maximize, as much as possible, individual's preferences. But given that one person's aims will no doubt conflict with another's, democracy calls for some way in which to compromise or aggregate preferences while treating every individual as an equal, respecting the preferences of all. Though aggregating, e.g., voting, seems to be a very democratic decision procedure, it has its problems, especially when individuals rankings of options are somehow incoherent (for example, ranking a conservative option first, a liberal one second, and a moderate one third) or when a group of individuals rankings show no clear winner (for example, when one person prefers A to B, another B to C, and a third C to A).

Social choice theorists have tried to solve such problems, attempting to see how social or public policies can be devised that respect and preserve the preference rankings of the individuals within a polity. There are two sides of social choice theory: first, the aspect of individuals ranking their preferences between two or more policy options; second, that of social planners devising ways to meld these numerous, individual rankings into one rank ordering of policy options. Yet social choice theorists have yet to find a nonproblematic way to turn a set of individual preferences into a social preference order.[5] Most agree that people's individual, given preferences should be aggregated in some way; but how? What kind of voting system would ensure that the will of the people really does emerge, especially when there is no clear first choice? For example, what happens when the option that got the second amount of votes is nearly everyone's last choice? Our winner-takes-all system leads to all kinds of counterintuitive inconsistencies and difficulties, and social choice theorists have taken it upon themselves to try to solve these problems, often by mustering intricate formalisms and tackling logical minefields. Yet decades of failure have led to the view that there is no will of the people that can be objectively put forward. Any aggregation scheme introduces its own shape to what this will seems to be. Moreover, no scheme seems to do a good job of illuminating social preference without being vulnerable to individual voters manipulating the system to get their favorite candidate chosen. Perhaps the whole enterprise of trying to develop a public policy that is consistent with individual preferences is doomed, along with democracy in general.[6]

Certainly by the 1970s, this is where the science of politics had led: to the view that democracy is a vain hope, inconsistent and absurd. This was an odd place for a discipline to land, especially one that began in part as an attempt to understand the mostly American democratic project.[7] Perhaps in response to this pessimism, a more optimistic area of study has emerged in political science departments since about the mid-1980s: deliberative democratic theory. Social scientists who have taken the deliberative turn reject the following views: (1) that individual preferences are fixed prepolitically; (2) that they are primarily self-regarding; (3) that individuals are rational to be ignorant and hence their preferences ill-informed; and (4) that each individual set of preferences will likely remain incoherent. Jon Elster has argued that deliberation is a means for transforming individual preferences.[8] Fishkin and his colleagues argue that deliberation can help people develop opinions that are more informed, reflective, and considered.[9] Because their views retain the social science focus on individual opinions and preferences, I call this model the preference-based view. Still, as I am noting, there are key differences between *deliberative* theories of preference and the old classical economists' notions. The old view holds that preferences are given in advance of the political process and that each individual's preferences are primarily self-regarding, that individuals tend to put their own desires before others. Hence politics is an arena for getting what one wanted before entering into the political arena. From a deliberative standpoint, preferences are not fixed in advance; they can be informed with balanced briefing materials and expert knowledge and transformed through deliberations with others, making them other-regarding, not just self-regarding. In short, these deliberative theorists think that people can transform their preferences for the better during deliberative, informative discussions with others, making them more collective, informed, and cognizant of the concerns of others in the community.[10] Such preferences would not be so difficult to aggregate rationally and democratically. Hence democracy becomes a possibility, democracy being a kind of governance in which preferences transformed through deliberation become the basis for public policy.

In this view, though, public policy is not formed in these deliberations. Given that deliberators will rarely unanimously agree on what policy is best, a deliberative polity still needs some kind of external decision-making procedure.[11] This might be a direct vote or it might be a matter of transmitting up the political ladder the new, improved set of individual preferences. Unlike conventional democratic politics, where policymakers make policy on the basis of unreflective preferences captured in standard public opinion polls, this model offers policymakers a snapshot of what a deliberative public thinks. That is how John Dryzek characterizes deliberative polling:

> From the point of view of deliberative democracy, ordinary opinion polls are pointless because they register only unreflective preferences. The idea of a deliberative poll is to assemble a random sample of members of the public, have them deliberate about the key issues of the election, poll them on their positions on the issue, and publicize the results. The intent here is to model the distribution of opinions that the general public would hold if they were able to engage in genuine deliberation, a far cry indeed from the unreflective preferences which ordinary opinion polls register.[12]

Through deliberation, participants turn their unreflective preferences into what Fishkin calls "considered judgments,"[13] but ultimately these are still judgments that will be framed as a policy after the deliberations have concluded. As Dryzek notes:

> The opinion poll administered at the conclusion of deliberation requires the analyst to summarize and aggregate opinions, so it is not clear how this particular transmission mechanism solves the problems of aggregation as defined by social choice theory except by handing them back to the institutions of government.[14]

Without diminishing the importance and usefulness of deliberative polling, I do want to highlight one of its self-imposed limitations (which others might take to be a benefit): it truncates the *political* task of trying to turn individual views into public judgments. The end result of a deliberative poll is not a public expression about what might be the best course of action. It is a *poll*, one that shows the distribution of individual opinions. However considered these are, they do not equal an integrated policy. Even aggregating the results does not lead to a coherent, democratic policy, or even the will of the people, as social choice theorists well know. A legislature might take on the political task of trying to integrate the various needs, aims, and constraints into something like a coherent public policy. If it does so on the basis of individuals considered judgments, so much the better. But we should be keenly aware that the political work occurs at this higher level, not at the level where deliberators work on transforming their own preferences. At this level, they stop short of the task of trying to decide what we, as a polity, should do. The preference-based view shows how individual opinions are transformed into superior opinions, but not into public policy.

Why is this? Why do deliberative polls shun any deliberation aimed at developing a public voice on an issue? Like other deliberative theorists, preference-based adherents are committed to democracy. Their commitment is shaped by the views that democracy calls for respecting individual preferences and that anything that exerts any untoward (e.g., coercive) force on individual preferences is undemocratic. Such forces include factions, the tyranny of the majority, social pressure, and the like. Hence there is some tension inherent in an individualist, preference-based model of *deliberation*, for the more people deliberate in public with others, the more likely they are to be moved by these others in their midst. Therefore, preference-based deliberative theorists try to guard against public pressure on individual deliberations, a real problem in the setting of public deliberation. Their goal is for participants to use deliberative settings to transform their preferences without being unduly swayed by others. In their view, deliberations should be geared toward giving participants full information and a clearer picture of how each option on the table would or would not satisfy each participants preferences.[15] Deliberations should supply expertise and an appreciation of others concerns, not social suasion. These theorists tend to worry that deliberations might lead participants to conform to others' expectations rather than to refine their own preferences.[16] They think this phenomenon would result in a kind of false consciousness where participants are not fully aware of their own, true self-interests and opinions. For them, democracy means rule by fully informed individuals. *Autonomy equals not being unduly influenced by anyone else.*

The social scientists' approach to deliberative theory goes a long way toward turning *homoeconomicus* into an other-regarding democratic citizen. But at the end of their deliberations, there is no discernible *public* transformation. Each individual might transform his or her individual views, in light of more information and exposure to others views; but there is no expectation that the result might be public views; they will just be more rational and considered views. At the end of the deliberations, individuals' views still have to be transformed into some kind of social ordering. If everyone were to agree on the nature of a problem and what policy is best, there would be no difficulty. But most anyone steeped in the facts of public life, Elster included, thinks this is unlikely (only the normatively oriented, whom I turn to in the next section, think this is a possibility). Given the fact of disagreement, some way needs to be found to make collective decisions. If the way is through voting, then the preference-based theorists have come full circle to the problem of articulating "the will of the people" out of a set of individual preferences. Bound to individualism, preference-based thinkers still face the challenge of social ordering.

The Rational Proceduralist Model

The second model I want to lay out here comes from a different direction, not the supposedly empirical and normatively agnostic orientation of the social scientist, but the normatively steeped orientation of the philosopher.[17] The second model sets a very high bar on what kinds of reasons deliberators should offer and accept: participants should deliberate upon the basis of reasons that are rational and acceptable to all. This view specifies what can count as a good reason and what kind of procedures should be in place to ensure a good outcome. Accordingly, I call this view the rational proceduralist model of deliberation.

In this second model, citizens are guided by a will to come up with universalizable norms or at least norms that are acceptable to all those affected by any given policy. This view can be traced back to both the social contract tradition of consent theory and to the Kantian normative claim that we, as rational individuals, can act rationally by only acting on the basis of maxims (or policies) that can be rationally universalized, i.e., applied to all equally and without contradiction. Here we have an explicitly philosophical conception of autonomy: autonomy means acting and choosing on the basis of universalizable norms; true self-rule is to live by rules that hold for all, not just for oneself. Rational deliberators offer arguments concerning justice and the public good. In this view, motivations of self-interest stand in the way of developing legitimate public policies, for these policies should be good for all. This theory encourages deliberators to opt an impartial, objective point of view and to offer reasons (not rhetoric) that all others would find compelling. Otherwise, a policy would not attract general consent and here I mean consent of all those rational agents affected by a policy. Irrational agents need not be heeded; in fact, according to Gutmann and Thompson, they should not even be in the room.[18] Though this view sees deliberators as always already in a community, it does tend to think of deliberators as capable of imagining themselves stripped of their affective and communal associations, roles, and conventions so that they might be able to deliberate objectively and impartially. They need to use their reason so as to imagine how a policy would affect anyone else. They are rational agents.

In this model, *deliberation is a way in which individuals collectively decide whether a policy is legitimate.* A policy or law is just only if (1) all those affected by it have an opportunity to consider, collectively, whether or not the policy or law is just; and if (2) all those affected assent to the policy. Deliberation, then, is the process through which people decide whether a proposal is normatively or ethically right. Participants decide this through the back and forth of argumentation, with everyone having an equal opportunity to put forward his or her own case. Ultimately, the unforced force of the better argument will prevail; that is, all the participants should ultimately agree upon which proposal is most rational and right. The rational proceduralist model considers deliberative democracy as a way to create legitimate public policy, that is, policies that all citizens would, under ideal conditions, have authored themselves.

Both Habermas and the political philosopher John Rawls contribute to this approach.[19] As Elster writes, the arguments advanced by Habermas and Rawls do seem to have a common core: political choice, to be legitimate, must be the *outcome of deliberation about ends among free, equal, and rational agents.*[20] It is no wonder then that Habermasians like Seyla Benhabib and Rawlsians like Joshua Cohen arrive at roughly the same philosophical position on deliberation.[21] Whether one adopts the Habermasian regulative ideal of the ideal speech situation or the Rawlsian regulative ideal of the original position, in democratic deliberations all those affected should recognize the outcome as in keeping with what they would have chosen had they had an opportunity to participate.

For Habermas, the operative form of reason in this democratic setting is communicative, internal to discursive practices. Though Habermas' theory of communicative action draws heavily on American pragmatist conceptions of self, truth, and action, ultimately it looks very much like Enlightenment rationality with its claims to universality, impartiality, and, in Benhabib's hands, reversibility of perspectives.[22] Habermas' theory of communicative action and allied theories of public reason-giving are put to use in deliberative theory, laying out the limits of the kind of talking out loud that ought to occur in a deliberative forum. For example, Joshua Cohen writes:

> In an idealized deliberative setting, it will not do simply to advance reasons that one takes to be true or compelling: such considerations may be rejected by others who are themselves reasonable. One must instead find reasons that are compelling to others, acknowledging those others as equals, aware that they have alternative reasonable commitments, and knowing something about the kinds of commitments that they are likely to have.[23]

In this model, partiality is a serious fault. One should be able to see the whole picture, not just one's own arena. It seems that one need not actually consult others to find out what the world looks like from their perspective; each sovereign citizen should have a mental map of the whole. Accordingly, the ideal deliberator reasons publicly with others not in order to get more information about how policies would affect others but rather to get their consent. This model holds out hope that decisions can be reached by consensus. If all agree on what policy is best, then there will be no need for social-choice type aggregation, bargaining, or voting.

In its search for unanimity, deliberation becomes a contest, a battle of arguments, in which the best argument wins. To be a contender, a policy needs to get universal consent. This kind of deliberation does not try to piece together second-best alternatives into something with which most everyone could live. It looks for policies that are simply the best. As a result of these stakes, it is possible that the participants in such deliberative ventures are more interested in winning a contest than in solving problems. This model seems to lose sight of the reason people enter into public deliberations because their communities are wracked by problems that politicians cannot seem to solve. In actual community deliberations, participants are not looking for which claim is normatively right but which picture of the problem is most telling and which courses of action have promise. Yet even though universality may be the guiding ideal, most deliberative proceduralists realize that consensus is rarely reached and that some kind of vote will be needed. As a result, this view runs into the very same problems that social choice theory does: finding the best way, short of consensus, to articulate the will of the people.[24]

The Integrative Model

Anyone familiar with deliberative theory probably recognizes the above two models readily, especially with the little bit of detail that I have provided. The third model I sketch here has not been discussed in the literature, or certainly not to any great extent. It is the model that I came to know firsthand through observing the deliberative forums that are part of the network known as the National Issues Forums, which has developed with some behind-the-scenes help (meaning intellectual but not financial) from the Charles F. Kettering Foundation in Dayton, Ohio, and Public Agenda in New York City.[25] Some of the intellectual founders of this approach include Kettering's president, David Mathews; the survey researcher Daniel Yankelovich; and the political theorists Benjamin Barber and Harry Boyte. Also instrumental have been the works of Hannah Arendt and John Dewey.

While NIF now has many sister organizations around the world, I trace the intellectual roots of this model to an American pragmatist tradition that is concerned more with what works than what is true. This model does have some roots in the civic republican tradition as well, though its normative conceptions are not as strong as those criticized in Habermas.[26] For one, this model sees the public as heterogeneous, not the collective actor of a Rousseauian model. This model is empirically observable, but one observes that participants have normative concerns: when people deliberate together about public matters they develop an interest in the public welfare (in solving public problems) that may override their particular preferences.

Yet even with all these theoretical resources, NIF is primarily driven by the way people actually deliberate and what their aims and concerns seem to be when they sit down together and try to solve problems that resist solution. These deliberators are motivated by the need to find a way forward on problems that affect them and their communities. Here the reader might recall E. J. Dionne's book of a decade ago, aptly titled *Why Americans Hate*

Politics.[27] Its main point is that Americans do not care about ideology, which seems to be the currency of conventional politics; rather they want solutions to problems. This is an insight that has long steered NIF. I spent a few years writing guides for deliberation with David Mathews, guides used by NIF convenors and moderators. We oriented our texts according to a framework we called "choice work." The aim was for citizens to consider an array of policy options and, on each one, to spell out the costs and consequences of each approach as well as the trade-offs that would need to be made if any one approach were adopted. Only by working through the various choices, grappling with what must be abandoned in order to proceed in a particular direction, only with this kind of struggle do deliberators begin to develop a public judgment as to what policy might be best. Though it often evokes the language of finding common ground for action, this approach does not aim for happy consensus. Rather, choice work engages deliberators in the pragmatic task of delineating what courses of action might work given polity members many aims and constraints.

According to the integrative model, *deliberation is a process through which people grapple with the consequences of various public problems and proposals*. Participants focus on solving public problems in ways that are consistent with their publicly formed understandings and ends. Instead of narrowly focusing on autonomy, this model sees democratic choice and action as practices that involve people considering how various options would affect their communities. They do not separate political ends from the fact that they are living with other people who are also affected by these policy choices. The public dimension of deliberation is indispensable to the task of fathoming problems and forming a public that can respond. Instead of seeing politics as bargaining about preferences, they see politics as a difficult matter of deciding what kinds of communities they are making for themselves. Instead of merely *preferring*, deliberators *choose*.

At the outset of this essay, I called this model "quasi-Deweyan." By this I do not mean that Dewey spawned the integrative model but rather that his observations mesh with it uncannily well. I have recently returned to his book, *The Public and Its Problems*,[28] and noted how much his observations intersect with the integrative model.[29] Both Dewey and NIF hold that public communication can be a way in which citizens simultaneously develop an understanding of public problems and of themselves as a public that can and should develop sound and effective public policies. Having defined the public as all those indirectly and seriously affected for good or evil by the human collective action of some particular group of people, Dewey understood the centrality of deliberating on public matters, both to define the matters and the public: An inchoate public is capable of organization only when indirect consequences are perceived, and when it is possible to project agencies which order their occurrence. In keeping with Dewey's insight, actual public deliberations usually spend a great deal of time developing a public picture of what a problem is and how it affects those in the room and others throughout the political community. As deliberators develop a public understanding of the nature and the many aspects of the problem at hand, they also begin to see themselves as a public.

This view distinguishes itself by aiming for *integration* of multiple, heterogeneous views. Unlike the second model, which expects deliberators to act according to the Enlightenment, universalizing ideal, this model accepts and makes use of citizens' particular perspectives. Because each starts out with a limited picture of how a policy under consideration might affect others, participants deliberate in order to learn. They seek information, not so much about facts but about the consequences of various policies. In this model, citizens' partial perspectives can be *integrated* into a viable, sound policy choice, one that is always provisional and subject to change.

When people come together to deliberate on matters that affect their polities, they seem to transform personal concerns and interests into public ones. To understand this phenomenon, observers and political theorists need to move beyond the tired dichotomy between egoism and altruism. It is not that public deliberations turn participants into altruists. Rather, public deliberations help forge an immediate interest in matters public, conjuring up the history of the term *interest* itself, *inter-esse*, a way of being between and with others. Participants develop an interest in the welfare of their political communities.

Moreover, this model attends to the problem over which both the first and the second models stumble: how to set policy direction when there is not full, or even much, agreement. Participants use their disagreements as productive constraints, helping them identify in which, albeit few, possible directions the polity might move. In the many deliberations that my colleagues at the Kettering Foundation and I have observed, participants leave saying that even when they did not agree with other participants, they did come to see why the others held the views they did. They came to change their views of others' views. Even in the face of trenchant disagreement, participants would focus on coming up with a direction that would accommodate the plural concerns in the room. Unlike the first model, which leaves the aggregation problem to social planners, this integrative model understands that deliberators want to have a hand in shaping policy, indeed that this shaping is central to deliberation itself. They do not want to just be preference inputs into some social utility function. They want to help decide what the policy should be in the very process of trying to understand what the problem is, how it affects all those concerned, and what kind of polity they want to forge.

Of the three, this view is the least idealistic. It has the most communal understanding of human psychology, seeing people and publics as constituted through their common language, customs, norms, relationships, and communities. It does not call on participants to imagine themselves stripped of affective and social associations in order to deliberate well. People do, and should, bring their particular concerns to the table when they deliberate with others. In practice, in this view, moderators try to ensure that all participants have an equal opportunity to speak, that no speakers dominate the deliberations, and that other factors in keeping with Habermasian speech-setting ideals are in place. But moderators also try to elicit stories from deliberators, using prompts such as tell us how you came to hold the view that you have. (This prompt usually brings forth a story that helps make sense of why someone would hold a view that others might find objectionable or unreasonable, in the process showing another aspect of an issue that others might not have considered.)

This model aims at getting participants to arrive at a choice that takes into consideration other participants' concerns, aiming for a choice that reflects a considered, public judgment on the issue. Through their deliberations, deliberators come to see possible outlines for public action. And they come to see themselves as part of a public, as public actors with considered judgments and purposes who can help shape public policy. In this view, the goal is not *rationality* per se but the possibility of understanding the public dimensions of problems and identifying what, if any, sound and sustainable directions there are in which the public might move. At the very least, it sets the boundaries of what Daniel Yankelovich calls "public permission."

Theories in Practice

These three definitions certainly do not exhaust the alternatives, but they do capture what seem to be the three most prevalent views. All three views have their virtues. But unless the different emphases between these views are made clear and unless their tensions are addressed then deliberative practice can falter. With this in mind, I close with some thoughts on how these themes manifested themselves in the National Issues Conventions, sometimes undercutting the potential of the event. I do think that deliberative polling and its National Issues Conventions are tremendously valuable political events. I simply want to show why its proponents should move closer to an integrative model.

The role of experts: Drawing primarily on the preference-based model of social choice, Fishkin and his colleagues take one of the central tasks of deliberation to be a matter of informing participants' discretion, giving them the means and the opportunity to develop opinions worth listening to. As Luskin, Fishkin, and Jowell write, the scientific value of the Deliberative Poll is that it provides a way of addressing the effects of information (and thought and involvement) on policy preferences.[30] To this end, deliberative polling relies heavily on panels of experts and policymakers to answer questions that arise during deliberations. During the last NIC, participants worked through two policy choices and then stopped to select questions for experts. They then went into plenary sessions to listen to how the experts answered their questions. Afterward, they returned to their small groups, deliberated a bit more, and worked on developing more questions for the experts. They ended the afternoon with another plenary session with experts. Before dinner, they met again to come up with questions for policymakers. The Sunday morning session was devoted to policymakers taking citizens' questions. By the end of the weekend, much more time was taken up with either formulating or asking questions of experts, and listening to experts, than was taken up by deliberating. Observers noted that through the course of the weekend participants took much care in how they worded the questions, more it seemed for the benefit of getting the panelists' attention than for their own benefit of getting information. Despite the organizers' intentions, the experts did not seem to be there in service to the deliberators and the participants felt frustrated when, because there was never enough time to address all the questions, their own questions did not get posed.

Expertise plays a much smaller role in the NIF or integrative style of deliberation. NIF does use issue books, balanced and informative guides to an issue that offer three or four policy choices, discussions of pros and cons, trade-offs, and other data. NIF deliberations tend to focus more on how various proposals will affect participants and their communities' ends and purposes. Questions of fact arise far less than do questions of value and consequence. In my observations, deliberations proceed quite differently depending on whether they see expertise in the service of deliberation (as NIF tends to do) or as something to aim for (which deliberative polling inadvertently does). Deliberative polls could improve by lowering the profile of the experts treating them as interested parties (which they usually are) who have some knowledge of how proposed policies fit into the larger political picture. Instead of panels taking up large portions of the program, these parties could be available in the background to answer any questions that spontaneously arise.

The meaning of politics: Finally, note that the three models I have described here have radically different conceptions of politics. The first holds that politics is the practice, exogenous to public deliberation, of turning deliberative preferences into public policy. Politics is the province of government. The second and third models expand the arena of politics beyond government to include the deliberations that go on within civil society.[31] The second hopes that the deliberative public can engage in policymaking, to the extent that it is able to reach rational agreement. The third is more forgiving of disagreement, in fact recognizing that politics begins because there is disagreement, and it puts what is obvious first: that people enter into politics to solve problems. Of course, the first two models might want to lay claim to that purpose as well. But they limit public problem solving to, respectively, the use of individual preferences and rationality. In the integrative model, participants are motivated by their sociality to meet with others they may neither like nor understand in order to find solutions to problems that vex what they do care about dearly, the public world that they inhabit, the world they will leave for their children and future generations. They are motivated to fashion a new *public* world, which is like putting together a puzzle: trying to see what all the pieces are, especially the pieces held by other participants, and then seeing how they might be able to fit them all together, however imperfectly and provisionally.

None of the above is meant to suggest that there is anything intrinsically wrong with deliberative polling. To the contrary, I think it is a tremendously important advance in democratic practice. My concern in this paper has been that deliberative polling has been too informed by a preference-based model of democratic deliberation and not informed (nor as a result formed) enough by an integrative model. In its concern to help individuals deliberate and refine their opinions, it has overlooked the public task of politics. Yet while many of the theorists behind the scenes might think they are culling well-formed individual preferences, deliberators in the rooms steadily set about integrating their many perspectives, experiences, and purposes into potential policies that are decidedly public. Each deliberative polling experiment ends with an individual survey of each individual's views. Participants each retreat to a secluded spot in the room to take the after survey, a survey they are to take without consulting anyone else. Afterward, the survey researchers gather and compare the pre- and post-deliberation responses. Then they hold a press conference and public television airs a program revealing the extent to which individual opinions changed. The results, it is thought, when aggregated, will point to what public opinion would look like if people were to think about the issues. But back in that same room, at the end of the deliberative poll, just before the surveys are distributed, there is another public voice to be heard. It is the voice of the people comparing notes, trying to piece together all the moving and conflicting and unsettling matters they have deliberated on while they were together; it is the voice of people trying to take account of and integrate their own and their fellow deliberators' perspectives, concerns, and desires. The question they return to is, on this matter at hand to us now, what shall we do? In these rooms the people know that, in politics, at the end of the day, our task is not to decide what each of us wants, but to decide what we as a polity should do.

EDITORS' NOTE

This chapter was originally published as Noëlle McAfee, "Three Models of Democratic Deliberation," *Journal of Speculative Philosophy* 18:1 (2004): 44–59. Reprinted by permission of The Pennsylvania State University Press. Minor stylistic changes have been made for the purposes of this volume.

NOTES

1. In keeping with this paper's spirit, the author is indebted to a great many colleagues for their helpful comments in response to earlier versions of this paper, including Michael Briand, David Crocker, John Dedrick, Stephen Elkin, James Fishkin, Robert Kingston, Peter Levine, David Mathews, Keith Melville, Henry Richardson, and Claire Snyder.

2. James S. Fishkin, *Democracy and Deliberation: New Directions for Democratic Reform* (New Haven, CT: Yale University Press, 1991); James S. Fishkin, *Voice of the People: Public Opinion and Democracy* (New Haven, CT: Yale University Press, 1995).

3. Please note that NIF and NIC refer to two different entities: the National Issues Forums (NIF) and the National Issues Convention (NIC). The former is a network of civic organizations in the United States (with sister networks in many countries throughout the world) that periodically hold deliberative forums in their own organizations and communities, using briefing materials produced by the Kettering Foundation and Public Agenda. These issue books lay out three or four possible courses of action on a given problem, drawing out the costs and consequences of each approach. For more information, consult their website at http://www.nifi.org/. The National Issues Convention is the name of two deliberative polls conducted by James Fishkin in the United States, the first in 1996 in Austin, Texas, and the second in 2003 in Philadelphia, Pennsylvania. To make matters a bit more confusing, both NIC events employed veteran moderators from the National Issues Forums, though these moderators were explicitly briefed beforehand on the need to moderate according to the precepts of the first model of democratic deliberation, as I am laying it out here. Additionally, both NICs, and many other deliberative polls, have provided issue briefing materials drafted in line with the same principles of the NIF issue books, though the NIC briefing materials avoid any language of working toward common ground.

4. I am a bit suspicious of the claim that social science research is primarily empirical, as opposed to work in the humanities, philosophy included. The social scientists focus on the individuals and their preferences, as discussed here, does betray a strong philosophical commitment.

5. Jon Elster and Aanund Hylland, eds., *Foundations of Social Choice Theory* (Cambridge: Cambridge University Press, 1986), 2.

6. A more thorough overview of the social choice project can be found in Kenneth J. Arrow, *Social Choice and Individual Values*, 2nd ed. (New York: Wiley, 1963); John Dryzek, *Deliberative Democracy and Beyond: Liberals, Critics, and Contestations* (Oxford, UK: Oxford University Press, 2000); Elster and Hylland, *Foundations of Social Choice Theory*.

7. Rogers Smith, "Still Blowing in the Wind: The American Quest for a Democratic, Scientific Political Science," in *American Academic Culture in Transformation: Fifty Years, Four Disciplines*, eds. Thomas Bender, Carl E. Schorske, and Stephen R. Graubard (Princeton: Princeton University Press, 1997).

8. Jon Elster, ed., *Deliberative Democracy* (Cambridge, UK: Cambridge University Press, 1998), 1.

9. Robert C. Luskin, James S. Fishkin, and Roger Jowell, "Considered Opinions: Deliberative Polling in Britain," *British Journal of Political Science* 32:3 (2002): 455–487.

10. In a public deliberation, the search to maximize one's own preference for X may entail offering generally acceptable reasons for others also to prefer X. If preferences are transformed to the point that individual

preference disappears or when the deliberator's focus is on seeking agreement then we are no longer in the realm of model one but have moved into model two. At a certain point, the line between models one and two has to do with perspective: the first focuses on individual preference, the second with individuals offering reasons they hope would be acceptable to all.

11. David Miller, "Deliberative Democracy and Social Choice," *Political Studies* 40: Special Issue (1992): 54-67.

12. Dryzek, *Deliberative Democracy and Beyond*, 55.

13. Fishkin, *Voice of the People*.

14. Dryzek, *Deliberative Democracy and Beyond*, 55.

15. Some preference-based theorists have a very narrow view of how preferences are transformed. Adam Przeworski argues that deliberation informs participants about which kind of means will satisfy their given preferences or that their preferences might change to be in keeping with what they really wanted. Adam Przeworski, "Deliberation and Ideological Domination," in *Deliberative Democracy*, ed. Jon Elster (Cambridge: Cambridge University Press, 1998). There is little room in Przeworski's picture for Luskin, Fishkin, and Jowell's broader notion that people change their individual preferences to more considered judgments that take into account the needs and concerns of others. Luskin, Fishkin, and Jowell, "Considered Opinions: Deliberative Polling in Britain."

16. Elster, *Deliberative Democracy*, 15; Cass Sunstein, "The Law of Group Polarization," in *Debating Deliberative Democracy*, ed. James S. Fishkin and Peter Laslett (Malden, MA: Blackwell Publishing, 2003).

17. See note 3.

18. Amy Gutmann and Dennis Thompson, *Democracy and Disagreement* (Cambridge, MA: Belknap Press, 1996). John Dryzek rebuts this view perfectly. Usually in the course of deliberations, participants can unmask bigoted views and show how illegitimate they are. Exogenous constraints are not needed. Dryzek, *Deliberative Democracy and Beyond,* 45 n.47. I have seen this at work in my own observations.

19. Jürgen Habermas, *Between Facts and Norms*, trans. William Rehg (Cambridge, MA: MIT Press, 1996); John Rawls, *Political Liberalism* (New York: Columbia University Press, 1993).

20. Elster, *Deliberative Democracy*, 5.

21. Seyla Benhabib, *Democracy and Difference* (Princeton, NJ: Princeton University Press, 1996); Joshua Cohen, "Deliberation and Democratic Legitimacy," in *Deliberative Democracy: Essays on Reason and Politics*, eds. James Bohman and William Rehg (Cambridge, MA: MIT Press, 1997).

22. Noëlle McAfee, *Habermas, Kristeva, and Citizenship* (Ithaca, NY: Cornell University Press, 2000).

23. Joshua Cohen, "Procedure and Substance in Democratic Legitimacy," in *Deliberative Democracy: Essays on Reason and Politics*, eds. James Bohman and William Rehg (Cambridge, MA: MIT Press, 1997), 414.

24. Dryzek, *Deliberative Democracy and Beyond*, 38-41.

25. Further discussions of NIF can be found in John Gastil, *By Popular Demand* (Berkeley, CA: University of California Press, 2000); David Schoem and Sylvia Hurtado, *Intergroup Dialogue* (Ann Arbor, MI: University of Michigan Press, 2001); Carmen Sirianni and Lewis A. Friedland, *Civic Innovation in America: Community Empowerment, Public Policy, and the Movement for Civic Renewal* (Berkeley, CA: University of California Press, 2001); Daniel Yankelovich, *Coming to Judgment: Making Democracy Work in a Complex World* (Syracuse, NY: Syracuse University Press, 1991).

26. Jürgen Habermas, *The Inclusion of the Other: Studies in Political Theory*, eds. Ciaran P. Cronin and Pablo De Greiff (Cambridge, MA: MIT Press: 1998), 244-249.

27. E. J. Dionne Jr., *Why Americans Hate Politics* (New York: Simon & Shuster, 1991).

28. John Dewey, *The Public and Its Problems* (Athens, OH: Swallow Press, 1927, 1991 ed.).

29. Noëlle McAfee, "Public Knowledge," *Philosophy and Social Criticism* 30:2 (2004): 139-157.

30. Luskin, Fishkin, and Jowell, "Considered Opinions: Deliberative Polling in Britain."

31. Dryzek, *Deliberative Democracy and Beyond*.

Rhetoric and Public Reasoning: An Aristotelian Understanding of Political Deliberation

by Bernard Yack

Since Aristotle defines human beings as both rational and political animals, you would think he would be eager to join the current celebration of public reason and political deliberation. But when you compare Aristotle's ideas about political deliberation to their counterparts in recent philosophical discussions, it quickly becomes clear that there is "no Aristotelian equivalent" to the notion of public reason that inspires currently popular models of deliberative democracy.[1]

Public reasoning in these contemporary models is a practice that sharply limits both the form and substance of political argument in order to facilitate cooperation among free and equal individuals.[2] Aristotelian public reasoning, in contrast, lacks such constraints. It draws its premises from the whole range of "reputable opinion," rather than from the limited number of premises that could, at least in principle, command reasonable assent of all members of the community (*Rhetoric* 1355a; *Topics* 101a). And it relies heavily on appeals to character and emotion as well the giving of reasons. In short, Aristotle places rhetoric, the art of identifying and employing "the available means of persuasion" (*Rhetoric* 1355b), at the heart of political deliberation. That makes the Aristotelian model of public reasoning much closer to the actual practice of political deliberation in our world as well as his. But it distances his model from approaches to political deliberation theories that are designed to correct the deficiencies of the past and present practice of democracy.

Why would Aristotle, certainly no friend to unlimited democracy, resist the idea of making public reasoning more reasonable? He is quite eager, as we shall see, to restrict the impact of forensic rhetoric on our legal judgments. Why not make a similar effort to improve the quality of our judgments about the making of law and policy, where the stakes are so much higher?

This paper answers these questions by reconstructing and defending a distinctly Aristotelian account of political deliberation. A number of Aristotle's recent commentators have shared these goals.[3] But while they narrow the gap between the *Rhetoric* and the rest of Aristotle's works by identifying the moral service that they believe that Aristotelian rhetoric performs, my paper closes this gap by moving in the opposite direction. For it argues that a relatively unconstrained form of public reasoning is precisely what is called for by the vision of political life developed in Aristotle's ethical and political writings. This is not to deny that Aristotle expects the use of deliberative rhetoric to improve political morality in subtle and significant ways.[4] It merely reflects my judgment that the overly moralistic view of politics shared by many of both Aristotle's interpreters and current defenders of political deliberation stands in greater need of correction than their under-moralized view of rhetoric.

Aristotle, I shall argue, is a political realist, at least in the sense that the late Bernard Williams gives to that term: someone for whom political morality is grounded in the basic social relationships and expectations that structure political life.[5] But because he insists that the good life of active virtue is the final end of politics, he is often mistaken for what Williams calls a political moralist: someone for whom political morality is determined by the application of independently derived moral standards to the making of political decisions or the formation of the basic structure of political institutions. Correcting this misimpression not only clears up an apparent inconsistency in Aristotle's political philosophy, it gives us access to a more realistic understanding of some of the most important practices in everyday political life.

An Aristotelian Account of Political Deliberation

Political deliberation is a social practice in which citizens communicate with each other about how they should direct the actions of their political communities. As such, it has two basic elements: some form of public reasoning, some way in which citizens exchange their views about matters of common interest and an opportunity to consider together this exchange of opinion and argument in reaching decisions about which collective action to support. Supporters of political deliberation argue that political communities make better political choices when the judgment of citizens is informed by the public exchange of views in this way.

It is important at the outset to emphasize that, contrary to much of the recent literature on deliberative democracy, political deliberation is not a form of collective decision making.[6] Political deliberation informs and prepares collective decisions by helping individual citizens determine which collective action to support. But it takes a second social practice, the implementation of a collective decision rule, such as majority rule or consensus, to turn this set of individual choices into a collective choice. For this reason, it is a mistake to contrast political deliberation with voting as one of a number of means of reaching collective decisions, as is often done by proponents of deliberative democracy.[7] Political deliberation is more properly contrasted with other means of shaping individual judgments about the proper collective action to take, such as bargaining or, to invoke an important ancient Greek practice, divination.

Although Aristotle never devotes the kind of sustained attention to political deliberation that he devotes to the deliberation of individuals, he does provide us with the building blocks with which to construct an account of the phenomenon—which is why I am comfortable describing the following account of political deliberation as Aristotelian. This account of political deliberation has three key components: the analysis of individual deliberation in Book 3 of the *Nicomachean Ethics*; the account of deliberative rhetoric in Book 1 of the *Rhetoric*; and the theory of political community introduced in Book 1 of the *Politics* and elaborated throughout his political writings. The first explains the goals of deliberation. The second describes the means by which we deliberate together in a political community. And the third explains why political deliberation leans so heavily on rhetoric, in particular, on the form of rhetoric in which we seek to persuade each other that one action rather than another best serves the common good or advantage.

By recalling the conclusions of his analysis of individual deliberation in his account of deliberative rhetoric in political assemblies (*Rhetoric* 1357), Aristotle makes it clear that most of what he says about individual deliberation pertains to political deliberation as well. Like the deliberation of each individual, political deliberation seeks to determine which acts will most contribute to the ends that we seek to achieve.[8] It deals with contingencies rather than necessities, since no one deliberates about things that cannot be done or actions that we cannot avoid performing. And, most important, it focuses on the consequences of future acts rather than, as in our judgments about justice and injustice or praise and blame, on our assessment of acts that have already been performed (*Nicomachean Ethics,* afterwards *NE,* 1112-1113; *Rhetoric* 1357-1358).

The obvious difference between individual and political deliberation lies in the communal or collective character of the latter. As an individual I deliberate about how best to pursue my happiness. As members of a political community we deliberate how best to work together to pursue our common ends. Since we are, according to Aristotle, political animals, my happiness as an individual depends to a great extent on what happens in my community. But the Aristotelian citizen is no Rousseauian *citoyen,* no mere fraction whose value is determined by his or her communal denominator.[9] The ends of the two forms of deliberation, individual flourishing and the shared or common good of the political community, remain distinct and potentially in conflict.

Individual deliberation is an interior monologue in which an inseparable mix of desire and intellect that leads to choice (*NE* 1139b, 1113a). We often express part of that monologue out loud when we seek help from others in thinking through important questions (*NE* 1112b). But individual deliberation need not involve verbal expression at all. Political deliberation, in contrast, necessarily involves speech and argument because it requires the sharing of our reasoning. That is why it makes sense to talk about "public reason" and public reasoning when talking about Aristotle's understanding of political deliberation, even though these are not Aristotle's own terms. Without the capacity to make our reasoning publicly available to each other, there would be no shared deliberation.

For Aristotle, the means by which we communicate our reasoning to each other in political deliberation is the particular form of persuasive speech he calls deliberative rhetoric. We deliberate together in political communities by making and listening to each other's attempts to persuade us that some future action will best serve the end that citizens share with each other, the common good or advantage of the political community.

It is this shared goal that distinguishes deliberative rhetoric, and therefore public reasoning, from the other forms of rhetoric and political judgment that Aristotle examines. When we make legal judgments forensic rhetoric seeks to persuade us of the justice or injustice, the guilt or innocence, of the people that we put on trial. When we make judgments about rewards and censure epideictic rhetoric seeks to persuade us of the honorable or dishonorable character of the individuals under consideration. And when we make judgments about the making of law and policy deliberative rhetoric seeks to persuade us that one course of action rather than another will best serve the common good or advantage (*Rhetoric* 1351b). Aristotle, it seems, reserves the term *deliberative* for the last of these three forms of rhetoric and public judgment because, like individual deliberation, it focuses on the choice of future action rather than on the assessment of past actions and character.[10]

The pursuit of the common good or advantage structures public reasoning in a number of significant ways. First of all, it rules out explicitly self-serving arguments. People who try to persuade us to do something that serves their own rather than the common advantage will have to find a way of portraying what's good for them as good for the other members of the community as well. This is a point on which Aristotle agrees with contemporary defenders of political deliberation, though as we shall see, they make rather more of it than Aristotle would think appropriate.[11]

Second, the pursuit of the common advantage significantly constrains the aims of public reasoning. In a courtroom or in private relations one might demand justice, the consequences be damned. But *fiat justitia, pereat mundus* is almost impossible to sell in political deliberation—unless one is speaking to a group that shares a set of religious convictions that makes the end of the world seem like a means to a transcendently good end. Similarly, insisting that, like Achilles, we should choose a short but glorious life might be a great way of celebrating an individual. And it may even inspire other individuals to emulate that noble hero. But proposals to sacrifice—as opposed to risk—the life of our community are almost impossible to defend in political deliberation, no matter how noble they may sound.[12]

Third, the pursuit of the common advantage constrains the kind of character and emotions that public reason appeals to as well as the kind of arguments it features. Impartiality and disinterestedness recommend individuals to us as judges, but not as political deliberators, since deliberators are supposed to be pondering our fate and theirs, not the disputes and interests of others. If they seem disinterested in the outcome, then that suggests that the matter really does not have any importance for them—or perhaps that they are hiding their true interests. For this reason political leaders seek to establish a reputation for public-spiritedness, rather than a reputation for impartiality and disinterestedness. Telling people that I make public judgments by asking myself what I would do if I could view the world from some impartial standpoint, like Rawls' original position, might enhance my reputation as an appeals court judge; but it is bound to undermine my reputation as a senator, a president or any other kind of political leader. And if I then went on to suggest that everyone else should accept my view because they would come to the same conclusion if they too took such an impartial view of the subject, that would probably inspire cries like "who's he trying to fool with such a line, as if he lacks any interest in the outcome!" or "what makes him think he's better than us!"

These limitations on public reasoning are structural rather than normative in character. In other words, they are derived from the structure of political relationships that leads us to engage in public deliberation and makes the common advantage our goal, rather than from the imposition of social norms on our habits of speaking. We deliberate in political communities because we have the capacity for reasoned speech, a capacity that, unlike mere voice, allows us to communicate to each other what we think is "advantageous and harmful, and therefore just and unjust." That is why Aristotle concludes that it is "community in these things," reasoned speeches or arguments about the advantageous and harmful, the just and unjust, that makes the political community (*Politics* 1253a). The political community is a relatively self-sufficient group of individuals that, among other things, shares in argument about what constitutes the common advantage.

Because Aristotle is so insistent that the political community exists for the sake of the good life of virtuous activity (*Politics* 1252b, 1278b, 1281a), his talk of the common advantage as the end of deliberative rhetoric strikes many readers as a "deeply provocative, even shocking" departure from the high-mindedness of the rest of his political philosophy.[13] But this impression, I believe, reflects an overly moralistic image of Aristotle's conception of political community. Once we correct that impression, it becomes clear that his description of deliberative rhetoric follows directly from his understanding of the nature of the political bond.

The political community, Aristotle famously declares, "comes into being for the sake of living, but exists for the sake of living well" (*Politics* 1252b, 1278b, 1281a). And "living well" means engaging in the life of active virtue that Aristotle associates with the good life. That does not mean, however, that while shared interests inspire us to form political communities, sharing in virtuous actions is our primary reason for sustaining them. It means, instead, that while political communities are established to serve our shared interest in staying alive and comfortable, they come to serve our shared interest in establishing the conditions—laws, moral habituation, opportunities for the exercise of prudence and the other virtues—that make it possible to lead the Aristotelian good life.[14] However high we reach in this community, it is our shared interest in making it possible to lead such a life that keeps us together. The members of a political community are bound by ties of friendship, but their friendship is a shared advantage friendship rather than the more perfect friendship of shared virtue that Aristotle celebrates in the *Nicomachean Ethics*.[15]

The partners in virtue friendships may well propose to abandon future well-being in the name of the noble and honorable life. After all, it is precisely their desire and ability to share a life of active virtue that brings such individuals together. But while virtue friends may sacrifice all for the sake of an honorable and noble life, a constitution, as Justice Holmes is said to have declared, is not a suicide pact. It is a political structure that makes it possible for large numbers of people to cooperate in projects of shared and common advantage. Aristotle has a much loftier version than Holmes and most contemporary political philosophers of the common advantage we seek in political deliberation. But it is, nonetheless, the pursuit of the common advantage that defines and structures political deliberation, as he understands it. People who propose that we abandon concerns about our future well-being are betraying the ties of friendship that bring us together as members of a political community.

Of course, there is much room for disagreement about what most contributes to the common good or advantage. Short-term gains in wealth, prestige, and power may, if achieved in dishonorable ways, undermine our long-term interests in sustaining the kind of decent and lawful community that promotes the Aristotelian good life. So when they appeal to the common good Aristotelian orators need not dress up their proposals as means of filling the city's treasuries or extending its power over its neighbors. But they do need to find ways of persuading us that their loftier vision of the common good is worth some sacrifice of wealth and power. Like opponents of torture who worry about the way it brutalizes the character of our fellow citizens or undermines our commitments to domestic restraints on political authority, they need to argue that the short-term gain is not worth the long-term risk to the institutions that nurture us. Rather than defend the right against the expedient, Aristotelian orators argue about more or less lofty conceptions of the shared interests that bring us together. That said, they cannot simply subordinate our interest in wealth and security, or in the maintenance of an imperfect regime, to our interest in maintaining the conditions of the Aristotelian good life. For without some degree of security and political stability that life is impossible. Their task is to help us make the difficult judgments about how to balance and prioritize these different components of the common good, rather than to urge us to behave in the noblest and most honorable way.

The Aristotelian Account Defended

Viewed from the perspective of recent theories of deliberative democracy, the Aristotelian understanding of political deliberation I have just outlined is bound to seem rather thin and underdeveloped. For it seems to ignore the most pressing issue for any advocate of political deliberation: the possibility that public reasoning might diminish rather than enhance the rationality of political decision making.

A defense of the Aristotelian understanding of political deliberation must therefore begin by addressing concerns about his seemingly naïve reliance on deliberative rhetoric as the characteristic form of public reasoning. If Aristotle recognizes the irrationality wrought by unconstrained forensic rhetoric, why is he not equally concerned about the potential for mischief in deliberative rhetoric? If it makes sense to try to minimize appeals to character and emotion in legal deliberation, why not try to do the same in political deliberation? In short, why does Aristotle not make more of an effort to make the form of public reasoning that he endorses more reasonable? Aristotle does not address these questions directly, since he seems to take it for granted that deliberative rhetoric as ordinarily practiced will be the form that public reasoning takes in political communities. But we can construct some reasonably Aristotelian answers in his name by reflecting on what he says about the structure and character of deliberative rhetoric.

For Aristotle public reasoning takes the form of deliberative rhetoric.

A relatively small subset of the political community take it upon themselves to persuade the rest of its members about what best serves their shared or common good.[16] As such, public reasoning rests on a crucial, but rarely examined social relationship between public speakers and their audience. For, as Susan Bickford reminds us, without public listeners as well as public speakers there can be no political deliberation. In other words, unless someone is paying attention to the arguments of public speakers and is open to the possibility of being persuaded by them, then public reasoning has no impact on deliberations about the collective actions of the political community. In public reasoning we members of a political community open ourselves up to the possibility of being persuaded by something said by the small subset of community members who compete to advise us about how to pursue our common good.[17]

The potential for irrationality on both sides of the practice of public reasoning, so understood, should be clear. Persuasive speech, as Aristotle emphasizes, is persuasive to someone (*Rhetoric* 1357a). If we are an ignorant and disorderly audience, then even the most admirable and trustworthy speakers will have to lower their sights in order to persuade us. And if public reasoning requires that we open ourselves to being persuaded by something that we hear, then it requires that even the most public-spirited among us make ourselves vulnerable to the possibility of being carried away against our interests and better judgment by the eloquence of public speakers.[18] At its best, political deliberation helps guide a public-spirited citizenry through complex and ambiguous issues. At its worst, it is a matter of the crooked leading the blind, as Plato was eager to point out.[19]

Why then is Aristotle so reluctant to impose formal and substantive constraints on the practice of deliberative rhetoric? One reason might be the threat that they pose to the social relationship upon which public reasoning rests. Public speakers make the effort to communicate their views because they believe that we are open to the possibility of being persuaded by them. Unlike the professionals that we often pay to advise us, they share with us an interest in the outcome of the issue-at-hand, and therefore seek to persuade us to do something, rather than merely lay out the options before us.[20] If they thought we were not open to the possibility of being persuaded by their arguments, then they would probably stay silent or seek coercive and/

or covert means getting their way. Similarly, as public listeners we listen to public speakers because we often need help in deliberating about important and uncertain matters (*NE* 1112b), and we are willing to make ourselves vulnerable to their rhetorical abilities to get it, at least as long as they recognize that we remain the final judges of what counts as a persuasive argument. If we thought the very act of listening to public proposals might entail their approval in some way, even when we find them unpersuasive, then we might not be so willing to offer ourselves as an audience for public reasoning. In other words, public reasoning, as Aristotle understands it, only works when we are open to persuasion by a group of public speakers who are willing to take no for an answer to their efforts.

Norms that limit the kind of arguments and proofs that should count in public reasoning threaten this social relationship between public speakers and public listeners. First of all, they undermine the openness to persuasion that encourages public speakers to speak, rather than seek more covert or coercive means of getting their way. For they suggest that we will listen to public speakers only when they argue in what we deem as a "reasonable" way. Since we listeners have no less of an interest in the outcome of political deliberations than the speakers who seek to persuade us, then the latter are bound to suspect that we are employing these standards of reasonable argument to keep the community from even considering their side of the issue.[21]

Second, the imposition of these rhetoric-limiting norms threatens to undermine our willingness to listen to public speakers by weakening their acceptance of our judgment of what counts as a persuasive argument. For they suggest that public speakers will accept our judgments of their arguments and look for ways of persuading us only when we reject their arguments in what they deem a "reasonable" manner, which suggests that we may have to *defend* our rejection of public speakers' proposals, rather than simply declare them unpersuasive. And since public speakers are no less prone to deficient and one-sided pictures of the common good than we are, we are bound to suspect that they are looking to coerce rather than persuade us when they insist that our rejection of their proposals must be reasonable. Such suspicions would only be deepened by the discovery that many of the proponents of these restraints on deliberative rhetoric identify justice and other moral norms in terms of propositions "which no one could reasonably reject"[22]—a formula that in the context of public argument might sound suspiciously like being made "an offer you can't refuse."

Arguments that no one could reasonably support or refuse a particular proposal have an important part to play in public reasoning, but as part of a practice of persuasion, not as its precondition or regulatory principle. In other words, it does not disrupt the relationship between speakers and listeners in public reasoning to complain about each other's unreasonable behavior. But it does threaten that relationship and the practice it sustains when we demand some norm of reasonableness as a condition of public engagement.

Even if I am right about the problems with introducing standards of reasonableness into the arguments made by public speakers, one might still seek to diminish public irrationality by curtailing appeals to character and emotion, the non-argumentative forms of proof. But Aristotle resists even this more limited means of improving the rationality of public reasoning. Indeed, Aristotle goes so far as to describe the appeal to character as the most effective of the three forms of proof (*Rhetoric* 1356a), a statement that I suspect many American politicians would endorse. For they know very well the advantage that reputation for good character lends to their arguments; they know how appeals that fall flat when attributed to some obscure academic can soar when they invoke Martin Luther King Jr. or the founding fathers or the wisdom of the American people.[23]

Few contemporary proponents of deliberative democracy share their enthusiasm for such appeals. Rawls takes the lead here by insisting that public reason should be governed by "precepts of reasonable discussion" that enjoin its participants from, among other things, accusing "one another of self- or group interest, prejudice or bias and of such deeply entrenched errors as ideological blindness and delusion." Attacks on character, he declares, amount to "an intellectual declaration of war" that undermines the assumption of "a certain good faith" without which we cannot deliberate together[24]—a point that Diodotus makes powerfully against Cleon in Thucydides' rendering of the Athenian debate about the fate of the Mitylenians.[25] Why does Aristotle leave room in his account of political deliberation for such a potentially disruptive practice?

First of all, it is not at all clear that Aristotle believes we can start with the assumption of a "certain good faith" on the part of citizens in most regimes.

Friends who share virtues and personal intimacy can make that assumption and therefore dispense with rhetorical celebration and unmasking of each other's character. Indeed, it would be a betrayal of their friendship, of their shared concern for each other's well-being, for intimate or virtue friends to seek to persuade each other of their good will. But the members of political communities have little reason to expect or display especially deep and genuine concern for each other's well-being. (That is not to deny that pretending that such mutual concern exists can be an extremely effective rhetorical pose, as when a speaker declares: "My friends, I have thrown away my prepared speech tonight so we can reason quietly here together, as good friends should!") What brings them together is shared advantage, the shared benefits of pooling their resources and cooperating, rather than shared virtues or mutual concern about their well-being.

If we were in a position to judge public proposal by its fruits, i.e. by its actual consequences, then abstracting from the character of its advocate would probably improve our deliberations. But since political deliberation deals with questions that, like the future consequences of our collective actions, inevitably involve uncertainty and imprecision, the character of the proposer may provide us an indispensable piece of evidence about the quality of the proposal (*Rhetoric* 1356a). For if an examination of competing proposals is not sufficient to distinguish the truly advantageous proposals from those that merely mask the self-interest of their advocates, then we are going to want to know something about the character of the people who are urging us to support them. Alcibiades was better informed and made much better judgments about political and military strategy than any of his contemporaries. But only a fool would trust him, given his extraordinarily ambitious and self-indulgent character. One wants to say, with Rawls, let us act as if Alcibiades were acting on good faith and judge his proposals on their merits—trust, but verify, to quote a more hard-headed version of the Rawlsian principle. But given the uncertainties of war and politics we can never reach definitive conclusions about such proposals, especially when we have reason to suspect that we lack some knowledge that the advocate possesses. In such circumstances, we would be foolish not to take the advocate's character into consideration, even if it sometimes leads us, as it led both the Athenians and the Spartans, to reject perfectly sound advice when it came from the mouth of someone like Alcibiades.[26]

As for appeals to the emotions, they threaten the impartiality that makes public reason reasonable for most contemporary proponents of democratic deliberation.[27] Public reason, according to their theories, should consist of propositions that "all can accept as valid,"[28] of "reasons that can be accepted by others who are similarly motivated to find reasons that can be accepted by others."[29] Emotional appeals, especially in heterogeneous communities, not only fail to meet that standard. They deflect our attention from those propositions that could meet that standard, thus deepening disagreement and social conflict. In private reason may be passion's slave, but in public impartial reasons must rule.

There is one arena in which Aristotle agrees that, for the most part, impartial reason should rule: the law court. But I would suggest that this endorsement of impartiality for adjudicators reflects his understanding of the peculiar structure of legal judgment, rather than his understanding of the practice of public reasoning in general. As already noted, legal judgment deals primarily with assessments of what others have done as opposed to judgments about what we should do in the future. And it is exercised by third parties who have no direct interest in the outcome rather than, as with political deliberation, by a group of people who share an interest in the outcome. For these reasons Aristotle urges judge and juror to ignore extraneous appeals to character and emotion, and apply the law as impartially as possible. In the law, Aristotle famously declares, reason operates without the passionate element of the soul (*Politics* 1286a). In order to apply the law to particular cases adjudicators, he suggests, should try to abstract from their passions and minimize their own judgments about the right thing to do.

But deliberation about future action is a completely different matter than deliberation about how to characterize what was done in the past. Decisions about future action, as Aristotle insists in the *Nicomachean Ethics* (1139b, 1113a), draw on an inseparable mix of desire and intellect, emotion and reason. In other words, it requires a live reason propelled by desire out into the world, rather than the dead, emotionless reason that best serves legal judgment.[30]

Aristotle underlines this point in a striking passage near the beginning of the *Rhetoric*. He suggests there, among a list of reasons that adjudicators should stick to the law and ignore the extraneous rhetoric of legal advocates, that the relative disinterestedness of adjudicators makes them the wrong people to decide what laws and actions would best serve the common advantage (*Rhetoric* 1354b).[31] Contemporary philosophers have gone to great lengths to invent and defend "devices of representation," like Rawls' original position, which are designed to help us occupy a more impartial perspective on contested political issues.[32] But Aristotle seems to believe that the occupation of this kind of impartial perspective weakens rather than improves political deliberation. For he argues that people who, like the third parties we ask to adjudicate in legal cases, lack a direct interest in the result of their deliberations are willing to entertain frivolous and illogical proposals that they would reject out of hand if they thought that they would have to live with the consequences of their decisions (*Rhetoric* 1354b).

It might seem, on the basis of the Rousseauian and Kantian precepts that inspire most contemporary theories of deliberative democracy, that the best way to identify what truly serves the common good is to abstract from our own distinctive needs and emotions and seek an impartial standpoint from which to judge the issues-at-hand—just as Aristotle recommends to adjudicators. But the application of that impartial standpoint in legal deliberation depends upon the backward looking nature of legal judgment and the existence of a preexisting rule or principle to apply to specific cases. Political deliberation lacks both of these structural features. It considers future actions and their consequences, rather than the conformity of past actions to general rules and principles. And it judges the value of different rules and principles, their contribution to the common good, rather than how to apply them to a particular set of cases. Dead reason, impartial reasoning without emotion, may be worth trying to re-create when adjudicating cases. But deliberation about what serves the common advantage requires a living reason, reasoning informed by the emotions that interest us in the consequences of our decisions. Since we need to call on our emotions help us judge the value of competing proposals, we must be willing to accept the risks that they will mislead us as well.

Conclusion

Political realists, like Aristotle, sometimes sound as if they are merely repeating "platitudes about politics." But, as Bernard Williams suggests, "that is just the point" of their approach to political theory. For they believe that "political theory should shape its account of itself more realistically to what is platitudinously politics," that the issues of political morality are structured by the social relationships and expectations that make political life possible.[33] The problem with political moralism, from this point of view, is not that it asks moral questions of politics, but that it asks the wrong moral questions.

The Aristotelian account of political deliberation developed in this paper is inspired by an insight into the nature of political community and the distinctive forms of social engagement it promotes. Most recent theories of deliberative democracy, in contrast, are inspired by the use of hypothetical and idealized processes of deliberation—as advocated in Habermas' discursive ethics or Rawls' version of social contract theory—to help us identify and justify principles of justice and other moral norms.[34] From the perspective of these theories of deliberative democracy, the Aristotelian theory is bound to look a little complacent, a little too much like a platitudinous description of the status quo. From the Aristotelian perspective, however, these theories seem insufficiently attentive to the needs and relationships that bring people together in the first place to engage in political deliberation. In particular, they fail to note the absence in political deliberation of the structure of relationships that makes impartiality a virtue in legal judgment. When we are asked to make legal judgments we are usually asked to do so as third parties judging competing characterizations of past actions. When, in contrast, we deliberate on political matters, we do so as interested parties trying to figure out the best way of achieving our shared goals. What contributes to good judgment in one case does not necessarily do so in the other. Indeed, when dealing with the uncertainties of what might most contribute to the common good, the virtues associated with impartiality may impede good judgment and threaten the relationships that allow us to deliberate together.

Such is the challenge that an Aristotelian account of political deliberation poses to contemporary theorists of deliberative democracy. Cutting out the appeals to character and emotion that loom so large in everyday deliberative rhetoric could, it suggests, undermine the very practice that these theorists seek to improve.

EDITORS' NOTE

This chapter was originally published as Bernard Yack, "Rhetoric and Public Reasoning: An Aristotelian Understanding of Public Deliberation," *Political Theory* 34:4 (2006): 417-438. Reprinted by permission of Sage Publications, Inc. The piece has been edited for length and format.

NOTES

[1.] Stephen Salkever, "The Deliberative Model of Politics and Aristotle's Ethic of Natural Questions," in *Aristotle and Modern Politics*, ed. Aristide Tessitore (South Bend, IN: University of Notre Dame Press, 2002), 342-374, 344.

[2.] Such constraints, inspired by Rawls' concept of public reason, are developed most systematically by Amy Gutmann and Dennis Thompson, *Democracy and Disagreement* (Cambridge, MA: Harvard University Press, 1996).

[3.] See Danielle Allen, *Talking to Strangers: On Little Rock and Political Friendship* (Chicago: University of Chicago Press, 2004), Chapters 9-10; Bryan Garsten, *Saving Persuasion: A Defense of Rhetoric and Judgments* (Cambridge, MA: Harvard University Press, 2006), Introduction and Chapter 5; and Paul Nieuwenberg, "Learning to Deliberate: Aristotle on Truthfulness and Public Deliberation," *Political Theory* 32:4 (2004): 449-467.

[4.] Garsten's argument (*Saving Persuasion*, Chapter 5) that Aristotle is trying to improve public reasoning by drawing our attention away from the exaggerated claims of forensic rhetoric seems quite persuasive to me, as does Nieuwenberg's point ("Learning to Deliberate," 450-452) about the way in which Aristotle relies on shame to improve the quality of deliberative rhetoric.

[5.] Bernard Williams, *In the Beginning Was the Deed: Realism and Moralism in Political Argument* (Princeton, NJ: Princeton University Press, 2005), 1-3. Realism, in this sense, refers to the social structures that make possible practices like political deliberation, rather than to Machiavellian notions about the primacy of self-interest in political life.

[6.] On this point, see Judith Squires, "Deliberation and Decision-Making," in *Democracy as Public Deliberation*, ed. Maurizio Passerin d'Entrèves (Manchester, UK: University of Manchester Press, 2002), 133-156; and Thomas Christiano, "The Significance of Public Deliberation," in *Deliberative Democracy*, eds. James Bohmann and William Rehg (Cambridge, MA: MIT Press, 1998), 243-277.

[7.] This mistake is made even by empirically focused supporters of deliberative democracy like Jon Elster. See Jon Elster, "Introduction" in *Deliberative Democracy*, ed. Jon Elster (Cambridge: Cambridge University Press, 1998), 5-6.

[8.] There is no need here to get into the controversy about exactly what Aristotle means when he suggests that deliberation concerns things that contribute toward the ends we pursue. For my own part, I agree with David Wiggins' interpretation that Aristotle is talking about things that constitute as well as produce ends. See David Wiggins, "Deliberation and Practical Reason," in *Essays on Aristotle's Ethics*, ed. Amélie O. Rorty (Berkeley, CA: University of California Press, 1980), 224-228.

[9.] Jean-Jacques Rousseau, *Emile* (New York: Basic Books, 1979), 39-40.

[10.] No doubt, when we decide what to do about our assessments of the guilt or praiseworthiness of actions, i.e. how to punish or reward individuals for what they have done, we do deliberate about the choice of future collective actions. Aristotle's point seems to be that we listen to forensic and epideictic rhetoric primarily to help us in our assessment of past behavior and character, while we listen to deliberative rhetoric primarily to help us determine the best course of action in the future.

11. Paul Nieuwenberg makes an interesting argument (in "Learning to Deliberate") about how Aristotle counts on shame as the psychological mechanism that produces improvements in the moral character of public speakers. Nieuwenberg notes how the reliance on this kind of heteronomous motive conflicts with the Kantian inclinations of most current defenders of deliberative democracy.

12. The Melians' defiance of the Athenian demand that they join the Athenian empire or face certain death might seem an exception, until one recalls that the Melians were unwilling to let the Athenians present this proposal for public debate in the assembly, for fear that it would win majority approval. (See Thucydides, *History*, Book 5, paragraphs 84-86.) Their defiance takes place, instead, in a parley of a few Melian representatives with the Athenians.

13. Robert Wardy, "Mighty Is the Truth and It Shall Prevail," in *Essays on Aristotle's Rhetoric*, ed. Amélie O. Rorty (Berkeley, CA: University of California Press, 1980), 56.

14. I defend this reinterpretation of Aristotle's understanding of political teleology in Bernard Yack, *The Problems of a Political Animal*, (Berkeley, CA: University of California Press, 1993), Chapter 3.

15. This is a controversial, though not uncommon interpretation of Aristotle's understanding of political community and political friendship, one that I develop at length in my book on conflict and community in Aristotle's political thought (Ibid., Chapters 2-4). For a critique of this interpretation, see Barbara Koziak, *Retrieving Political Emotion: Thumos, Aristotle, and Gender* (State College, PA: Penn State University Press, 2000), 110-114. For an alternative interpretation of political friendship as an advantage friendship, one that makes it less distant from Aristotle's understanding of virtue friendship than my own, see Jill Frank, *A Democracy of Distinction: Aristotle and the Work of Politics* (Princeton, NJ: Princeton University Press, 2005), Chapter 5.

16. As Gary Shiffman notes, our practice of public reasoning seems to rely on something like a norm of dissensus, the expectation that speeches will be opposed or challenged by other speeches. See Gary Shiffman, "Construing Disagreement: Consensus and Invective in 'Constitutional' Debate," *Political Theory* 30:2 (2002): 175-203. In order to make clear how much we rely on such a norm, imagine how suspicious we would become if political leaders with very different backgrounds and interests were always agreeing with each other publicly: their agreement would suggest that some conspiracy was afoot, that they're not doing the job we sent them there to do.

17. Susan Bickford, *The Dissonance of Democracy* (Ithaca, NY: Cornell University Press, 1996), 4-5. Bickford develops this important argument partly through an interpretation (in Chapter 1) of Aristotle's understanding of political deliberation.

18. Ibid., 48.

19. Plato makes this case in his famous turn on the "ship of state" metaphor in the *Republic*, 488-489.

20. So while Harvey Yunis, *Taming Democracy* (Ithaca, NY: Cornell University Press, 1996), 12-13, is right to describe Aristotelian orators as advisors, it is important to note they are advisors who share our interest in outcome of the issue at hand; hired advisors, like lawyers and other consultants, do not share our interest in this way. The former therefore have an interest in persuading us that the latter do not.

21. See Stanley Fish, "Mutual Respect as a Device of Exclusion," in *Deliberative Politics: Essays on Democracy and Disagreement*, ed. Stephen Macedo (Oxford: Oxford University Press), 88-102, 90-91.

22. As in T. M. Scanlon's influential reformulation of Rawlsian contractualism, "Contractualism and Utilitarianism," in *Utilitarianism and Beyond*, eds. Amartya Sen and Bernard Williams (Cambridge: Cambridge University Press, 1982).

23. Similarly, they know the value of negative character appeals, as when someone invokes Hitler's campaigns against smoking to undermine support for regulation of the tobacco industry. In *Natural Right and History* (Chicago: University of Chicago Press, 1953), 42-43, Leo Strauss dubs this rhetorical move the "*reductio ad Hitlerum*."

24. John Rawls, "The Domain of the Political and the Overlapping Consensus," *NYU Law Journal* 64 (1989): 233-255, 238-239.

25. Thucydides, *History*, Book 3, paragraphs 32-34.

26. The Athenians' difficulty with getting sound advice from their leaders, given their well-justified suspicions of their leaders' motives is an important theme in Thucydides' *History*.

27. On this point, see especially Melissa S. Williams, "The Uneasy Alliance of Group Representation and Deliberative Democracy," in *Citizenship in Diverse Societies*, eds. Will Kymlicka and Wayne Norman (Oxford, 2000), 124-146, 128-129.

28. Ibid., 127.

29. Gutmann and Thompson, *Democracy and Disagreement*, 52-53.

30. See Martha Nussbaum, "The Discernment of Perception: An Aristotelian Conception of Private and Public Rationality," in *Love's Knowledge* (New York: Oxford University Press, 1990), 54-105; and Gisela Striker, "Emotions in Context: Aristotle's Treatment of the Emotions in the *Rhetoric* and his Moral Psychology," in *Essays on Aristotle's Rhetoric,* ed. Amélie O. Rorty (Berkeley, CA: University of California Press, 1996), 286-302, 297-298.

31. Bryan Garsten presents an especially insightful discussion of this passage in *Saving Persuasion* (125-129), where he defends Aristotle's view of what he describes as "situated judgment."

32. See Michael Saward, "Rawls and Deliberative Democracy," in *Democracy as Public Deliberation*, ed. Maurizio Passerin D'Entrèves (Piscataway, NJ: Transaction Publishers, 2006), 112-132, for a good discussion of how these impartiality inducing devices of representation color contemporary visions of deliberative democracy.

33. Williams, *In the Beginning Was the Deed*, 13.

34. As Michael Saward suggests, were it not for the connection to these two highly influential philosophical theories, it is not at all clear that democratic deliberation would be on the agenda for contemporary moral and political philosophers. See Michael Saward, "Rawls and Deliberative Democracy," 112.

Difference Democracy: The Consciousness-Raising Group Against the Gentlemen's Club

by John S. Dryzek

Large sections of the intellectual left of the English-speaking developed countries turned in the 1990s to the politics of identity and difference, which could find support from postmodern thinking in social theory and literary criticism. This turn coincided with an increasingly bleak assessment of the prospects for socialism, or even substantial material redistribution, in any foreseeable future. Progressive politics could, however, be redefined in terms of the emancipation of a growing list of excluded minorities, defined on the basis of gender, race, ethnicity, sexuality, age, disability, as well as social class. The agents of oppression were often treated in cultural terms, but political (and occasionally economic) structures could also be condemned. Much to the surprise of its proponents, deliberative democracy too came to be accused of complicity in the oppression of difference.

Difference democrats are those who stress the need for democratic politics to concern itself first and foremost with the recognition of the legitimacy and validity of the particular perspectives of historically oppressed segments of the population. Quite what form this politics should take is a matter of continuing debate, as we shall see shortly. Thus the difference democrats are not a self-consciously unified school of thought (a uniformity which would in any case subvert their emphasis on variety). Some stress isolated acts of resistance, others want to replace class struggle with an oppositional politics of unity in diversity. Some propose reform of governmental structures of representation, others scorn the state. Some are self-consciously postmodernist or poststructuralist, others eschew high theory. What they all share is a stress on the variety of oppressions and so subject-positions, leading them to oppose ostensibly neutral rationalistic practices that in practice exclude or silence particular kinds of oppressed subjects.

The case against deliberative democracy here is that its focus on a particular kind of supposedly reasonable political interaction is not in fact neutral, but systematically excludes a variety of voices from effective participation in democratic politics. This charge is the opposite of that made by social choice theorists, who fear that deliberative democracy opens the door to an unmanageable proliferation of participants and positions. Where social choice theorists sees dangerous variety, difference democrats see dangerous uniformity. Before I address their critique in a bit more detail, let me lay out in a bit more detail what difference democracy means, and how it relates to the politics of identity.

Models of Difference Democracy

The question of difference as it arises in politics is normally paired with the concept of identity: individuals and groups find their identity only in establishing their differences with others who represent what the individual or group in question is not.[1] In this light, questions of identity and difference can extend to religious fundamentalism and even ethnic warfare, but difference democrats have in mind much more civil and constrained processes. The identities at issue generally relate to social class, culture, nationality, ethnicity, sexuality, and gender, though the list is open-ended.

A case that processes oriented to the exploration of identity and difference should encompass pretty much all we mean by democracy is made by William Connolly.[2] Connolly operates within a postmodern idiom, and so opposes any tendency to assertion or recognition of any fixed and timeless identities (of the sort that fundamentalists and essentialists from many points on the political spectrum, not just the religious or nationalist right, trade in). Instead, identities and their associated differences should be treated as a matter for continuous exploration, receiving at best only conditional and contingent statement. Democratic politics in this light should involve the creative questioning of identities through encounter with disparate others. This is not a deadly struggle, more a matter of play; what matters is that the game never ends. Thus a ludenic attitude on the part of participants is crucial: they must be prepared to question the complexities and ambiguities of their own identities as well as those of others.

Connolly is realistic enough to recognize that such an attitude is not widely shared in a world where the assertion of identity and questioning of the identity of others is frequently treated in deadly serious terms, even within developed liberal democracies. "Only when both of the hands holding our necks in the grip of resentment are loosened can the politics of agonal democracy be enhanced. Today existential resentments and resentments against injustice in the social distribution of opportunities, resources, sacrifices, and burdens combine to tighten the grip of dogmatism upon the life of identity."[3] To former US Secretary of the Interior James Watt, one could not be an environmentalist and an American; ultimately Watt averred that environmentalists should be defeated using the cartridge box rather than the ballot box or jury box.[4] To conservative Christians, denial of feminist and gay identities is integral to their own identity, an article of dogma.

In addition to such obstacles in the world as it stands, Connolly allows that there are material inequalities that have to be remedied before the desired democratic attitudes can be activated. Thus Connolly in the end regards his prescriptive democratic theory as a hope for a better world, but of little contemporary practical applicability. Perhaps the experience of American university life in the 1990s bears Connolly out. The politics of identity and difference pervades campus life, but it is generally accompanied by dogmatism and resentment, on the part of those asserting identities as well as those denying them.

Other difference democrats share Connolly's interpretation of the democratic life, but not his resignation in the face of a recalcitrant world. Instead, they link the negotiation of identity and difference to resistance to a dominant political order that represses difference. Such theorists often write in the shadow of socialism, while recognizing that struggles must be plural, as opposed to socialism's one big struggle. Yet if there is no longer one big struggle, there remains for these theorists one big opponent: the liberal capitalist political order. Thus the politics of identity and difference are played out not just in the unconstrained open-ended interaction of a variety of selves, their identities, and their others, but rather in a conflict with this one opponent.

Marxists would have conceptualized this struggle in material terms; post-Marxists such as Chantal Mouffe conceptualize it in discursive terms.[5] Mouffe identifies herself as a poststructuralist (as well as a postmodernist) and so a supporter of Michel Foucault. To Foucault, the established order is at any particular time represented by discourses which condition the way people communicate and think. Foucault himself elucidated in great detail the history (or genealogy) of discourses surrounding sexuality, criminality, health, disease, and mental illness, with the intent of exposing the way these discourses simultaneously both constitute and oppress subjects. But oppressive discourses make themselves felt in different ways in different situations. Thus for Foucault there is no hope for any grand project of resistance (of the Marxist sort), only for local resistances; for example, for a group of individuals to refuse their categorization as mentally ill.

Mouffe has greater hopes for the summation of local resistances into some larger radical politics that opposes the discursive order of liberal capitalism. This politics would constitute what she and Ernesto Laclau call a "radical and plural democracy" composed of the variety of self-defined struggles and movements that respond to the multiple oppressions generated by the dominant order.[6] Such a democracy would pervade social and cultural life, rather than orient itself exclusively to the state.[7] At the heart of this democracy would be a politics of identity and difference that contests any attempts to impose universal identities, including supposedly "rational" and "neutral" ones advanced by liberal political theorists such as Rawls.[8] Less neutral but still rational and universal identities such as those once sought by Marxists are also ruled out. There is an irony here, because the realization of "radical and plural democracy" would seem to require the persistence of the unified dominant liberal capitalist order and its multiple oppressions. No liberal capitalism means no oppressions means no radical and plural democracy.

Not all difference democrats connect their efforts to radical resistance to the liberal capitalist order; some believe this order can be reformed from within to better accommodate difference. Thus Anne Phillips calls for a "politics of presence" as opposed to a "politics of ideas," in which efforts are made to ensure the presence of members of disadvantaged groups in the institutions of liberal democracy, such as parliament.[9] Such presence is needed because only members of these groups have the capacity to give authentic voice to the exclusions and oppressions they have experienced. Attuned to the danger of essentializing particular identities, in the end Phillips is confident enough only to recommend quotas in parliament for women, on the grounds that "women" is an inclusive category that itself contains a number of different identities.[10] Women who thus enter parliament are not constrained to be only women in terms of what they represent; they can also be working class women, or middle-class women, or black women, or white women, and so forth. Phillips also endorses Lani Guinier's suggestions for an electoral system with multi-member constituencies and a system of cumulative voting, with a quota much less than 50 percent of the total votes needed to elect a candidate.[11] Each citizen would have a number of votes that he or she could divide among candidates, or cast them all for a single candidate. By concentrating their votes on a single candidate, members of a minority group could get a representative elected.

Guinier's proposals constitute a better response to the charge of essentializing identity than do Phillips's quotas. While Guinier is interested mainly in promoting the organization and representation of racial and ethnic minorities, the system of cumulative voting itself is actually neutral when it comes to the kinds of groups that will be induced to mobilize for representation (indeed, it could promote the mobilization of racists and rednecks). This system would encourage the formation of groups in general, also of coalitions that transcend traditional group boundaries (for example, when two ethnic minorities are too small to mobilize enough votes for a representative each, but together could mobilize the threshold number of votes). Thus as identities change, the character of the representatives can change too.[12] If particular differences, for example class differences, are ever erased, then groups representing those differences will simply fade from view.

More substantial adjustments to representation within the liberal state are advocated by Iris Young, who argues that disadvantaged groups should have not just representatives, but also guarantees of consultation, and veto power over policies that affect them.[13] Any suggestion of veto power should be greeted with alarm by anyone who has contemplated the workings of voting systems. If group A is allowed to veto policy X while group B is allowed to veto policy "not X" then the result is deadlock that privileges the status quo, which is presumably not what Young has in mind. Thus some means of softening the idea of veto needs to be found if group representation is to have any practical purchase.

For Young, the politics of difference involves recognition of the group by the state, as well as respect and affirmation across groups in civil society. Like Mouffe, Young begins with a critique of liberalism's universalizing tendencies that in practice repress group difference and mask exclusions. The list of repressed groups to be granted privileged representation will vary for different societies and times. For her own United States circa 1990, it encompasses "women, blacks, Native Americans, old people, poor people, disabled people, gay men and lesbians, Spanish-speaking Americans, young people, and nonprofessional workers."[14] Aware of postmodern warnings against essentializing group identity, Young emphasizes the fact that (oppressive) circumstances beyond its own choosing create the category from which the group then springs.[15] Thus people need not adopt any essential and fixed identity, but only respond to the shared histories and circumstances in which they find themselves. Indeed, Young resists the use of the term *identity* because it connotes an assertion of essential and unshakeable characteristics, as opposed to the multiple possibilities with which individuals may be faced by virtue of the circumstances into which they are thrown. "I have only my own identity, fashioned in relation to my multiple group positionings."[16] Like most difference democrats, Young believes that particular identities should be validated. But it is important to recognize that some differences are disabling, so that they merit elimination rather than validation. Class differences would be the obvious example here.[17]

Does Deliberation Repress Difference?

Support for difference does not have to entail hostility to deliberation. For example, Anne Phillips embraces deliberative democracy, while recognizing the tension between the group interests she believes should always be present and the idea that deliberators should be compelled only by what they hear in the forum.[18] However, the difference democrats' suspicion of universal rationality claims has led some of them to attack deliberative democracy. It is these critics I will focus on here. I shall begin with a poststructural critique of democracy in general, for it is this which acts as the outer boundary for the difference democracy critique of deliberation in particular, and so puts the latter in particularly sharp focus.

Poststructuralists follow Michel Foucault in their suspicion of any dominant discourse, because they believe that discourses are the taken-for-granted assumptions that constitute subjects and so subjugate them to power. Fewer discourses today seem more dominant than that of democracy, not just among political thinkers, but also within nearly all the world's regimes, including some very dubious ones. Concerning the way Western political systems have come to be ordered, Foucault himself stressed the idea of a "governmentality" which constitutes subjects in ways that make them amenable to government control.[19] Such control comes not through overt coercion or compulsion of any sort, simply through the basic assumptions about politics that people come to share which make them compliant subjects of political regimes. In this light, the contemporary hegemony of the discourse of democracy is just the latest phase of governmentality.

Taking a look at the rise of democracy in the modern era, Barry Hindess believes that modern political thought and practice could only let go of absolute monarchy once the people were suitably subdued.[20] The threat of force or legal sanction is not crucial here, because the practice of democracy itself contains a variety of mechanisms for taming people. One prominent strand in democratic thinking associated with John Stuart Mill stresses the developmental or educative benefits of participation. But on Hindess' interpretation, these developmental effects have a disciplinary function. For example, individuals called upon to chair meetings must set aside personal convictions; and a quorum will discipline attendance. When it comes to deliberation in particular, "actual participation in … deliberations often requires a considerable degree of self-restraint, an ability and a willingness to conceal one's own views and a capacity to deal peacefully with periods of boredom and intense frustration."[21] Thus deliberation promotes oppressive self-control.

In this light, democracy acts as a disciplining force by constructing individual identities in ways that make individuals willing participants in and supporters of political systems which can in the end only foreclose their opportunities. Connors applies this kind of analysis to democratic reform in Thailand. Such reform, he argues, is designed to create new kinds of "democratic" subjects, more conducive to a liberal constitutionalist political order.[22] This order in turn finds its real justification in being functional for the liberal capitalist political economy developing in Thailand, replacing older traditions of clientelism and deference. Individuals have the impression of choice and participation in control, but they are being constituted to behave in a particular fashion.

Hindess for his part intimates no escape from the disciplinary discourse of democracy, and in this he is arguably more Foucauldian than Foucault. In his later years, Foucault became increasingly attuned to the possibility of

reflective choice across discourses, and that some discourses were more con-
sensual and less oppressive than others.[23] But for Hindess, all that seems to
remain is a resigned acceptance of the status quo, which can be condemned
but not changed.

While Hindess emphasizes the universally oppressive character of participation in deliberation and democratic processes more generally, he allows
that some people are disciplined more than others, such that deliberation
can reinforce existing political hierarchies. Critiques of deliberative democracy that build upon this claim are developed by the difference democrats
Lynn Sanders and Iris Young. Their basic charge is that deliberation represents a particular kind of communication: dispassionate, reasoned, and logical. The problem is that "some citizens are better than others at articulating
their arguments in rational, reasonable terms."[24] Young for her part allows
that deliberative democrats have stressed the importance of incorporating
as wide as possible a variety of individuals in deliberative processes (Sanders
is not so generous), but nonetheless argues that deliberative democrats have
ignored what she calls the "internal exclusion" entailed by an emphasis on
deliberation.[25]

How do exclusion and oppression work within the deliberative setting?
To Sanders, it is partly that some people are good at making arguments
and so likely to be heard, while others are less likely to be listened to.[26] She
points to work on American juries which suggests that when their compo-
sition is mixed they tend to be dominated by white, well-educated men.[27]
Sanders argues that "Prejudice and privilege do not emerge in deliberative
settings as bad reasons, and they are not countered by good arguments. They
are sneaky, invisible and pernicious for that reasonable process." But her essential argument need not rest on such questionable empirical assertions.
Rather, the key is that deliberative virtues of civility have a sedative effect
that curbs unruly behavior on the part of the disadvantaged. "Deliberation
is a request for a certain kind of talk: rational, constrained, and oriented to a
shared problem." Moreover, she argues, public reason's emphasis on interests
that can be shared or at least understood by all in practice universalizes the
interests of the wealthy and powerful, while simultaneously erasing the particular experiences and interests of poor and powerless minorities. In short,
"learning to deliberate in America might be inseparable from indoctrination
in familiar routines of hierarchy and deference."[28]

In reading Sanders it is sometimes hard to disentangle the critique of deliberation as such from the critique of how deliberation plays out in the context of a particular unjust political system, that of liberal democracy in the United States. Iris Young's critique is more sharply focused on deliberation as such. Invoking Lyotard's postmodern concept of "différence," she argues that deliberative frameworks for conflict resolution are systematically skewed when they operate in the idiom of one of the parties to the conflict, while the suffering of the other cannot even be expressed in that idiom.[29] The problem here, then, is one of deliberation requiring common premises; but in a world of difference, neutral shared premises are hard to find. Those liberals from Kant to Rawls who have articulated such supposedly neutral premises have in fact only reproduced the standards of a particular political order.[30] Deliberative democracy is charged by Young with privileging certain kinds of speech and so certain kinds of power: speech that is "assertive and confrontational," "formal and general," "dispassionate and disembodied." The first of these in particular advantages stereotypically male as opposed to female speaking styles. Deliberation is not in this light open problem solving, but a confrontation in which there are winners and losers. For all three kinds, "these differences of speech privilege correlate with other differences of social privilege," while disadvantaging "the speech culture of women and minorities."[31]

The other main problem with deliberative democracy for Young is its impetus toward unity. For communitarians, that unity is specified in advance by a common tradition. For liberals and critical theorists, the unity is more likely to be reasoned toward rather than specified in advance. Young believes that the former is vitiated by the fact of difference, the latter likely to reach a definition of the common good that favors the privileged.[32]

The force of all these criticisms of deliberation remains something of an open question pending sustained empirical investigation of the degree to which the claims about what actually happens in deliberation actually do describe reality. Are particular kinds of people in reality better than others at arguing in rational terms? Is it really the case that prejudice and privilege are never uncovered and opposed by good argument? Is learning to participate in deliberation really the same as indoctrination in hierarchy? Is an individual's capacity to deliberate really directly proportional to social standing? Is Young's "speech culture of women and minorities" really disadvantaged in deliberation? The answer to all these questions is that we do not know. So however plausible these claims might seem, their assertion on the part of theorists is no substitute for their empirical investigation in the context of actual cases of deliberation. A body of work does exist that investigates talk in groups, looking at issues such as who talks most, who interrupts most and gets interrupted most.[33] But to the best of my knowledge none of this work addresses directly the propositions advanced by difference democrats about deliberation in particular.

Sanders and Young both argue for kinds of communication other than deliberation. For Sanders, the ideal is testimony, or telling one's own story in one's own language, rather than in the constrained language of deliberation. Rap music is one such kind of testimony. She claims that testimony is "radically egalitarian," though presumably some people are capable of giving better testimonials than others.[34] Testimony is similar to one of Young's three alternative forms of communication, storytelling. Storytelling "reveals the particular experiences of those in social locations, experiences that cannot be shared by those situated differently but that they must understand in order to do justice to the others" and "exhibits subjective experience to other subjects."[35] Examples here would include women's' stories about the sexual harassment they have experienced.

Young's other two forms of alternative communication are greeting and rhetoric. Greeting involves more or less elaborate recognition of the presence of others, not just at the outset of an encounter, but in expressions of politeness and concern for the well-being of others as the encounter proceeds. In this way, others can be welcomed into the communicative circle, and trust established.[36] Greeting means that the individuals in question can henceforth be treated as subjects in debate, rather than objects of discussion. Greeting resonates with the difference democrats' concern with recognition of identity of the other; it also plays a large part in international diplomacy.[37]

Rhetoric involves context-specific attention to the way points are made, with the intention of reaching the perspective of particular listeners and persuading them. Speech without rhetoric can be flat, unpersuasive, boring. Speech with rhetoric can involve jokes, anger, laughter, ridicule, flattery, and hyperbole.[38] Some contemporary deliberative democrats, notably Chambers, Spragens, and Habermas, do indeed want to purge rhetoric from deliberation, on the grounds that rhetoric can open the door to demagogues, manipulators, deceivers, and flatterers.[39] Young argues in contrast that rhetoric can be used to draw attention to previously marginalized concerns, to reach categories of people traditionally excluded from discussion by couching points in terms familiar to them, and to force action on a problem or issue.[40]

If greeting, rhetoric, and storytelling are to meet Young's great expectations of them, then it needs to be demonstrated that they do not simply generate other kinds of hierarchy. Young argues that some people are better at argument than others; in the societies with which she is familiar, she believes that the best arguers are well-educated white males. Yet similar differentials can conceivably apply to these other three types of communication. Demagogues might on average be the best rhetoricians. Public relations experts and extrovert Americans who have read books on the habits of highly effective people might be the best greeters. Graduates of creative writing programs and those with lots of accumulated experience might be the best storytellers. The empirical validity of Young's claims about the degree to which these three forms of communication equalize across difference depends on the hierarchies within argument, greeting, rhetoric, and storytelling compensating for, rather than reinforcing, one another.

Any such hierarchies associated with alternative forms of communication notwithstanding, difference democrats have placed some serious question marks next to deliberative democracy. Thus we need to determine the degree to which deliberative democracy must stress rational argument, and the extent to which it can and should admit alternative forms of communication. This will help determine how deliberation might best accommodate the fact of radically different identities and subject positions. I will now try to show that effective responses to the difference democrats' critique can be crafted.

Deliberating across Difference

If the recognition of difference means simply the recognition of the different kinds of communication enumerated by Young, then the solution might at first sight appear to be simple: let them in! For greeting, rhetoric, and storytelling on the one hand and familiar forms of argument on the other are not mutually exclusive, and can coexist in any real discursive setting.[41]

This accommodating reaction is in fact too easy. A more defensible response is that all forms of communication should only ever be admitted conditionally. There are two tests that can be applied. First, any communication that involves coercion or the threat of coercion should be excluded. Second, any communication that cannot connect the particular to the general should be excluded.[42] These two tests can be applied to any form of communication, be it storytelling, testimony, rhetoric, greeting—and even argument. My introduction of these tests for the various kinds of communication is not to rule any of them out in blanket terms. To use the language of Foucault, "My point is not that everything is bad, but that everything is dangerous."[43] Advocates of the alternative forms are generally blind to the dangers. So let me give some examples of how each form of communication can fail on the two tests, and consider what might be done about such failure.

Storytelling and Testimony

Storytelling is a coercive form of communication when group norms constrain the range of acceptable stories. For Young, the paradigm of a forum hospitable to storytelling is the consciousness-raising group, in which members "identify one another, and identify the basis of their affinity" through telling stories about their own experience.[44] But there is a danger that such groups will require correct storylines, and punish incorrect ones which cannot easily withstand the normalizing gaze of the group. The storyline must begin with oppression whose character is not recognized by the victim, and proceed through recognition of the oppression to the search for a need to contextualize that realization in a more general framework. Such disciplining of story lines is not of course unique to consciousness-raising groups.[45] It can be found equally in fundamentalist religions, where the newcomer to the group must offer a story based on past sin leading to realization of God's mercy and the hope for redemption; and the bigger the sin, the better the story. Disciplined stories may also be required in particular kinds of therapy, in order to fit the theoretical framework of the therapist.

Turning to the second test, if an individual's story is purely about that individual then there is no political point in hearing it. The reason the consciousness-raising group or the religious sect wants to hear stories is because they illustrate the general situation of those in the group. When it comes to deliberation beyond the particular group the tests are a bit more demanding: the story must be capable of resonating with individuals who do not share that situation—but do share other characteristics (if only a common humanity). Thus a truly effective story about a particular repression will also involve implicit appeal to more universal standards. The story of a refugee from a war zone may be full of harrowing episodes particular to the conflict in question, perhaps the repression of a particular ethnic group. But such stories are moving precisely because they involve gross violation of more general standards of human dignity, not because listeners have to identify with the oppressed ethnicity in question. The latter is likely only to perpetuate cycles of revenge.

Greeting

Greeting at first sight might seem an innocuous form of communication, perhaps even a necessary beginning for the recognition of other parties to communication. Yet greeting too can be coercive. Think, for example, of the bone-crushing handshake. The New Zealand national rugby team, the All Blacks, always precedes its matches with the *haka*, a Maori greeting ceremony designed to intimidate opponents. Greeting can also fail to connect the particular to the general. For example, the secret handshakes of Freemasons are presumably designed to mark them off immediately from other people, and establish an exclusive communicative relationship (in some cases, such as the British police and judiciary, or the P2 Lodge that was long part of Italy's "invisible government," one with real political force).

Rhetoric

Rhetoric can be coercive when it is deployed by demagogues and emotional manipulators, which is precisely why some deliberative democrats (such as Habermas, Chambers, and Spragens) wish to purge it. Think, for example, of the power of Nazi rhetoric, and the fate awaiting those who were not swayed by it. Rhetoric can raise the emotional stakes by casting issues in terms of threats to the core identity of the group, especially when it is defined on ethnic or national lines. Less dramatically, when an expert recites his or her credentials in order to silence lay criticism, that is also rhetorical coercion.

According to Miller, rhetoric requires a context of a community of like-minded people, taking force only "when people are united in their aims," igniting their passions and making it less likely that their differences with those outside the group can be resolved.[46] If so, then by definition rhetoric must always fail in its capacity to connect the particular with general. However, rhetoric can also be effective in making appeals across different frames of reference, perhaps with a view to their reconciliation, or the expansion of a particular frame. Good rhetoric on behalf of the disadvantaged can induce a sense of the need for redress on the part of the powerful. The rhetoricians of the Civil Rights Movement in the United States in the 1960s, notably Martin Luther King Jr., deployed exactly this kind of rhetorical capacity to good effect. Rhetoric oriented to reciprocal understanding is often essential in reaching others when simple argument cannot. One of the most important "others" to be reached will often be those with access to the levers of governmental power. Rhetoric can enable transmission to the state of public opinion formed in the public sphere, without that transmission requiring subordination to strategic action, such as that entailed in voting and elections.

Argument

At first, it is perhaps less easy to see how argument can be coercive. If an argument is backed by a threat, then it is not really argument at all. For if only one side can make credible threats, then the kind of communication at issue is more like command, while if both sides can make threats, then the situation is one of bargaining rather than arguing. Habermas speaks of "the forceless force of the better argument," which is why he values argument above other forms of communication. Yet argument is only forceless if all the individuals involved share an equal communicative competence: the capacity to raise and challenge validity claims. When such equality does not hold, then in practice some individuals will be able to make their arguments prevail as a result of denial of access to the premises of argument to other individuals. Indeed, this is the basic worry of the difference democrats who first challenged deliberation's stress on argument: that *in practice* it involves communication in the terms set by the powerful, who almost by definition are those best able to articulate their arguments in terms of the dominant speech culture of a society. It is this speech culture that will often be embedded in the informal and formal rules of dominant institutions.

Coercion in argument occurs as a result of failure to connect the particular to the general—or, rather, the suppression of any challenge to the particular. For example, if a supreme court rules that a law must be struck down because it contravenes the constitution, that is an argument in terms of the particular. The constitution may be unfair to a particular group in society— for example, if it specifies the sanctity of private property, thus disadvantaging those who have little or no property. If deliberation ends with "because this is what the constitution says," rather than allowing the challenge "but should the constitution mean this?" then it has failed the second test. Legalistic forums are especially problematic in the restrictions they impose upon admissible argument and so free dialogue. But similar logic can be applied to argument that ends with appeal to the authority of tradition, precedent, or supposed laws of nature. Of course, this does not mean that to pass the test of connecting the particular to the general argument must always be taken to philosophical first principles. All it means is that challenges should not be foreclosed.

Argument too can, then, be coercive, and fail to connect the particular to the general. Yet argument is also capable of exposing these failings—in itself, but also in testimony, greeting, and rhetoric. If a group censors storylines, the way to overcome that censorship could be to tell an unacceptable story—but if impasse then results, argument can break the logjam through discussion of the grounds for admitting stories. If a greeting is aggressive, it can be challenged with a hug; or by an argument about aggression. If rhetoric whips up passion directed against an out-group, that can be challenged by more inclusive rhetoric—but also by an argument pointing to the consequences of exclusion.

When it comes to the key question, what is to be done? about communicative failures of the kind I have discussed here, argument always plays a central role. When it comes to what is to be done? in terms of collective action in response to a social problem, argument also must enter. Thus argument always has to be central to deliberative democracy. The other forms can be present, and there are good reasons to welcome them, but their status is a bit different because they do not *have* to be present.

At this juncture I conclude that deliberative democracy can cope with the issue of difference by conditionally admitting a variety of forms of communication, as well as being attuned to plurality in subject positions and associated ways of life. Thus critics who charge that deliberative democracy "posits a simplistic opposition between private interest and general interest" are mistaken;[47] partial interests intermediate between the private and the general can be recognized. Deliberative democrats themselves have long recognized and grappled with the issue of plurality.[48] Thus Iris Young's observation that for all such theorists "the goal of deliberation is to arrive at consensus" is simply wrong.[49] Even Habermas, who has clung to the ideal of consensus longest and hardest, long ago recognized the practical difficulties that precluded the realization of consensus in practice.[50] (Young's observation also fits oddly with her claim on the very next page—equally mistaken in my view—that "Deliberation is competition. Parties to dispute aim to win the argument, not to achieve mutual understanding."[51] This claim grounds deliberation in strategic rationality, as opposed to the communicative rationality that underwrites discursive democracy.) Some notion of reasoned agreement that allows for different individuals to retain different reasons for subscribing to an agreement is widely held among deliberative democrats. However, this notion of reasoned agreement as opposed to consensus does call into question Rawls' reliance on a unitary public reason.[52] In this Rawlsian language, Bohman points out that the solution is to think of public reason as itself "plural," such that "agents can come to an agreement with one another for *different* publicly accessible reasons."[53]

Deliberative democracy need not fear difference, let alone repress difference. Indeed, were it not for difference, deliberation would be a very dull affair, a conversation among those who had already settled upon basics. As Phillips puts it, "Deliberation matters only because there is difference."[54] Many of the most fundamental questions confronting a polity entail confrontations with difference of some kind, be it in terms of nationality, social class, gender, ethnicity, or ecological situation. Schlosberg can argue with justification that "Deliberative democracy is the procedure of a revived pluralism. As such, I read much of the literature of deliberative democracy as designs for the intersubjective banquet that both James and Connolly imagine."[55] The kind of pluralism to which Schlosberg is referring here is the critical strand, that begins with William James' century-old account of how the variety of ways in which human beings can experience the world must be accommodated in an open and evolving political order. This strand covers William Connolly's more recent pluralism of agonistic respect across difference. (Such critical pluralism is very different from the mid-century celebration of the range of competing interest groups in the United States by pluralists such as David Truman, Edward Banfield, Nelson Polsby, and Robert Dahl—who later changed his mind.) While endorsing Schlosberg's observation here, I would note in passing that deliberative democracy is more interested in the production of collective outcomes in problem-solving contexts than is Connolly, such that the fit may not be quite as comfortable as Schlosberg believes.

Conceiving of deliberative democracy in terms of an intersubjective banquet should also help allay the fears of Foucauldians such as Barry Hindess, which I introduced earlier, even though it could never banish those fears entirely (nor could any political theory). Hindess, recall, portrays deliberation in the image of a committee meeting in which individuals restrain themselves, conceal their views, and subject themselves to boredom and frustration. Deliberation may have moments like this; but then all forms of political life fall short of a perpetual carnival. An expansive notion of deliberation across difference is probably better than most kinds of politics at constituting subjects in non-oppressive ways.

Difference as the Contest of Discourses

Deliberative democrats should not simply rest here and congratulate themselves on their ability to accommodate difference. James' intersubjective banquet serves only diners who will not throw food at each other or seek to banish beggars from the table.[56] Similarly, Connolly's hopes for agonistic respect extend to people differently situated—but who are enlightened enough to reject dogmatism and sectarianism, and to open themselves to engagement with others. That is why Connolly sees little possibility for the adoption of his prescriptive model of democracy in contemporary circumstances, where identities linked to the denial of respect loom large.

Here, it is noteworthy that Schlosberg's paradigm for deliberation across difference is the US environmental justice movement and its network form of organization.[57] Yet whatever the differences the movement accommodates when it comes to race, urban/rural location, ethnicity, or even social class, the recognition and respect that the movement achieves is, at least in the first instance, among those with a common interest in fighting the environmental risks imposed upon them. Unlike many difference democrats, Schlosberg also highlights the character of the interactions that the movement seeks to establish with governmental and corporate actors with no commitment to or interest in communication across difference. Here the record is more mixed. Participants in the movement have often insisted on interactions with such actors that involve mutual respect rather than condescension, substantive rather than symbolic participation in decisions. Such insistence often meets with resistance from state and corporate actors. This situation illustrates the fact that there is another half to the problem of identity and difference: what to do in deliberative terms about oppressive identities and discourses, and those that appear in locations other than the "progressive" end of the political spectrum. Difference democrats invoke the image of the gentlemen's club in criticizing the excessively civil image of deliberation. If they have replaced the gentlemen's club only with the consciousness-raising group, that is not good enough.

A serious response to the challenge of difference requires an account of democracy that can address difference across repressive and emancipatory identities and discourses, both of which will populate political life for the foreseeable future. Here I believe it is useful to introduce the account of the public sphere, which highlights contestation across discourses rather than engagement across identities, and so establish a link to discursive democracy as opposed to liberal constitutionalist deliberative democracy. There is of course a tight connection between discourses and identities, which are constituted in whole or part by discourses. Discourses, recall, are shared sets of assumptions and capabilities that enable their adherents to assemble bits of sensory input into coherent wholes, or organize them around coherent storylines. One way of interpreting the whole idea of difference is therefore in terms of discourses rather than identities.

A hard-line Foucauldian usage of the discourse concept (as deployed, for example, by Hindess) treats discourses in hegemonic terms. In this light, a discourse is not just a partial view of the world, but something that constitutes even seemingly competing views (such as, for example, market liberal and social democratic viewpoints on capitalist political economy). Yet however hegemonic discourses may have been historically, *our* age—enlightened in part by Foucauldian exposés of the power of particular discourses!—is home to a variety of discourses about which people can be aware. This awareness does not mean that Foucauldian hegemony must be discarded in favor of an Enlightenment universalism that can scrutinize all assumptions and storylines. Rather, it recognizes that discourses are powerful because they can and do constitute identities; yet reflective comparisons across discourse boundaries can, if only occasionally and with some effort, be made.[58]

This interpretation of the public sphere in terms of the contestation of discourses has the advantage of being able to address the question of what to do about repressive or recalcitrant discourses. Think, for example of the discourse of market liberalism, which constructs individuals as consumers, profit-maximizers, and rent-seekers. Or racist discourses with elaborate constructions of reasons for the denial of interracial equality. Or Leninist discourses which subordinate absolutely everything to the strategic struggle for revolution, with a grim fate for deviants from the party line. Or a "realist" discourse of anarchy in international relations, which constructs actors only as states always at the edge of violent conflict with one another. The presence of these discourses drives home the point that it is a mistake to conceptualize the public sphere or civil society only in terms of a set of progressive discourses or groupings (such as new social movements).

There are, then, many discourses that provide little grist for agonistic respect of the sort that difference democrats favor. But they do have a place in the public sphere thought of in terms of contestation across discourses. This latter model is not in the first instance a prescriptive one: it is an interpretation of the way the world is. Market liberalism does contest more social democratic and interventionist discourses. Racist discourses do contest alternatives that stress tolerance or affirmation of other races, and also discourses that deny the relevance of race as a category. Leninism (inasmuch as it exists still) contests more libertarian approaches to radical politics. Hobbesian anarchy as an interpretation of international relations is contested by a liberal discourse which stresses the possibility of cooperative institutional construction. So the issue is not whether to welcome or bemoan such contestation of discourses, but what to do about it.

A prescriptive model of the public sphere in terms of contestation, of publics rather than discourses, is advanced by Nancy Fraser.[59] Fraser believes that contestation is different from deliberation: "the discursive relations among differently empowered publics are as likely to take the form of contestation as that of deliberation."[60] But this contrast holds only to the extent deliberation is characterized in the narrow terms criticized by difference democrats. Deliberative authenticity exists to the extent that communication induces reflection on preferences in noncoercive fashion. Provided that this standard is met, the kinds of communication admissible can be quite wide-ranging, and contestation in particular should be welcomed for its ability to induce reflection. Contestation also helps respond to those who believe that deliberation will produce only a conformist "groupthink."[61]

Discursive contestation can proceed in more or less democratic terms; the mere fact of contestation does not signal the presence of democracy. Contestation is undemocratic to the extent it is controlled by public relations experts, spin doctors, and demagogues. Contestation is democratic to the extent that it is engaged by a broad variety of competent actors under unconstrained conditions of the kind that deliberative democrats, or at least those discursive democrats influenced by critical theory, have always championed.

In this light, the real democratic contribution of the network form of organization celebrated by Schlosberg lies less in its internal relations of agonistic respect across difference, more in its capacity to promote dispersed control over the terms of discourse.[62]

The US environmental justice movement analyzed by Schlosberg is indeed an exemplary network. It arose in the 1980s and flourished in the 1990s as a result of the mainstream environmental organizations' perceived indifference to the distribution of environmental risks on the basis of race and social class. The movement grew out of a series of local actions against waste dumps, incinerators, pesticides, uranium mining, and other hazardous activities. These local actions eventually grew into the sharing of information and resources through networks coordinated by bodies such as the Citizens' Clearinghouse on Hazardous Wastes and the Southwest Network for Environmental and Economic Justice. But the organization has always been bottom-up rather than top-down; there is no hierarchy and central leadership of the sort characterizing the mainstream groups.

This movement and its networks have been successful in reframing environmental issues related to risk and social justice, and so extending deliberative democratic control on these issues. Its discursive contests have been with more entrenched environmentalist discourses that conceptualize risks in terms of their collective and common character, as well as with industrialist discourses that deny the severity of risk, or subordinate risk to the pursuit of material prosperity. The environmental justice discourse is not organized and promoted centrally. Instead, it emerges from a wide variety of local struggles that together help to define what environmental injustice and justice can mean. Those schooled in social choice theory might look at the emergence of this movement and see only potential trouble for tractable social choice, inasmuch as the movement increases the number of subject positions that have to be addressed in collective choices. A series of localized "not in my back yard" actions would seem to have this effect. Yet the emergence of the network form and its associated discourse actually presents a coherent perspective on issues of environmental risk; in the terminology of Maarten Hajer, the movement has constituted a discourse coalition organized around a common storyline about the generation and distribution of environmental hazards.[63] The picture here is one of struggle between the environmental justice discourse coalition and an industrialist discourse coalition, with a more established mainstream environmentalist discourse coalition also involved. What we see is a relatively small number of competing discourses, rather than a wild proliferation of subject positions of the sort that would alarm social choice theorists.

The environmental justice movement has also succeeded in affecting the content of public policy—for example, through an executive order on environmental justice signed by President Clinton in 1993, and the establishment of an Office of Environmental Justice in the United States Environmental Protection Agency in 1992. This success highlights a further advantage of thinking in terms of the contestation of discourses rather than the engagement of identities: the recognition of difference can coexist with an orientation to collective decision. One of the standard criticisms of deliberative democracy is that it is radically incomplete as a model, because it specifies no mechanism for collective choice; we deliberate, and then what? Difference democracy is still more subject to the same criticism. In the hands of Connolly, for example, democracy is redefined as the creative interplay of subject positions. There is no suggestion that there are collective decisions to be made, social problems to be solved. Sanders' emphasis on testimony suffers from the same difficulty: individuals testify—and then what?[64]

Democratic life is not just the endless interplay of discourses. There have to be moments of decisive collective action, and in contemporary societies it is mainly (but not only) the state that has this capacity. Discourses and their contests do not stop at the edge of the public sphere; they can also permeate the understandings and assumptions of state actors. Yet it is important to maintain a public sphere autonomous from the state, for discursive interplay within the public sphere is always likely to be less constrained than within the state. It is within the public sphere that insurgent discourses and identities can first establish themselves. In this light, liberal statist difference democrats such as Phillips can be over-optimistic about the capacity of the state to promote difference, at least in terms of anything more than limited corrections to mechanisms of representation.[65]

I have tried to show that a conceptualization of democracy that empha-sizes the contestation of discourses in the public sphere enables discursive democrats to reply effectively to the criticisms of both social choice theorists and difference democrats. Yet is such a conceptualization vulnerable to the charge frequently leveled at postmodernists and poststructuralists who de-ploy the discourse idea that an overemphasis on language means that the in-fluence of governmental structure, political power, and material interest are ignored? Moreover, can there not be moments of decisive collective action that do more than simply confirm the power of the dominant discourse?

To Foucault and Foucauldians, discourses are the prime causal factors in human affairs, including politics. My account of the contestation of dis-courses is quite different, because it allows that there is much more to life and politics than discourses. The claim is only that the contestation of dis-courses in the public sphere is the most defensible way to think about dis-cursive democracy on a society-wide basis. The outcome of this contesta-tion is in reality not always decisive; in authoritarian states, for example, it might even be irrelevant in affecting public policy outcomes. Even in liberal democracies, the outcome may well be overridden by the exercise of po-litical power by dominant interests tied to government, or by government's need to maintain investor confidence and keep the markets happy. However, the same might be said for deliberation of any kind.

Still, there are times when discursive shifts do make a difference, and are decisive in changing the content of public policy.[66] Civil rights legislation in the United States in the 1960s marked a demise of a discourse that saw little wrong in denying individuals full humanity on the basis of skin color. The flurry of environmental legislation, administrative action, and institution-building around 1970 was evidence of the sudden arrival of the discourse of environmentalism. At this time environmental groups were not a significant presence in terms of exerting pressure on policymaking, nor were environ-mental issues especially contentious in election campaigns.

A skeptic might still argue that such influence of discourse shifts is spo-
radic and indirect. Yet the same might be said of elections—especially in
light of their distortion by money, and the arbitrariness revealed by social
choice theory. And interest-group influence can be just as tenuous. Pluralists
who once pinned their hopes on interest groups as more effective channels
of influence than elections eventually conceded the systematic dominance
of particular kinds of groups, especially corporations.[67] Democracy as discursive contestation should be compared with these real and so defective
alternatives, not with some unattainable ideal of how the will of the people
can take effect directly in policymaking.

EDITORS' NOTE

This chapter was originally published in *Deliberative Democracy and Beyond* by John Dryzek (2000), Chapter 3 (pp. 57-80), © John Dryzek 2000.
Reprinted by permission of Oxford University Press. The piece has been
edited for style. Minor deletions have been made for the purposes of this
volume.

NOTES

1. See, for example, Seyla Benhabib, "Introduction: The Democratic Moment and the Problem of Difference," in *Democracy and Difference: Contesting the Boundaries of the Political*, edited by Seyla Benhabib (Princeton:
Princeton University Press, 1996), 3-4. Iris Young resists the pairing of difference and identity, but her objection is only to sectarian assertions of identity in fixed and unassailable terms. Iris Marion Young, "Difference
as a Resource for Democratic Communication," in *Deliberative Democracy*, eds. James Bohman and William
Rehg (Cambridge, MA: MIT Press), 385.

2. William E. Connolly, *Identity/Difference: Democratic Negotiations of Political Paradox* (Ithaca, NY: Cornell
University Press, 1991); William E. Connolly, *The Ethos of Pluralization* (Minneapolis, MN: University of
Minnesota Press, 1995).

3. Connolly, *Identity/Difference*, 211.

4. Mark Dowie, *Losing Ground: American Environmentalism at the Close of the Twentieth Century* (Cambridge,
MA: MIT Press, 1995), 97.

5. Chantal Mouffe, "Democracy, Power, and the Political," in *Democracy and Difference: Contesting the Boundaries of the Political*, ed. Seyla Benhabib (Princeton: Princeton University Press, 1996), 245-256.

6. Ernesto Laclau and Chantal Mouffe, *Hegemony and Socialist Strategy: Towards a Radical Democratic Politics*
(London: Verso, 1985).

7. Kirstie McClure, "On the Subject of Rights: Pluralism, Plurality, and Political Identity," in *Dimensions of
Radical Democracy*, ed. Chantal Mouffe (London: Verso, 1992), 108-127.

8. Mouffe, "Democracy, Power, and the Political," 248-250.

9. Anne Phillips, *The Politics of Presence* (Oxford: Oxford University Press, 1995).

10. See also Anne Phillips, *Democracy and Difference* (State College, PA: Pennsylvania State University Press, 1993), 96-99.

11. Lani Guinier, "The Politics of Tokenism: The Voting Rights Act and the Theory of Black Electoral Success," *Michigan Law Review* 89 (1991): 1077-1154; Lani Guinier, *The Tyranny of the Majority* (New York: The Free Press, 1994).

12. See Susan Bickford, "Reconfiguring Pluralism: Identity and Institutions in the Inegalitarian Polity," *American Journal of Political Science* 43:1 (1999): 86-108.

13. Iris Marion Young, "Polity and Group Difference: A Critique of the Ideal of Universal Citizenship," *Ethics* 99 (1989): 250-274; Iris Marion Young, *Justice and the Politics of Difference* (Princeton: Princeton University Press, 1990).

14. Young, "Polity and Group Difference," 265.

15. Young, "Difference as a Resource for Democratic Communication," 385-393.

16. Ibid., 393.

17. Val Plumwood, "Inequality, Ecojustice, and Ecological Rationality," in *Debating the Earth: The Environmental Politics Reader*, eds. John S. Dryzek and David Schlosberg (Oxford: Oxford University Press), 578. Postmodernism's stress on multiple and contingent differences is reconciled to liberalism still more thoroughly in the hands of Richard Rorty, a self-proclaimed "post-modernist bourgeois liberal." Richard Rorty, "Post-Modernist Bourgeois Liberalism," *Journal of Philosophy* 80 (1983): 583-589. Rorty believes that the variety and fluidity in subject positions and their associated differences that postmodernism has highlighted can be negotiated quite adequately through the existing institutions of liberal democracy. Richard Rorty, *Contingency, Irony, Solidarity* (Cambridge: Cambridge University Press, 1989). In his (postmodern) hostility to the idea that philosophical foundations can be specified for these institutions, Rorty differs profoundly from most liberal political philosophers—but ends up justifying the same institutions nonetheless. He thinks that the world, or at least the American left, needs less philosophy (including postmodern philosophy) and more action to pursue the pluralistic dreams long associated with American thinkers, such as Whitman and Dewey. Richard Rorty, *Achieving Our Country: Leftist Thought in Twentieth Century America* (Cambridge, MA: Harvard University Press, 1998). Still, Rorty is an outlier among difference democrats, most of whom believe that the contemporary liberal state requires either thorough reform or radical opposition.

18. Phillips, *The Politics of Presence*, 145-165.

19. Graham Burchell, Colin Gordon, and Peter Miller, eds., *The Foucault Effect: Studies in Governmentality* (Chicago: University of Chicago Press, 1991).

20. Barry Hindess, "Representation Ingrafted Upon Democracy?" *Democratization* 7:2 (2000): 1-18.

21. Ibid., 9.

22. Michael Connors, "Democracy and National Ideology in Thailand" (PhD thesis, University of Melbourne, 2000).

23. Michel Foucault, "On the Genealogy of Ethics: An Overview of Work in Progress," in *The Foucault Reader*, ed. Paul Rabinow (New York: Pantheon, 1984), 343.

24. Lynn Sanders, "Against Deliberation," *Political Theory* 25:3 (1997): 348.

25. Iris Marion Young, "Communication and the Other: Beyond Deliberative Democracy," in *Democracy and Difference: Contesting the Boundaries of the Political*, ed. Seyla Benhabib (Princeton: Princeton University Press, 1996), 120-135; Iris Marion Young, "Inclusive Political Communication: Greeting, Rhetoric, and Storytelling in the Context of Political Argument" (paper presented at the Annual Meeting of the American Political Science Association, Boston, MA, 1998).

26. See also Susan Bickford, *The Dissonance of Democracy: Listening, Conflict, and Citizenship* (Ithaca, NY: Cornell University Press, 1996).

27. Sanders, "Against Deliberation," 362-369.

28. Ibid., 353, 356, 370, 359-362, 362.

29. Young, "Inclusive Political Communication," 6-7.

30. See, similarly, Mouffe, "Democracy, Power, and the Political," 249-252.

31. Young, "Communication and the Other," 123-124.

32. Ibid., 125-126.

33. See, for example, Rose Barbour and Jenny Kitzinger, eds., *Developing Focus Group Research* (London: Sage, 1999).

34. Sanders, "Against Deliberation," 372.

35. Young, "Communication and the Other," 131.

36. Ibid.,129-130.

37. Young, "Inclusive Political Communication," 15.

38. Young, "Communication and the Other," 130-131.

39. Simone Chambers, *Reasonable Democracy: Jürgen Habermas and the Politics of Discourse* (Ithaca, NY: Cornell University Press, 1996); Thomas Spragens, *Reason and Democracy* (Durham, NC: Duke University Press, 1990).

40. Young, "Inclusive Political Communication," 23-27.

41. This is recognized, for example, in Patsy Healy's deliberative approach to public planning, which, though based on a Habermasian framework of the sort Young finds objectionable, is open to "the power of ideas, metaphors, images, and stories." Patsy Healy, "Planning Through Debate: The Communicative Turn in Planning Theory," in *The Argumentative Turn in Policy Analysis and Planning*, eds. Frank Fischer and John Forester (Durham, NC: Duke University Press, 1993), 244.

42. Miller applies this second test, but only to testimony. David Miller, "Is Deliberative Democracy Unfair to Disadvantaged Minorities," in *Democracy as Public Deliberation: New Perspectives*, ed. Maurizio Passerin d'Entrèves (Manchester, UK: Manchester University Press, 2002), 39-52.

43. Foucault, "On the Genealogy of Ethics," 343.

44. Young, "Inclusive Political Communication," 32.

45. For some cautionary cases, see Daphne Patai and Noretta Koertge, *Professing Feminism: Cautionary Tales from the Strange World of Women's Studies* (New York: Basic Books, 1994).

46. Miller, "Is Deliberative Democracy Unfair to Disadvantaged Minorities."

47. Joseph Femia, "Complexity and Deliberative Democracy," *Inquiry* 39 (1996): 359-397.

48. For example, James Bohman, "Public Reason and Cultural Pluralism: Political Liberalism and the Problem of Moral Conflict," *Political Theory* 23:2 (1995): 253-279; John S. Dryzek, *Discursive Democracy: Politics, Policy, and Political Science* (New York: Cambridge University Press, 1990), 16-19; Russell L. Hanson, *The Democratic Imagination in America: Conversations with Our Past* (Princeton: Princeton University Press, 1985); Stephen K. White, *The Recent Work of Jürgen Habermas: Reason, Justice, and Modernity* (Cambridge: Cambridge University Press, 1988), 70.

49. Young, "Communication and the Other," 122.

50. Jürgen Habermas, *Communication and the Evolution of Society* (Boston, MA: Beacon Press, 1979), 90; Jürgen Habermas, "A Reply to My Critics," in *Habermas: Critical Debates*, eds. John Thompson and David Held (Cambridge, MA: MIT Press), 257-258.

51. Young, "Communication and the Other," 123.

52. John Rawls, *Political Liberalism* (New York: Columbia University Press, 1993).

53. James Bohman, *Public Deliberation: Pluralism, Complexity, and Democracy* (Cambridge, MA: MIT Press), 83-85, emphasis in original.

54. Phillips, *The Politics of Presence*, 151.

55. David Schlosberg, "Resurrecting the Pluralist Universe," *Political Research Quarterly* 51:3 (1998): 605.

56. William James, *The Will to Believe and Other Essays in Popular Philosophy* (Cambridge, MA: Harvard University Press, 1979 [1896]).

57. Schlosberg, "Resurrecting the Pluralist Universe.

58. As I noted earlier, this position is consistent with remarks Foucault himself made toward the end of his life.

59. Nancy Fraser, "Rethinking the Public Sphere: A Contribution to the Critique of Actually Existing Democracy," in *Habermas and the Public Sphere*, ed. Craig Calhoun (Cambridge, MA: MIT Press), 109-142.

60. Ibid., 125. For Fraser, contestation is engaged by "subaltern counterpublics" which constitute "parallel discursive arenas" (123) within which similarly situated individuals can find their voices. They are publics rather than enclaves because their members "aspire to disseminate [their] discourse to ever-widening arenas" (124). Her paradigm is the feminist movement in the United States.

61. Femia, "Complexity and Deliberative Democracy," 386-387.

62. Schlosberg, "Resurrecting the Pluralist Universe"; David Schlosberg, *Environmental Justice and the New Pluralism: The Challenge of Difference for Environmentalism* (Oxford: Oxford University Press, 1999).

63. Maarten A. Hajer, *The Politics of Environmental Discourse: Ecological Modernization and the Policy Process* (Oxford: Oxford University Press, 1995).

64. Iris Young is careful to specify that she does not want to banish argument about what is to be done from deliberation—simply to supplement rational argument with other kinds of communication that better represent difference. Thus she can present her own model of communicative democracy as a development of the deliberative model, rather than a negation of it, and so she is no more subject to the charge of incompleteness than is deliberative democracy.

65. Phillips, *Democracy and Difference*; Phillips, *The Politics of Presence*.

66. See, for example, the case studies of Hajer, *The Politics of Environmental Discourse*; Karen T. Litfin, *Ozone Discourses: Science and Politics in Global Environmental Cooperation* (New York: Columbia University Press, 1994).

67. Charles E. Lindblom, *Politics and Markets: The World's Political-Economic Systems* (New York: Basic Books, 1977).

Deliberation in Complex Systems: Everyday Talk and De-centered Democracy

Everyday Talk in the Deliberative System

by Jane Mansbridge

What I will call "everyday talk" does not meet all of the criteria implicit in the ordinary use of the word *deliberation*. It is not always self-conscious, reflective, or considered. But everyday talk, if not always deliberative, is nevertheless a crucial part of the full deliberative system that democracies need if citizens are, in any sense, to rule themselves. Through talk among formal and informal representatives in designated public forums, talk back and forth between constituents and elected representatives or other representatives in politically oriented organizations, talk in the media, talk among political activists, and everyday talk in formally private spaces about things the public ought to discuss—all adding up to what I call the deliberative system—people come to understand better what they want and need, individually as well as collectively. The full deliberative system encompasses all these strands.[1]

If a deliberative system works well, it filters out and discards the worst ideas available on public matters while it picks up, adopts, and applies the best ideas. If the deliberative system works badly, it distorts facts, portrays ideas in forms that their originators would disown, and encourages citizens to adopt ways of thinking and acting that are good neither for them nor for the larger polity. A deliberative system at its best, like all systems of democratic participation, helps its participants understand themselves and their environment better. It also helps them change themselves and others in ways that are better for them and better for the whole society—though sometimes these goals conflict. How one judges a deliberative system thus depends heavily on what one believes to be a "good" or "bad" way of thinking or acting and what one judges to be a better or worse understanding of self and environment. Such judgments will always be heavily contested.

This chapter has two aims. First, it argues that theorists of deliberation ought to pay as much attention to citizens' everyday talk as to formal delib-

eration in public arenas. Although talk intended to conclude with a binding
decision differs from talk that has no such intention, that difference is not
significant for judging the quality of the deliberation for democratic purposes. Second, it argues that existing criteria for judging democratic talk are
inadequate and need revision. The analysis calls throughout for a democratic
theory that puts the citizen at the center.

One of the major aims of Amy Gutmann and Dennis Thompson's *Democracy and Disagreement* is to widen the scope of public reason to include
not only its judicial exemplifications but also the democratic deliberations
characteristic of legislatures at their best.[2] Indeed, they extend the concept of
public forum to include meetings of grassroots organizations, hospital committees, and sports and professional associations (113, 359). I see no reason
not to widen the scope still further, to include in the arena of democratic
deliberation what I call everyday talk, as well as the media, interest groups,
and other venues of discussion.

Everyday talk anchors one end of a spectrum at whose other end lies the
public decision-making assembly. Everyday talk produces results collectively,
but not in concert. Often everyday talk produces collective results the way
a market produces collective results, through the combined and interactive
effects of relatively isolated individual actions. A decision-making assembly,
by contrast, produces results in concert, usually through the give-and-take of
face-to-face interaction. Everyday talk is not necessarily aimed at any action
other than talk itself; deliberation in assembly is, at least in theory, aimed at
action.

Everyday talk may be almost purely expressive; deliberation in the assembly, being aimed at action, is usually intentional. Deliberation in a public
assembly is often aimed at creating a collectively binding decision. It may
seem, then, that everyday talk and decision making in an assembly differ in
kind rather than in degree, because only a governmental assembly aims at
and creates a collectively binding decision. Yet everyday talk among citizens
on matters the public ought to discuss prepares the way for formal governmental decisions and for collective decisions not to "decide." One can trust
formal governmental decisions to reflect the considered will of the citizenry
only insofar as that will has gone through a process of effective citizen deliberation—in the everyday talk of homes, workplaces, and places where a few
friends meet, as well as more formal talk in designated public assemblies.[3]

Few of the standards that various theorists have offered for judging deliberation map onto the one great difference between governmental assemblies and other forms of deliberation: that such assemblies (including the governing bodies of grassroots organizations, hospital committees, and sports and professional associations) aim at producing a decision binding on the participants and other venues for talk do not. I conclude, both from this lack of fit and from analyzing the features of everyday talk directly, that the larger deliberative system (including everyday talk) should be judged by much the same standards as classic deliberation in assemblies. Those standards must be loosened to accommodate the more informal character of the nongovernmental parts of the deliberative system, but in this loosening they do not lose their character.

In both legislative bodies and the rest of the deliberative system, the concept of "public reason" should be enlarged to encompass a "considered" mixture of emotion and reason rather than pure rationality. The standards of publicity and accountability, which in Gutmann and Thompson's presentation are designed primarily for representative assemblies, have counterparts elsewhere in the deliberative system, including everyday talk. Reciprocity applies well to everyday talk. So do the standards of freedom, equality, consideredness, accuracy in revealing interests, and transformative capacity that arguably apply to the deliberations in assembly whose procedures democratically legitimate their conclusions.

In the full process of citizen deliberation, the different parts of the deliberative system mutually influence one another in ways that are not easy to parse out. Television, radio, newspapers, movies, and other media both influence their intended audiences and are influenced by them. So too in social movements, which work as much by changing the way people think as by pressuring governments to enact legislation, the intentionally political talk of political activists both influences and is influenced by the everyday talk of nonactivists.[4]

The interaction between activists and nonactivists in a social movement, for example, combines the dynamics of a market and a conversation. In a market, entrepreneurs put forth a product, which consumers then buy or do not buy. By making this binary choice, to buy or not to buy, consumers shape what the entrepreneurs produce. In an ideal market, entrepreneurs try to understand the present and potential desires of the consumers in order to produce a product the consumers will buy; entrepreneurs who offer an undesired product will go out of business. Conversations, by contrast, do not depend on binary signals. An ideal conversation, like Jürgen Habermas' ideal speech situation, aims at understanding. But even a conversation has a component that works a little like a market: Each partner advances words, which the other does or does not understand, does or does not find interesting. Even a partner who does not speak can shape what the other says by nonverbally indicating understanding or confusion, interest or boredom. Nonactivists affect what activists say and think in part by being speaking partners in conversation with the activists or intermediate actors and in part by responding to those offerings with understanding or confusion, interest or boredom, appropriation or rejection. The interaction of activists and nonactivists only begins the real work of nonactivists. In everyday talk and action the nonactivists test new and old ideas against their daily realities, make small moves—micronegotiations—that try to put some version of an idea into effect, and talk the ideas over with friends, sifting the usable from the unusable, what appears sensible from what appears crazy, what seems just from what seems tendentious. In their micronegotiations and private conversations, nonactivists influence the ideas and symbols available to the political process not only aggregatively, by favoring one side or another in a vote or in a public opinion survey, but also substantively, through their practice. They shape the deliberative system with their own exercise of power and reasoning on issues that the public ought to discuss.

The activism of nonactivists, which has its greatest effect through everyday talk, includes even the snort of derision one might give at a sexist television character while watching with friends. That snort of derision is, in my analysis, a political act.

Once More into "The Personal Is Political"

Outside the discipline of political science, the subfield of political theory, and the subculture of certain activist groups, the label "political" may have little relevance or laudatory power. Inside that discipline, subfield, and subculture, however, the label has a legitimating function for objects of study, a normative function in bringing into play criteria of judgment specific to political things, and a valorizing function in marking a particular activity as "serious." The reader who balks at giving the label "political" to the kind of everyday actions and talk that this chapter describes may, for almost all of the purposes of this chapter, simply think of them as "prepolitical." But because I am interested in the normative criteria appropriate to political things, I will argue that these everyday, informal forms of action and deliberation are best understood as political.

I propose that we define as political "that which the public ought to discuss," when that discussion forms part of some, perhaps highly informal, version of a collective "decision."[5] As a collective, we the people (bounded by some large or small perimeter that we or our forebears have set) make many more "decisions" than appear in our formal state apparatus. Large numbers of mutually interacting individual choices, weighted unequally through patterns of domination and subordination, chance, and other justifiable and unjustifiable inequalities, together create a host of collective choices. Those collective choices, or "decisions," then affect, often substantially, the individual choices of each member of the collective. To "politicize" one of these collective choices—to make it "political"—is to draw it to the attention of the public, as something the public should discuss as a collectivity, with a view to possible change. What the public ought to discuss is explicitly a matter for contest.[6]

This process of bringing a collective "decision" to public attention, as something the public ought to discuss, need not involve the state. We may bring to public attention not a decision made in concert but rather one that has emerged from highly informal, unconscious, and aggregative processes. Nor need we involve (the state in the discussion or resolution of the issue. A medieval maxim concludes that "What touches all should be decided by all."[7] If that maxim means, as it seems to have been intended to, "decided by all" through formal government with its legitimate monopoly of force, I propose that it is simply wrong. A public might rightly decide, collectively but informally through the evolution of norms, that certain questions that affect all in a particular area should not be decided by all through formal government. My action as CEO of General Motors, or cardinal of the Catholic Church, or anchorwoman for NBC, or simply as a private individual might subtly affect literally everyone in the polity, but collectively though informally the public might decide not to allow formal governmental decision to touch the areas in which the CEO, cardinal, anchorwoman, or individual acts.

Too much has been written on the subject of "the political" to cover in any detail here.[8] For the moment, however, let me explain how I came to the definition I suggest, give some examples of what I want to cover and why, and explain why previous definitions do not seem to me fully satisfactory. Carol Hainisch first used the phrase "The personal is political" in print, expressing an idea developed in the group to which she belonged, New York Radical Women. In the article with that title, Hainisch explained to critics within the women's movement why consciousness-raising groups, which often discussed issues such as individual women's experiences with menstruation or sexual orgasm, were as "political" as more action-oriented groups.[9]

Hainisch argued that such issues as feeling ashamed of menstruation or believing incorrectly that vaginal orgasms were different from and better than clitotal orgasms were, in my terms, matters that the public should discuss. These feelings and beliefs require public discussion because they support a structure of male dominance that for reasons of justice ought to be changed. Although that change had to be collective in the broadest sense, it did not necessarily require action in concert or by a formal government. Indeed, many of these issues were almost certainly best left outside the realm of formal government. The personal became political once individual struggles were linked conceptually with a larger normative struggle for equal status in the polity as a whole.

By coining the phrase "The personal is political," feminists meant that a host of concerns, previously trivialized as "personal" and experienced as individual or idiosyncratic, we now saw as "political," experienced by women as a group or by subgroups of certain women, and deserving of collective discussion with a view to deciding whether or not it was appropriate to take collective (though perhaps informal and piecemeal) action. An issue becomes "political" when it deserves public discussion and possibly action. Defining the political as whatever involves "power," by contrast, includes too much and too little. It includes too much: All else equal, I exercise power but it is not "political" if I hold a gun to your head and demand your money, if I threaten anger when you want the last cookie, or if I constrain your ability to use the car because I took it to Wisconsin. More important, the definition includes too little: It excludes all that involves persuasion rather than power. It excludes all that creates and fosters commonality. In this vein, Jean Elshtain convincingly took to task several early feminist writers for concluding, as Kate Millet did, that power "is the essence of politics," or, as

Nancy Henley put it, that "the personal is political" means "there is nothing we do—no matter how individual and personal it seems—that does not reflect our participation in a power system."[10]

The opposite mistake is to say, with Hannah Arendt and Sheldon Wolin, that "the political" is only the ground of "commonality," when commonality excludes procedural arrangements, such as majority rule, for deciding matters of fundamentally conflicting interest through relatively legitimate forms of power, or as Arendt called it, "violence."[11] The political should neither exclude the grounds of commonality, the way a definition based solely on power is likely to do, nor be confined to commonality.

Finally, what the public ought to discuss is a matter of collective concern and in a sense a matter of collective "decision," but it is not always a matter for positive action. Whether or not to take action is one of the issues that the public ought to discuss. We might discuss an issue collectively (formally or informally) and decide collectively (formally or informally) that we ought not to take action on that issue, either through formal government or through the most informal, individual processes. In this I disagree with Benjamin Barber, who defines the realm of "politics" as "circumscribed by conditions that impose a necessity for public action."[12] I adapt the formulation of Ronald Beiner, who depicts "politics" as the medium in which human beings try to "make sense of their common situation in discourse with one another,"[13] adding that "making sense" almost inevitably has decisional implications for action, when "decision" and "action" are defined in the highly informal, weakly collective sense that I define them here.[14]

Does defining the political this broadly "[erode] the terms of the private sphere"?[15] I believe it does—in small part. To suggest that the public should discuss many intimate and familial matters, at least in general terms, destroys one strong defense against the invasion of the private world by the public. That strong defense is simply to say that what goes on in the family, or in the sphere of intimacy, is not for public discussion. Appropriate norms should put sexual orgasm or child-rearing practices, for example, simply off-limits. Informal prohibitions on public speech about these issues constitute one of the strongest defenses I can imagine against the invasion of the public into the private. I would argue, however, that the private sphere can be protected sufficiently against serious incursions from formal government without so limiting public discussion.

What the public ought to discuss is contested and essentially contestable. The question, is this political?, demands an argument aimed at convincing the interlocutor that an issue ought to, or ought not to, be discussed by the public. This kind of argument has to produce reasons why the matter in question should be of larger collective concern, why it should go beyond the two of us (or the four or ten of us).

An argument of this sort would not collapse the distinction between the public and private realms. It would not eliminate either or subordinate either to alternative concepts. It would not demand that the private be integrated fully within or subsumed by the public. It would not insist that the public realm be privatized. It would not devalue the private sphere or suggest that the relationships that characterize that sphere had little significance or value.[16]

But it would say that some matters, hitherto thought too intimate for the public to discuss, or of so little importance that they did not need to be discussed by the public, were matters on which the collective, the public, ought to deliberate.

Everyday Activism and Everyday Talk

Everyday activism occurs when a nonactivist takes an action in order to change others' actions or beliefs on an issue that the public ought to discuss. Much everyday activism takes place through talk. Here is an African American woman reporting an instance of everyday activism to other participants in a focus group:

> I was born and raised in Chicago, and I've never been south in all of my life. But all my in-laws are from the South. So I go to this big family dinner and I'm just waiting, you know, sitting at the table, waiting. And all of a sudden all the men shift [speaker makes a funny shifting noise; laughter from others] to one side of the room. And all of a sudden all of the women shift [makes another shifting noise] into the kitchen. And I'm sitting there at the table by myself scratching my head. And the women come out with the plates, handing out the plates, and my husband says: "You gonna fix my plate?" "I don't fix your plate at home. Why would I do it here?" Well, it ties in. It's a generation thing. It's a cycle, a never-ending

cycle. His father did it, and his father's father did it. They just sit there and wait while the women go [shifting sound] around.

[Others in the group chime in, ask questions.]

Well, what I did was I ended up like liberating the other women in the family and then all of a sudden they stopped serving them all of a sudden. [Others interrupt with their stories.][17]

With this small act—a combination of speech and, in this case, nonperformance of an expected action—the nonactivist intervened in her own and others' lives to promote a relatively new ideal of gender justice, exemplified by her verb *liberating*. She intended to affect the others by her actions and words. She undoubtedly also believed that the issues on which she acted were issues that the public ought to discuss.

On the issue I am currently studying—changing conceptions of gender justice—the everyday activism of the nonactivists I have met has relied less on power, that is, the threat of sanction or the use of force, than on influence, that is, persuading another of a course of action on its merits.[18] In one or two incidents that my informants described, a form of power did most of the work of social change—as when a woman phoned the company of a sexist window salesman to get him fired. In several other incidents, power in the form of a threat of personal anger and withdrawal played an important role. Yet even in those incidents in which power played the greatest role, persuasive appeals to justice underlay my informants' approach to the conflict.

Consider the act of calling someone a "male chauvinist." The hurling of an epithet, often in anger, surely ranks near the bottom of a scale of articulated, nonmanipulative, and humane forms of deliberation. It falls far short of the ideal that deliberation should be conducted in a context of mutual respect, empathy, and listening. It serves itself as a sanction, and it implicitly threatens further sanctions, thus fitting solidly within the particular constellation of causal effects that I call "power." Yet the summary indictment captured in the term *male chauvinist* also works as a crude and shorthand form of influence.

It inherently makes two claims—one structural, the other normative. Descriptively, it claims that the behavior in question results in part from a structure of gender relations that extends beyond the particular individuals engaged in this interaction. Normatively, it claims that the man's behavior is not merely disagreeable but also unjust. Persuading others to act or refrain from acting on the basis of shared and contested ideals of human interaction often takes just such a shorthand form.

Here is a professional-class woman, self-identified as "conservative" on a liberal-conservative spectrum, reporting that she had called her husband a male chauvinist.

JM: What was your husband's reaction to you saying something like that to him?

R: I remember him being surprised and then saying that he didn't think he was, but as he thought about he guessed he was a little. It never occurred to him that he was male chauvinist before I said it.

JM: Do you think he took it as a criticism?

R: Yes. I don't think he wanted to be that way—especially since he values my intelligence and that is why he married me. I think he has improved; I am looking back a couple of years, and he is better now.[19]

In some of the reported instances of women calling a man a "male chauvinist," the phrase sparked an interchange that led to changed behavior, primarily through persuasion based on an implicit appeal to justice. In many instances, men simply laughed the criticism off or got angry, and the women in the interaction thought there was no chance the men would change. In several instances the women did not challenge the men directly at all. Instead, they talked with one another "backstage," using the phrase and the analysis it embodies to reinforce one another in an emerging sense of injustice that they did not yet dare to bring into the open.[20]

In social movements, new ideas—and new terms, such as *male chauvinist* or *homophobia*—enter everyday talk through an interaction between political activists and nonactivists. Activists craft, from ideals or ideas solidly based in the existing culture, ideals or ideas that begin to stretch that base. Social enclaves in which activists talk intensely with one another foster this kind of innovation. The activists, along with others who for various reasons find themselves in these enclaves, discuss and try to put into practice these extensions and revisions of received ideas. In the protected space of the enclave, and also on the borders between that enclave and mainstream society, activists experiment with persuading others. They discover through empathy, intuition, logic, and trial and error which ideas move others to change their own ideas and behavior and which do not. The enclave nourishes the development of extreme ideas—such as that gun control advocates consciously intend to destroy citizens' capacities to resist government, or that babies should be produced in test tubes by cybernetricians. The enclave confirms some of its participants in the reality of their perceptions, both accurate and inaccurate. It stokes collective anger. It encourages creative, sometimes harebrained, solutions to collective problems. It helps remove the deadening conviction that nothing can be done. It stirs the intellectual and emotional pot. From the enclave crucible and the surrounding ferment emerge ideas that may or may not get anywhere in the larger society. To change the thinking and behavior of large numbers of people, an idea must be sufficiently congruent with existing ideas to find a niche in the schemas people already employ to interpret the world. It must explain hitherto unexplained phenomena or apply old lessons to something relatively new. A new idea will often emerge from a new material base. But the powerful role of interpretative schemas, both in the particular cultures of competing enclaves and in the often conflicting strands of mainstream thought, ensures that no new idea can be predicted simply from material change.

As the activists, with their many tendencies and factions, take their ideas out into the larger society, they become willy-nilly entrepreneurs, or carriers of infection, or participants in a somewhat one-sided conversation. Whether in the market many consumers buy the ideas, whether in the epidemic many become infected, or whether in the conversation many eyes light up or glaze over, depends on the activists, on translators with one foot in the enclave and one in the larger society, and on the needs and ideas of members of the society-at-large.

As new ideas enter the larger society, different kinds of people pick them up and try them on, for different reasons. Some find in these ideas a new club with which to beat old enemies, others an enticement with which to seduce would-be friends. Some find in them the answer to intellectual and emotional puzzles. Some see them as healthy extensions of ideals they already hold. Pundits weigh in. News magazines run side articles, then possibly lead articles or even cover stories. Television programs lightly air the new ideas, then drop or focus on them. If the ideas have relevance to the lives of ordinary citizens, those citizens begin to take positions and talk the ideas over with their friends.

Women may talk with their husbands and the other women in the family. They may stop fixing plates and may call the men they know "male chauvinists." If parts of the new ideals begin to win more general acceptance, many people, including nonactivists, begin changing their lives in order to live up to those ideals in a better way. Those whose material lives are improved by putting the new ideals into practice have incentives to promulgate those ideas.

Those whose material lives will be harmed have incentives to denigrate them. But material loss and gain do not fully explain adherence to or rejection of an idea. People are governed in part by their ideals, and they often want to act consistently. Showing that a new ideal is consistent with an old ideal, or that previous arguments for why the new ideal did not apply are wrong, can make at least some contemporary human beings change their ideas of right relationships, their ideas of right action, and their lives.

The ideas and ideals that generate and are generated by this process can be either good or bad. The process that generates, over time, a growing conviction that schools should be racially integrated is the same process, in its outlines, as the process that generates, over time, a conviction that Jews should be sent to concentration camps. But although the outlines may be the same, the process in its details may not be the same. The ideals of good deliberative process have been derived, in part, from long human observation of what procedures produce good decisions over time, as well as, in part, from understanding what procedures have elements that are good in themselves. The democrat's faith is that good deliberative systems will, over time, produce just outcomes. Yet what the criteria for good deliberation are is at the moment an open question. It is also unclear whether the criteria for good deliberation in a public assembly are the same as the criteria for a good deliberative system.

Criteria for Judging Deliberation and Everyday Talk

Gutmann and Thompson suggest the standards of reciprocity, publicity, and accountability as criteria for judging deliberation in a public assembly. These criteria apply in a modified manner to the larger deliberative system, including everyday talk. The criteria also need revision to capture adequately what distinguishes good democratic talk from bad in an assembly or in everyday talk.

Publicity, as Gutmann and Thompson present it, is primarily a virtue of representative assemblies, which typically produce a binding decision.

Jürgen Habermas and Immanuel Kant suggest that the deliberative system as a whole should also foster publicity in ideas.[21] Yet neither formal nor everyday talk should make a fetish of publicity. Secrecy often produces better deliberation than "sunshine." In a formal decision-making assembly, proceedings are often more productive if the doors are closed and members do not have to watch their words. Similarly, in the everyday talk of the larger deliberative system, creative thought often thrives in protected space. A better criterion than publicity pure and simple would be some mixture of protection and publicity in the early stages of a deliberative process, but maximum feasible publicity in the final stages.[22]

Accountability might seem, even more than publicity, the virtue of a representative body. Yet in a larger sense, all the citizens of a polity are accountable to one another. Because neither journalists nor ordinary citizens are formally accountable to their readers or fellow citizens, the standard of accountability must be interpreted broadly in the deliberative system as a whole.

In most instances of everyday talk it makes sense to mandate only an informal sense of responsibility to others, and it is worth discussing what that undoubtedly contested responsibility might be.[23] "Hate speech," for example, could usefully be analyzed in the larger frame of parsing out the forms of mutual accountability appropriate to good democratic talk. Beginning to do so raises the point, applicable as well to deliberative assemblies, that constant accountability to others does not always produce the most creative and authentic deliberation, or even a deliberation that is ultimately the most helpful to the polity as a whole. Human beings may sometimes need spaces protected from accountability as well as from publicity in order to think most freely about the problems that face them. Again, a good criterion for deliberation would not mandate full accountability in the creative stages of the process but only in the later most public stages.

The standard of reciprocity applies fairly unproblematically to everyday talk. Gutmann and Thompson group under the heading of "reciprocity" the values of mutual respect, the goals of consistency in speech and consistency between speech and action, the need to acknowledge the strongly held feelings and beliefs of others, and the values of openmindedness and "economy of moral disagreement" (seeking rationales that minimize the rejection of an opposing position). Gutmann and Thompson incorporate in reciprocity, by making it an early step in the deliberative process, Lynn Sanders' proposed alternative to deliberation of "testimony," or stating one's own perspective in one's own words, an action that both has expressive value and helps change others' interpretive schemas.[24] All of these values can apply straightforwardly to everyday talk.

Along the same lines, Benjamin Barber's discussion of "strong democratic talk" stresses the mandate to listen.[25] Amitai Etzioni proposes for informal moral dialogues among citizens rules of engagement that include appealing to an overarching or external value that might reconcile participants in a given conflict, not affronting the deepest moral commitments of others (including leaving some issues out of the debate), and when possible substituting for the language of rights the language of needs, wants, and interests.[26]

Daniel Yankelovich spells out some of the ways in which, ideally, public judgment should differ from a mere aggregation of preferences—including "working through" controversial public matters as one would work through grief after death.[27] Iris Young opens up the process of deliberation to participants disadvantaged by traditional elite understandings of "reason-giving" by adding the elements of "greeting" (explicit mutual recognition and conciliatory caring), "rhetoric" (forms of speaking, such as humor, that reflexively attend to the audience), and "storytelling" (which can show outsiders what values mean to those who hold them).[28] Young's suggestions apply easily to everyday talk; all of these other writers explicitly apply their expanded understandings of "reciprocity" to everyday talk.

Yet even interpreted so expansively, reciprocity cannot stand unchallenged as a criterion for judging either formal deliberation or everyday talk. Gutmann and Thompson insightfully conclude their section on reciprocity by commenting that "the politics of mutual respect is not always pretty." In order to attract attention to a legitimate position that would otherwise be ignored, they point out, citizens may need "to take extreme and even offensive stands . . . refuse to cooperate with opponents, and even threaten retaliation" (90). The same is true in everyday talk, and more so. Because public statements go on record, because being made to look a fool in public is more wounding than a comparable insult in private, and because the sequencing of interaction in an assembly of several speakers makes it harder to correct misinterpretation or soften a harsh remark with a subsequent compliment, speakers in a public forum must be particularly careful to weigh their words and give others at least formal respect. The looser and less accountable settings of everyday talk foster greater incivility.

Both in a public forum and in everyday talk, there are justifiable places for offensiveness, noncooperation, and the threat of retaliation—even for raucous, angry, self-centered, bitter talk, aiming at nothing but hurt. These forms of talk are sometimes necessary not only to "promote mutual respect in the long term" (90), but also to achieve authenticity, to reveal (as in "testimony") the pain and anger, hate, or delight in another's pain, that someone actually feels, when expression or knowledge of those feelings furthers the understanding that is the goal of deliberation. These uncivil forms of talk are also often necessary as means to the end of approaching both liberty and equality in deliberation. Sometimes only intensity in opposition can break down the barriers of the status quo. No one always listens attentively to everyone else, and members of dominant groups are particularly likely to find they do not need to listen to members of subordinate groups. So subordinates sometimes need the battering ram of rage.[29]

Everyday talk sometimes provides spaces, such as the arms of a best friend, in which the most corrosive and externally harmful words can be uttered, understood, assimilated, and reworked for more public consumption. The corridors of public forums provide the same function. Everyone who has deliberated frequently in a public forum, even if that forum is no bigger than the 25 or so members of an academic department, knows that good deliberation has to include what goes on before and after, as individuals talk over their positions with likeminded and opposing others, as anger is worked up against the enemy in order to provide the impetus to speak, and as tempers are cooled, misunderstandings explained, compromises brokered—or positions sharpened, obfuscations skewered, and shoddy attempts at consensus revealed as internally contradictory. These processes work best in groups of only two or three, where the flow of communication, both verbal and nonverbal, is relatively unfettered.[30] Everyday talk, the New England town meeting, the state legislature, and the US Congress are alike in these respects. They all require their spaces of unmediated authenticity, which sometimes require nonreciprocity toward the outside world. Both in public forums and in the deliberative system as a whole, therefore, the criterion for good deliberation should be not that every interaction in the system exhibit mutual respect, consistency, acknowledgment, openmindedness, and moral economy, but that the larger system reflect those goals.

Joshua Cohen was the first theorist to specify criteria by which one might judge the democratic legitimacy of deliberation, that is, the degree to which suitably structured deliberation generates the legitimate authority to exercise power.[31] His criteria for legitimate deliberation apply equally well to deliberation in public assemblies and to everyday talk, for the quality of everyday talk affects the normative legitimacy of our many informal collective "decisions."

Yet his criteria too require revision. Cohen's first criterion is that a deliberation be free. This criterion is best reinterpreted as the Habermasian ideal of "freedom from power," that is, freedom from the threat of sanction or use of force.[32] Although Foucault is right that no situation can be "free" from power, and each of us both is constituted by power and exercises power in every interaction, nevertheless, some spaces for talking and acting are, although never fully free, more free than others.[33] We seek out such spaces both in democratic constitution making and in our everyday search for self-understanding and the creation of commonality. Democratic constitutions often try to insulate public deliberative forums from the worst effects of external power: The US Constitution, for example, exempts congressional representatives from liability for their official acts. Negotiations are often arranged so that with two parties (such as labor and management) each side has an equal number of representatives and votes, allowing the formal power of each to cancel out the formal power of the other. To guarantee sufficient freedom for everyday talk, a polity must not only provide the specific liberties of speech, press, and association needed for good deliberation but also generate for all groups some spaces that are relatively free from power.[34]

Equality, another of Cohen's criteria, applies to judging both everyday talk and formal deliberation. Deliberation is never fully free of power. Therefore, Cohen points out rightly that the criterion of equality requires making participants "substantively equal in that the existing distribution of power and resources does not shape their chances to contribute to the deliberation."[35] Insofar as threats of sanction and force do enter the deliberative arena, each participant should have equal resources to use as the basis for the threat of sanction and the use of force. Asymmetries should not give unfair advantage to any participant.[36] When systemic power, derived from a history of domination and subordination, produces a set of naturalized expectations and norms that disadvantage subordinates, both classic deliberation and everyday talk must, in order to approach the condition of equality, draw from a stream of alternatives to those expectations. The need to solicit and encourage previously excluded constituents in order to come closer to equality does not mean that every forum need include all those affected, but rather that in the deliberative system as a whole no participants should have an unfair advantage.[37]

Yet the equality appropriate to either everyday talk or formal delibera- tion does not require equal influence. Although Cohen writes that each participant should have "an equal voice" in the decision, deliberative equal- ity should not mean that each participant ought to have an equal effect on the outcome. Rather, the force of the better argument (including, as we shall see, the force of good arguments based on emotion) should prevail, no matter from whom that argument originates or how frequently it originates from one or more participants.[38] In practice, influence is not easy to separate from power, but both a smoothly functioning public assembly and a group of friends in everyday talk will try to perform that separation as best they can. They will take a good idea from any source but will reject attempts to exercise power, particularly unequal power, in the sense of the threat of sanc- tion and the use of force.[39]

The criterion of equality also mandates some form of mutual respect among participants. Mutual respect, a major component of Gutmann and Thompson's reciprocity, requires listening.[40] It requires your trying, through imagination and empathy, to put yourself in another's place.[41] It also requires recognizing the differences between you and others that make it impossible for you fully to put yourself in their place (Young 1997).[42] Until the recent work of African American feminist and postcolonial writers (e.g., Harris 1990), theories of mutual respect did not emphasize, or even recognize, the need to honor those differences.[43] The criterion of equality in deliberation should therefore be modified to mandate equal opportunity to affect the outcome; mutual respect; and equal power only when threats of sanction and the use of force come into play.

Cohen's next criterion is that deliberative outcomes should be settled only by reference to the "reasons" participants offer. Yet requiring of legiti- mate deliberation that it be "reasoned" implicitly or explicitly excludes the positive role of the emotions in deliberation. Amélie Rorty and Martha Nussbaum point out the flaws in dichotomizing "reason" and "emotion."[44]

The emotions always include some form of appraisal and evaluation, and reason can proceed only rarely without emotional commitment, if only an emotional commitment to the process of reasoning. Nussbaum's positive account of the role of emotions in deliberation further singles out the emotion of compassion as an essential element of good reasoning in matters of public concern. Other emotions, such as solidarity, play equally important roles. Because making the best sense of what we collectively ought to do requires a finely tuned attention to both cognitions and emotions, the third criterion for normative legitimacy should be that a deliberation be "considered" rather than "reasoned."[45]

Cohen's fourth criterion is the degree to which deliberation "aims to arrive at a rationally motivated *consensus*."[46] This is not, in my view, an appropriate criterion for legitimate deliberation. Even at the formal assembly level, normatively legitimate deliberation should aim not only at consensus but also at clarifying conflict, sharpening that conflict if necessary. Similarly, Cohen's criteria for an "ideal deliberative procedure" include that it should be "focused on the common good" (19), but such a singular focus on the common good makes it harder to recognize that deliberation may legitimately conclude correctly that the interests of the participants are fundamentally in conflict (Mansbridge [1980] 1983, 1992; Knight and Johnson 1994, 1998; Young 1996; Sanders 1997).[47] The conscious or unconscious pressure to frame one's argument in terms of the common good can seriously distort participants' understandings of the issue, making it far harder to resolve it through legitimate bargaining (e.g., taking turns or equalizing outcomes with sidepayments).

For the same reasons, deliberation should not ideally shape the "identity and interests of citizens" only "in ways that contribute to the formation of a public conception of the common good."[48] Formal deliberation, everyday talk, and other forms of democratic participation should enable citizens to see conflict more clearly when that conflict has previously been masked (e.g., by elite "nondecisions" and by hegemonic definitions of the common good).[49] Women, for example, have often been socialized to put the interests of others ahead of their own in ways that interfere with understanding their own interests. The articulation of self-interest has a legitimate role in democratic deliberation, particularly in discussions of fair distribution.[50] A legitimate deliberation should therefore meet the criterion of helping citizens understand their interests better, whether or not these interests can be forged into a larger common good.

Revised in these ways, both Gutmann and Thompson's criteria for justifiable decisions in a public assembly and Cohen's criteria for legitimate decisions in a binding forum turn out also to be reasonable criteria for judging everyday talk. In settings of relative liberty and equality, considering both reason and emotion, both everyday talk and more formal deliberation should help participants understand their conflicts and their commonalities. I will not try to resolve here how we may judge formal deliberation and everyday talk on the basis of their capacity for transforming a participant from a "private person" to a "citizen."[51] In both venues, we should judge these transformations by the *kinds* of solidarity and commitment to principle they involve.[52]

A Range of Forums, a Range within Standards

The venues for deliberation fall along a spectrum from the representative assembly,[53] to the public assembly producing a binding decision,[54] to the "public sphere,"[55] to the most informal venues of everyday talk. Moving along this range entails moving along a similar range, from formal to informal, within the same standards for good deliberation.

Jürgen Habermas has drawn a bright line between the binding assembly, as the locus of "will-formation," and the rest of the deliberative system, as the realm of "opinion-formation."[56] But this line does not, I believe, imply any great difference in the standards for deliberation. Habermas' public sphere is not restricted to a binding forum. Nor do his two constitutive elements of the public sphere—that in it "the private people . . . come together to form a public" and that it evince critical reasoning—define or map onto the binding/nonbinding distinction.[57]

The criteria for judging deliberation thus fall along a continuum that may not break at the binding/nonbinding distinction. At the most stringent end should be the standards that help create political obligation.[58] Possibly less stringent, but possibly no different, are the standards that generate the legitimate authority to exercise power.[59] Less stringent still are standards that allow us to judge which arguments are "justifiable" to other citizens,[60] adequate for continued cooperation,[61] or simply productive of higher-quality decisions.[62] The line between the forums that produce binding decisions and all other venues does not correspond, Gutmann and Thompson contend, to the line between legitimacy and mere justifiability. Gutmann and Thompson avail themselves explicitly of the line between binding and nonbinding decisions, making their analysis apply only to binding decisions. Yet they also make it clear throughout that they are working not within the framework of legitimacy but within the far broader frame of justifiability.[63] If we do not draw from the distinction between binding and nonbinding forums qualitatively different standards for judging deliberation on either side of that line, we are left with one set of standards that simply apply more and more loosely as the participants in talk are less and less formally accountable to one another. Everyday talk in this respect differs from classic deliberation in an assembly not in kind but only in degree.

I do not deny that formal representation differs in important ways from informal accountability. Assemblies with the authority to produce binding decisions also differ from the informal conversations that comprise everyday talk. The outstanding question is whether any of the criteria for judging the quality of deliberation, with which Gutmann and Thompson and others concern themselves, change at the binding/nonbinding boundary or at the boundary between formal and informal representation. With the possible exception of accountability, which obviously becomes formal with the institution of formal representation, this analysis claims that these criteria do not change; they simply become looser in application. Public deliberation stretches across a spectrum in which the various divisional points—state/nonstate, representative, binding/nonbinding—have as yet no coherent relation to the criteria for deliberation. As we ask what can motivate good deliberation within our formal and binding assemblies we should also ask what can motivate good deliberation in our interest groups, our media, and our everyday talk. All of these constitute important parts of the larger deliberative system.

Everyday talk was once revered as the prime locus of the formation of public judgment. Today it appears too rarely in the theoretical literature on deliberation,[64] as theorists direct their attention primarily toward deliberation in formal and binding assemblies. It is time to broaden our descriptive and analytic horizons again and give adequate credit, as a critical component of democracy, to the entire deliberative system, including its centerpiece, the citizen's everyday talk.

EDITORS' NOTE

This chapter was originally published in *Deliberative Politics: Essays on Democracy and Disagreement*, edited by Stephen Macedo (1999): "Everyday Talk in the Deliberative System," by Jane Mansbridge (pp. 211–239), © 1999 by Oxford University Press. Reprinted by permission of Oxford University Press, Inc. We have made stylistic changes for the purposes of this volume.

NOTES

I would like to thank Michael Bratman, Kimberly Curtis, Jean Elshtain, Stephen Macedo, and Andrew Sabel for comments on all or parts of this chapter, and Kimberly Curtis, Marshall Ganz, and Amy Gutmann for conversations that persuaded me to change my earlier phrase *everyday deliberation* to *everyday talk*. This chapter was prepared while I was a fellow at the Center for Advanced Study in the Behavioral Sciences. I am grateful for financial support provided by National Science Foundation Grant #SBR-9601236.

1. By using the word *system* I do not want to imply that the parts of the whole have a mechanical or perfectly predictable relation to one another, although both of these attributes are connotations of the words *system* and *systematic* in ordinary speech. Rather, I want to imply an interrelation among the parts, such that a change in one tends to affect another. See Thomas Christiano, *Rule of the Many: Fundamental Issues in Democratic Theory* (Boulder, CO: Westview Press, 1996), for interest groups and political parties as part of what I call the deliberative system.

2. Amy Gutmann and Dennis Thompson, *Democracy and Disagreement* (Cambridge: Harvard University Press, 1996).

3. Although Habermas includes in his deliberative "public sphere" privately owned settings with restricted access, such as the coffeehouses in England in the late 17th century, he does not include the kitchens and bedrooms that often host everyday talk. Jürgen Habermas, *The Structural Transformation of the Public Sphere*, trans. Thomas Burger and Frederick Lattimore (Cambridge: MIT Press, 1989 [1962]).

4. In a 1989 representative survey, about a third of the US public reported not engaging in any political act beyond voting. Sidney Verba, Kay Lehman Schlozman, and Henry G. Brady, *Voice and Equality* (Cambridge, MA: Harvard University Press, 1996), 83. By "nonactivists" I mean people like these. By "activists" I mean people who identify with a social movement, who feel an obligation toward that social movement, that is, a commitment to pay some price to promote the ends of the movement, and who actively discuss, craft, and propagate the ideas of the movement as a major part of their identities and lives. The majority of citizens in the United States today falls somewhere between these groups. They may have moments of activism, but in most of their identities and actions they are nonactivists. My term *nonactivists* also applies to the nonactivist sectors of the lives of this great majority of partially active citizens. The analysis in this chapter does not, I believe, depend on the exact definition of either group. It also focuses on only one aspect of the deliberative system—the everyday talk of nonactivists—and not on other aspects of the deliberative system or on other ways nonactivists influence the political process.

5. This formulation is intended to be more specific than Habermas' "matters of general interest" or Benhabib's "matters of common concern." Jürgen Habermas, *Communication and the Evolution of Society*, trans. Thomas McCarthy (Boston: Beacon Press, 1979 [1974]), 49; Seyla Benhabib, "Deliberative Rationality and Models of Democratic Legitimacy," *Constellations* 1 (1994): 26. It is not intended to be much more specific, as all of these formulations leave open to contest the meaning of "general," "common," and "what the public ought to discuss." This formulation, however, tries to underline that openness to contest by making the "ought" explicit. Note that Habermas used the phrase *matters of general interest* to describe the "public," not the "political"; he wrote that citizens "behave as a public body when they confer in an unrestricted fashion

... about matters of general interest" (49). By contrast he used the adjective *political*, modifying "the public sphere," to designate discussion that "deals with objects connected to the activity of the state" (ibid.). The formulation I suggest does not restrict the meaning of the political to issues connected with the activity of the state. Other words, such as *state* and *governmental*, allow us to retain the important distinction between matters of state decision and matters of collective decision outside the state. Young quotes Hannah Pitkin and Roberto Unger as defining *politics*, respectively, as "the activity through which relatively large and permanent groups of people determine what they will collectively do, settle how they will live together, and decide their future, to whatever extent this is within their power," and the "struggle over the resources and arrangements that set the basic terms of our practical and passionate relations. Preeminent among these arrangements is the formative institutional and imaginative context of social life." These definitions are highly compatible with mine. Iris Marion Young, *Justice and the Politics of Difference* (Princeton: Princeton University Press, 1990), 9; Hannah Pitkin, "Justice: On Relating Public and Private," *Political Theory* 9:3 (1981): 343; Roberto Unger, *Social Theory: Its Situation and Its Task* (Cambridge: Cambridge University Press, 1987), 145.

6. Simply allowing certain issues, such as pedophilia, into public debate gives them a legitimacy grounded in the possibility that such debate might usher in approval. Jean Elshtain (personal communication) argues on these grounds for excluding such issues from public debate and therefore from the realm of the political. For different but parallel reasons, John Stuart Mill suggested keeping certain fundamental values "*above* discussion" (his emphasis). John Stuart Mill, "Coleridge," *London and Westminster Review* (March 1840): 272-273.

7. Cited in, e.g., Michael Walzer, *Spheres of Justice* (New York: Basic Books, 1983), 292. This is a relatively common understanding in modern theory as well. Dewey, for example, defined "public" matters as those whose consequences "affect the welfare of many others" and are "so important as to need control." He defined "the public" as "all those who are affected by the indirect consequences of transactions to such an extent that it is deemed necessary to have those consequences systematically cared for." John Dewey, *The Public and Its Problems* (Athens, OH: Swallow Press/Ohio University Press, 1994 [1927]), 12, 16. Leaving aside the problematic indefinite subject in "is deemed," this definition leaves unexplored the meaning of "control" and "systematically," in which much of the meaning must lie if the definition does not simply extend the boundaries of the public to anyone even indirectly (though "seriously") affected (35). See below, note 37 on the boundaries of the polity and note 51 on the normative dimensions of Dewey's "public."

8. Carol Hainisch, "The Personal Is Political," in *Notes from the Second Year: Women's Liberation, Major Writings of the Radical Feminists*, eds. Shulamith Firestone and Anne Koedt (New York: Radical Feminists, 1970).

9. On the private/public distinction, see, e.g., Jean Bethke Elshtain, *Public Man/Private Woman: Women in Social and Political Thought* (Princeton: Princeton University Press, 1981), 217-218, 331-353; Mary Dietz, "Citizenship with a Feminist Face: The Problem with Maternal Thinking," *Political Theory* 13:1 (1985): 19-37; Iris Marion Young, "Impartiality and the Civic Public," in *Feminism as Critique: On the Politics of Gender*, eds. Seyla Benhabib and Drucilla Cornell (Minneapolis, MN: University of Minnesota Press, 1987), 74; Seyla Benhabib, "The Generalized and Concrete Other," in *Feminism as Critique: On the Politics of Gender*, eds. Seyla Benhabib and Drucilla Cornell (Minneapolis, MN: University of Minnesota Press, 1987), 177, note 12; Susan Moller Okin, *Justice, Gender, and the Family* (New York: Basic Books, 1990), 124-133; Catherine A. MacKinnon, *Toward a Feminist Theory of the State* (Cambridge, MA: Harvard University Press, 1989), 120; Jane Mansbridge and Susan Moller Okin, "Feminism," in *A Companion to Contemporary Political Philosophy*, eds. Robert E. Goodin and Philip Petit (Oxford: Blackwell, 1993).

10. Elshtain, *Public Man/Private Woman*, 218.

11. Sheldon Wolin, *Politics and Vision* (Boston: Little Brown, 1960, 1996); Hannah Arendt, *On Revolution* (New York: Viking, 1965); Jürgen Habermas, "Hannah Arendt's Communications Concept of Power," in *Philosophical-Political Profiles*, trans. Frederick G. Lawrence (Cambridge: MIT Press, 1985 [1976]). For a critique of the position on this subject, and an argument for the democratic legitimacy of "power" defined as the threat of sanction or use of force, see Jane Mansbridge, "Using Power/Fighting Power: The Polity," in *Democracy and Difference*, ed. Seyla Benhabib (Princeton: Princeton University Press, 1995).

12. Benjamin R. Barber, *Strong Democracy: Participatory Politics for a New Age* (Berkeley, CA: University of California Press, 1984), 121, 137, 161, 174 passim.

13. Ronald Beiner, *Political Judgment* (London: Methuen, 1983), 148.

14. My definition is compatible with Barber's if one defines "action" to include the decision not to take action and "public" to include the informal collective processes with which I am primarily concerned as well as the formal processes of state action.

15. Elshtain, *Public Man/Private Woman*, 333.

16. These comments respond to arguments in ibid.

17. Focus group, 1994, drawn from a representative Chicago sample, of African American women who had said in an earlier survey that they had less than a college education and considered themselves "feminist."

18. For an elaboration of this distinction between power and influence, see Mansbridge, "Using Power/Fighting Power." I would like to avoid the purely rationalist implication of "persuasion on the merits" but cannot find in English a phrase that includes a legitimate appeal to the relevant emotions along with a legitimate appeal to the relevant reasons. For the legitimate appeal to relevant emotions, see below.

19. From a 1994 in-depth follow-up to a survey earlier in 1994, in which 63 percent of women in a representative sample of the Chicago area reported having used the phrase *male chauvinist*.

20. See James C. Scott, *Domination and the Arts of Resistance: Hidden Transcripts* (New Haven, CT: Yale University Press, 1990), for parallels.

21. Much of the late 18th- and early 19th-century literature extolling the virtues of "public opinion" applies specifically to what I call "everyday talk." Habermas, *The Structural Transformation of the Public Sphere*, 90-102. Habermas also supports the application of the criterion of publicity to everyday talk (100-101). Following Bentham on "the regime of publicity," he applies the criterion both "inside and outside the parliament," and quotes Kant on the importance to the development of public reason of "the course of conversation in mixed companies [including] . . . businesspeople or women" (106).

22. See Jon Elster, "Deliberation and Constitution Making," in *Deliberative Democracy*, ed. John Elster (Cambridge: Cambridge University Press, 1998), 117.

23. See Jane Mansbridge, *Beyond Adversary Democracy* (Chicago: University of Chicago Press, 1983), 248-251, for active citizens as informal representatives of the inactive, and Jane Mansbridge, "What Is the Feminist Movement?" in *Feminist Organizations: Harvest of the New Women's Movement*, eds. Myra Marx Ferree and Patricia Yancey Martin (Philadelphia: Temple University Press, 1995); and "The Many Faces of Representation" (working paper, Politics Research Group, John F. Kennedy School of Government, Harvard University, 1997), for informal accountability in the representative sector.

24. Lynn M. Sanders, "Against Deliberation," *Political Theory* 25:3 (1997): 347-376.

25. Barber, *Strong Democracy*.

26. Amitai Etzioni, *The New Golden Rule* (New York: Basic Books), 102-106. Gutmann and Thompson are rightly leery of this sometimes necessary solution, because it forestalls attempts to generate deliberation within disagreement.

27. Daniel Yankelovich, *Coming to Public Judgment* (Syracuse, NY: Syracuse University Press, 1991).

28. Iris Marion Young, "Communication and the Other: Beyond Deliberative Democracy." In *Democracy and Difference*, ed. Seyla Benhabib (Princeton, NJ: Princeton University Press, 1996).

29. Linguists point out that human cultures differ dramatically in the degree to which various forms of expression are permitted and how these forms are interpreted. See, e.g., Thomas Kochman, *Black and White Styles in Conflict* (Chicago: University of Chicago Press, 1981), on black/white differences in the United States. As theorists explore further the role of the emotions and uncivil acts in the democratic process, it will be important to distinguish those speech forms and actions that are likely to promote mutual understanding across cultures from those that simply reflect the cultural habits of the writer.

30. The backstage does not, however, solve the problems of deliberative inequality. In backstage action and in everyday talk as well as in the deliberative forum, members of the professional classes are more likely than working-class or lower-middle class participants to have the skills that generate greater influence. Mansbridge, *Beyond Adversary Democracy*, 201. How unfettered such talk should be is, again, a matter of contest. See Thomas Christiano, "Deliberative Equality and the Deliberative Order," in *Political Order: NOMOS XXXVIII*, eds. Ian Shapiro and Russell Hardin (New York: New York University Press, 1996), on the "inherent contestability of

deliberative equality"; Jack Knight and James Johnson, "What Sort of Political Equality Does Democratic Deliberation Require?" in *Deliberative Democracy*, eds. James Bohman and William Rehg (Cambridge: MIT Press, 1998), for a critique of Rawls' "precepts of reasonable discussion"; and Rawls himself on the conditions for legitimate civil disobedience, John Rawls, *A Theory of Justice* (Cambridge: Harvard University Press, 1971).

31. Joshua Cohen, "Deliberation and Democratic Legitimacy," in *The Good Polity: Normative Analysis of the State*, eds. Alan Hamlin and Philip Petit (Oxford: Basil Blackwell, 1989).

32. Cohen categorizes Habermas' concept not under the criterion of freedom but under the criterion of a reasoned decision. Cohen's own criterion of "freedom" includes not being "constrained by the authority of prior norms or requirements" (22). This condition seems problematic unless it means, as I assume Cohen intended it to mean, *absolutely* constrained by the *traditional* authority of prior norms or requirements. Our lives and selves have no meaning apart from prior norms and requirements. One might almost say that our lives and selves are made up of prior norms and requirements. Many of those norms and requirements are right and just. Some (like language) are in many ways merely convenient but also contain elements of the use offered against the interests of some, often subordinate, groups. Some of the norms and requirements are highly unjust. Deliberation, even in the ideal sense, should be constrained by these priors when they are neutral or just. It should not be absolutely constrained; nor should it be constrained merely by tradition or by other requirements that cannot stand up under scrutiny.

These considerations are included in my definition of freedom from power. Conceptually, what I call "freedom" has strong links to Bentham's and Kant's understanding of publicity. Habermas describes how Kant's principle, that political actions are "in agreement with law and morality only as far as their maxims were capable of, or indeed in need of, publicity," derived from his thinking about the role of giving reasons everyday talk. Habermas, *The Structural Transformation of the Public Sphere*, 108. Kant's conclusion that "the public use of one's reason must always be free" (quoted, 106), which animates his distinction between "private" and "public" reason, is fully appropriate as a regulative ideal in everyday talk.

All these criteria, including freedom, should be understood as regulative ideals, that is, as ideals that can never be fully achieved but serve instead as standards at which to aim. As such, the regulative ideals of deliberative democracy parallel the regulative ideals of aggregative (or "adversary") democracy, e.g., that in the aggregation each should count for one and none for more than one. In practice, neither deliberative democracy nor aggregative democracy can ever fully live up to its regulative ideals. This fact does not mean we should reject these ideals as goals, or fail to use them to judge the degree of legitimacy (which will never, therefore, be full) of existing democratic practice. It is therefore not an appropriate criticism of a regulative ideal (such as "love thy neighbor as thyself") to say with, e.g., Lynn Sanders, "Against Deliberation," that it cannot fully be reached in practice. It is an appropriate criticism of such an ideal to say that aiming at it produces ill effects in utility, justice, or other values, or that aiming at an ideal that cannot fully be achieved in practice itself produces ill effects. See Christiano, *The Rule of the Many*, for a good critique of making only deliberation the basis for legitimacy.

33. See Pamela Allen, *Free Space: A Perspective on the Small Group in Women's Liberation* (New York: Times Change Press, 1970); shorter version reprinted in Anne Koedt, Ellen Levine, and Anita Rapone, eds., *Radical Feminism* (New York: Quadrangle Press, 1973), 271-279, and Sara M. Evans and Harry C. Boyte, *Free Spaces* (New York: Harper and Row, 1986) on "free space"; Jane Mansbridge, "Feminism and Democracy," *American Prospect* 1 (1990): 127-136, and Mansbridge, "Using Power/Fighting Power," on deliberative enclaves; Nancy Fraser, "Rethinking the Public Sphere," in *Justice Interruptus* (New York: Routledge, 1997 [1992]), on subaltern counterpublics; Scott, *Domination and the Arts of Resistance*, on sequestered spaces; and James Johnson, "Communication, Criticism, and the Postmodern Consensus," *Political Theory* 25:4 (1997): 559-583, for an interpretation of Foucault as searching for spaces of concrete freedom.

34. Robert A. Dahl, *Democracy and Its Critics* (New Haven, CT: Yale University Press, 1989); Jack Knight and James Johnson, "Aggregation and Deliberation: On the Possibility of Democratic Legitimacy," *Political Theory* 22:2 (1994): 277-296. Freedom in deliberation might also include what John Rawls called "the worth of liberty," but I categorize those considerations under equality. Rawls, *A Theory of Justice*.

35. Cohen, "Deliberation and Democratic Legitimacy," 23.

36. Knight and Johnson, "What Sort of Political Equality Does Democratic Deliberation Require?" 293; Jane

Mansbridge, "The Equal Opportunity to Exercise Power," in *Equality of Opportunity*, ed. Norman E. Bowie (Boulder, CO: Westview Press).

37. Knight and Johnson, "What Sort of Political Equality Does Democratic Deliberation Require?"; Knight and Johnson, "Aggregation and Deliberation"; Iris Marion Young, "Justice, Inclusion, and Deliberative Democracy," in *Deliberative Politics: Essays on Democracy and Disagreement*, ed. Stephen Macedo (Oxford: Oxford University Press, 1999). Young, Fraser, and Mansbridge, among others, address the institutional requirements that usually increase equality in deliberation. Young, *Justice and the Politics of Difference*; Fraser, "Rethinking the Public Sphere"; Mansbridge, "Feminism and Democracy"; Mansbridge, "Using Power/Fighting Power." See Norman Maier, "An Experimental Test of the Effects of Training on Discussion Leadership," *Human Relations* 6 (1953): 161-173, and Reid Hastie, ed., *Inside the Juror* (Cambridge: Cambridge University Press, 1993), on encouraging minority voices in deliberation. The question of inclusion involves norms regarding the boundaries of the polity. Robert A. Dahl, *After the Revolution?* (New Haven, CT: Yale University Press, 1956), 64-67. Without putting bounds on the polity, the maxim "What affects all should be decided by all" could entail weighting the power of individuals in a decision (including their capacity to block consensus and therefore retain the status quo) by the degree to which the decision would affect them.

38. For the effect of equality in opening an arena for the authority of the better argument, see Habermas, *The Structural Transformation of the Public Sphere*, 36; for deliberation not requiring equal influence, see Mansbridge, *Beyond Adversary Democracy*, esp. 235-244, and more recently, Mark Warren, "Deliberative Democracy and Authority," *American Political Science Review* 90:1 (1996): 46-60; and Harry Brighouse, "Egalitarianism and the Equal Availability of Political Influence," *Journal of Political Philosophy* 4 (1996): 125. When Cohen uses the term *equal voice* as a requirement for participants in legitimate deliberation, he presumably does not mean to imply equal numbers of words from each participant or an equal effect on the outcome. Joshua Cohen, "Deliberation and Democratic Legitimacy," 22. The term *equal voice* does not as yet have an exact or even a frequently stipulated meaning in democratic theory. A new generation of theorists has recently begun to tackle the formidable problems involved in formulating a concept of equality congruent with deliberative ideals. In their excellent essay on the subject, Knight and Johnson's most challengeable argument is that "deliberation requires equal capacity to advance persuasive claims," including "the ability to reason, articulate ideas, etc." Knight and Johnson, "What Sort of Political Equality Does Democratic Deliberation Require?" 281. One could, it's true, argue for such an ideal, stressing its regulative and unachievable side, on the grounds of full agency, self-development, and the precisely faithful representation of one's interests in deliberation. But it is not clear that equality in these capacities is required for deliberation or even deliberative equality. Many participants in deliberation might prefer Christiano's formulation, in which although "I have a great interest in having my views expressed . . . it is not essential that I do the expressing." Christiano, "Deliberative Equality and the Democratic Order," 259. Christiano's further formulation, that for equality to prevail in deliberation "equal time should be given" to different opinions, is, however, overly mechanical, unsuited to how thinking and deliberation actually work (when one point may be made well in 5 words and another may require 500). Bohman's institutional suggestions for furthering equality in deliberation are more persuasive than his analysis of the normative ideal. James Bohman, *Public Deliberation* (Cambridge: MIT Press, 1996); see 107, 113, 122, 124, 126, 131, for differing formulations of that ideal.

39. Legitimate influence does not encompass manipulation (getting others to agree to positions against their deepest interests through persuasion that has the external form of "the better argument"). Manipulation is illegitimate in any democratic deliberation, including everyday talk.

40. Barber, *Strong Democracy*.

41. Bernard Williams, "The Idea of Equality," in *Philosophy, Politics, and Society*, eds. Peter Laslett and W. G. Runciman (Oxford: Blackwell, 1962); Martha Minow, "Foreword to the Supreme Court 1986 Term," *Harvard Law Review* 101:1 (1987): 10-95; Seyla Benhabib, *Situating the Self* (New York: Routledge, 1991).

42. Young, "Assymetrical Reciprocity."

43. E.g., Angela Harris, "Race and Essentialism in Legal Theory," *Stanford Law Review* 42:3 (1990): 581-616.

44. Amélie Oskenburg Rorty, "Varieties of Rationality, Varieties of Emotion," *Social Science Information* 2 (1985): 343-353; Martha Craven Nussbaum, "Emotion and Women's Capabilities," in *Women, Culture, and Development*, eds. Martha Craven Nussbaum and Jonathan Glover (Oxford: Oxford University Press, 1995).

45. See Jane Mansbridge, "Self-Transformation within the Envelope of Power" (paper delivered at the annual meeting of the American Political Science Association, Chicago, IL, September 2, 1992); Jane Mansbridge, "Activism Writ Small, Deliberation Writ Large" (paper delivered at the annual meeting of the American Political Science Association, Washington, DC, August 28, 1997); Charles E. Lindblom, *Inquiry and Change: The Troubled Attempt to Understand and Shape Society* (New Haven, CT:Yale University Press, 1990), 32; Barber, *Strong Democracy*; Knight and Johnson, "What Sort of Political Equality Does Democratic Deliberation Require?" 284.

46. Cohen, "Deliberation and Democratic Legitimacy," 23, emphasis in original.

47. Mansbridge, *Beyond Adversary Democracy*; Knight and Johnson, "Aggregation and Deliberation"; Knight and Johnson, "What Sort of Political Equality Does Democratic Deliberation Require?"; Young, "Communication and the Other"; Sanders, "Against Deliberation."

48. Cohen, "Deliberation and Democratic Legitimacy," 19.

49. See Peter Bachrach and Morton Baratz, "Decisions and Non-Decisions: An Analytical Framework," *American Political Science Review* 57:3 (1963): 632-642; Peter Bachrach, "Interest, Participation, and Democratic Theory," in *Participation in Politics, NOMOS XVI*, eds. J. Roland Pennock and John W. Chapman (New York: Lieber-Atherton, 1974). See also criterion of "enlightened understanding" in Robert A. Dahl, "Procedural Democracy," in *Philosophy, Politics, and Society*, eds. Peter Laslett and James Fishkin (New Haven, CT: Yale University Press, 1979), 104-105.

50. Jane Mansbridge, "A Deliberative Theory of Interest Representation," in *The Politics of Interests*, ed. Mark P. Petracca (Boulder, CO: Westview Press); Laura Stoker, "Interests and Ethics in Politics," *American Political Science Review* 86:2 (1992): 369-380; Knight and Johnson, "What Sort of Political Equality Does Democratic Deliberation Require?"

51. Habermas, *The Structural Transformation of the Public Sphere*. In *The Public and Its Problems*, Dewey also wanted "The Public" to "form itself" (31), "define and express its interests" (146), and become "organized" (28), in contrast to the "mass," which he saw as "scattered, mobile and manifold" (146), forming "too many publics" (126). See also Barber, *Strong Democracy*, 28.

52. For an invigorating skepticism on transformation, see Nancy Rosenblum, *Membership and Morals: The Personal Uses of Pluralism in America* (Princeton, NJ: Princeton University Press, 1998); also Knight and Johnson, "Aggregation and Deliberation."

53. Joseph M. Bessette, *The Mild Voice of Reason: Deliberative Democracy and American National Government* (Chicago: University of Chicago Press, 1994).

54. Cohen, "Deliberation and Democratic Legitimacy," Gutmann and Thompson, *Democracy and Disagreement*.

55. Habermas, *The Structural Transformation of the Public Sphere*.

56. By 1992, Habermas had borrowed from Nancy Fraser the idea that the "general" public sphere consists of both a "strong" public sphere that engages in making binding decisions and a "weak" public sphere that engages exclusively in opinion-formation and consists of "overlapping, subcultural publics" that can form "collective identities." Jürgen Habermas, *Between Facts and Norms*, trans. William Rehg (Cambridge, MA: MIT Press, 1996 [1992]), 307-308, esp. note 26; Fraser, "Rethinking the Public Sphere." I argue here that the weak public sphere should include the full range of everyday talk on matters that the public should discuss. This weak public sphere is responsible for the "informal opinion-formation that prepares and influences political decision making" (171). As the realm of "opinion-formation," it differs from the realm of "will-formation," that is, the formal arena making binding decisions (314).

57. Habermas, *The Structural Transformation of the Public Sphere*, 25. Although these two criteria of coming together to form a public and critical reasoning do not exclude nonbinding forums such as the coffeehouse, they might seem to exclude everyday talk. On the first criterion, informal everyday talk itself can "pull together the scattered critical potentials" of the public (382). Ideas, loosed upon a population by individuals linked with social movements, governments, a differentiated media, and other sources of intellectual ferment,

do some of the required "pulling together." Whether the group then forms a "public" raises a contested question. My portrayal of the public sphere intentionally blunts the critical edge of both Dewey's conception of the "Public" (see note 51 above) and Habermas' ideal public sphere (which should produce a transformation from "private person" to "citizen") on the grounds that if these concepts require the citizenry to aim at a common good (even while disagreeing, sometimes violently, on that good), they do not define the only appropriate ends and if they do not require such an aim their meaning is ambiguous. On the second criterion, "critical consideration" of appropriate reasons and emotions seems a better requirement for a public sphere (see above), particularly if that consideration encompasses forms of deliberative shorthand, such as entire arguments summed up in a word, rules of thumb, and other time- and cognition-saving heuristics. Samuel Popkin, *The Reasoning Voter* (Chicago: University of Chicago Press, 1991).

[58.] Arthur Isaak Applbaum, "Democratic Legitimacy and Official Discretion," *Philosophy and Public Affairs* 21:3 (1992): 240-274.

[59.] Bernard Manin, "On Legitimacy and Democratic Deliberation," *Political Theory* 15:3 (1987): 338-368; Cohen, "Deliberation and Democratic Legitimacy."

[60.] Gutmann and Thompson, *Democracy and Disagreement*.

[61.] Bohman, *Public Deliberation*.

[62.] David M. Estlund, "Who's Afraid of Deliberative Democracy? On the Strategic/Deliberative Dichotomy in Recent Constitutional Jurisprudence," *Texas Law Review* 71 (1993): 1437-1477.

[63.] Gutmann and Thompson do link the binding quality of decisions to their justifiability. The decisions they analyze "are collectively binding, and they should therefore be justifiable, as far as possible, to everyone bound by them" (13). However, how one comes to be "bound" is not fully clear. Gutmann and Thompson may, like Rawls, base a citizen's duty to obey the law solely on the near-justice of the overall constitutional system, provided that the law in question does not exceed certain limits of injustice. This stance would be congruent with their explicitly rejecting the idea that deliberative democracy will necessarily produce a just outcome (18), and also explicitly rejecting the idea that an outcome is legitimate if the process that produced it was legitimate (200). Most important, they reject the dichotomy that asks "whether democratic procedures have priority over just outcomes or just outcomes over democratic procedures" (27). Rather, "neither the principles that define the process of deliberation [the "conditions of deliberation," i.e. the principles of reciprocity, publicity, and accountability] nor the principles that constitute its content [the "content of deliberation," i.e. the principles of basic liberty, basic opportunity, and fair opportunity] have priority in a deliberative democracy. Both interact dynamically in ways that overcome the dichotomy between procedure and outcome" (27).

It is not easy to parse out the relation of these six dynamically interacting principles to whether or not a law that results from a given deliberation is justified. In most of the argument in the book, justifiability lies along a spectrum, so that the "more nearly the conditions [that is, the principles of reciprocity, publicity, and accountability] are satisfied, the more nearly justifiable are the results likely to be" (17). But some sections of the book suggest a more either/or structure, in which if one or more of any of the principles is violated, the results of the deliberation are not justified. For example, "liberty and opportunity join reciprocity, publicity, and accountability as the constitutional principles of a deliberative democracy" (199; also 201), while constitutional principles are "standards that public officials and citizens *must not* violate in the making of public policy in order that those policies can be provisionally justified to the citizens who are bound by them" (199, emphasis added). This sounds as if justifiability falls upon violation of any one of the six principles. This interpretation is strengthened by their statement that "public policies that violate [a constitutional principle] are *not justifiable*, even if they are enacted in a process that otherwise satisfies the conditions of deliberation" (199-200, emphasis added). On the other hand, these strong either/or sentences all appear in the section on liberty and opportunity. They may well therefore apply not to all six principles but only to the three principles that constitute the "content" of deliberation, namely liberty, opportunity, and fair opportunity. This counterinterpretation is strengthened not only by the context but also by recognizing that part of the role of these "content" principles is to act in analogy with rights or other forms of priority, constraining (199, 229, 354, 355), restraining (209), and ruling out (225) certain actions within and resulting from deliberation.

Yet if the second three principles (liberty, opportunity, and fair opportunity) have a stronger either/or role, making policies that violate them "not justifiable," this difference from the first three principles is not spelled out. Gutmann and Thompson state far more weakly that each of the six principles constrains and restrains all the others (355), although the content principles are "more constraining" than the conditions principles (199).

64. For past concern for everyday talk, see note 21 above. For the current literature on deliberation see citations in Gutmann and Thompson, and more recently, Paul H. Weithman, "Contractualist Liberalism and Deliberative Democracy," *Philosophy and Public Affairs* 24:4 (1995): 320-340; Bohman, *Public Deliberation*; James Bohman and William Rehg, eds., *Deliberative Democracy* (Cambridge: MIT Press, 1998); Jon Elster, ed., *Deliberative Democracy* (Cambridge: Cambridge University Press, 1998); and Don Herzog, *Poisoning the Minds of the Lower Orders* (Princeton, NJ: Princeton University Press, 1998), chap. 4.

De-centering Deliberative Democracy

by Iris Marion Young

In recent years, ideas associated with deliberative democracy have caught the imagination, not only of political theorists but also of many government and nongovernmental practitioners who wish to improve the quality of public discussion and decision making. As more professionals have endorsed deliberative democracy, the term has come most commonly to refer to practices of citizen dialogue in face-to-face groups. While promoting face-to-face discussion is usually a good thing in a democracy, I will argue in this essay that deliberative democracy ought not to be identified primarily with processes of discussion in face-to-face settings. Conceiving deliberative democracy in this way blunts its theoretical insight and critical force.

As an application of theory to the world of mass democracy, I suggest, deliberative democracy should be conceived primarily as "de-centered." I take this concept from Jürgen Habermas' theory of deliberative democracy and adopt elements of his normative model of democratic process. To consider deliberative democracy as de-centered means that we do not find the process of deliberation taking place in any single forum or bounded group, whether the entire polity considered as a whole or relatively small face-to-face groups. Instead we should understand processes of discussion and decision making that we evaluate under norms of deliberative democracy as occurring in multiple forums and sites connected to one another over broad spans of space and time. Considering the process of deliberative democracy as such a mediated relation among diverse sites, forums, and events magnifies the significance of the political issues deliberative democracy deals with beyond the primarily local issues that occupy most consultative practices that currently aim to adopt deliberative norms.

Theorizing deliberative democracy as de-centered, however, presents problems for the generation and application of criteria for evaluating the quality of public discussion and decision making. It is not obvious how criteria put forward by some deliberative theorists, such as publicity, political equality, inclusion, or accountability, should be applied to the evaluation of processes that take place across a society. This paper will take some steps toward applying such criteria to de-centered democratic processes. Before doing that, however, I will propose a criterion of "linkage" as necessary to evaluation, specifically of de-centered processes.

Critique of a Centered Concept of Deliberation

In *Between Facts and Norms,* Jürgen Habermas criticizes Joshua Cohen's conception of deliberative democracy for harboring what Habermas understands as an inappropriately centered view of the deliberatively democratic process. According to Habermas, Cohen sees the ideal process of deliberative democracy as involving the society as a whole in a political process steered through deliberative decision making.[1] On the contrary, Habermas asserts, modern societies are too complex ever to engage in a single process that can be moved in one direction or another. To the extent that democratic politics can be deliberative, its processes, even as ideal, are necessarily embedded in social processes that exceed political regulation. Democratic theory remains bewitched by a philosophy of consciousness that conceives of an agent from whom processes of deliberation originate. When conceiving of society as a whole, the people as sovereign, or their representative legislative body, this conception of democratic will formation assumes that there is a single collective whose will it is.[2]

Habermas recommends theorizing a de-centered conception of democratic process as against ideas of deliberation as centered in a unified process of will formation:

> The discourse theory of democracy corresponds to the image of a de-centered society, albeit a society in which the political sphere has been differentiated as an arena for perception, identification, and treatment of problems affecting the whole society. Once one gives up the philosophy of the subject, one needs neither to concentrate sovereignty concretely in the people nor to banish it in anonymous constitutional structures and powers.[3]

Habermas may not be fairly representing Cohen's position, for in the intervening years Cohen himself has promoted a de-centered conception of deliberative politics.[4]

More generally, however, Habermas is right that many conceptions of deliberative democratic politics point to a republican ideal in which the members of the society, as it were together, in a single process, make decisions that bind members of the collective. For some others, however, such a picture of a polity itself as a centered locus of deliberation is both unrealistic and disturbing. Many theorists of deliberation conceive democratic process as centered in a more mundane sense, in relatively small face-to-face groups. Some now tend to identify deliberative democracy with processes in which ordinary citizens meet to discuss and make recommendations on important issues. In these processes citizens are neither mere observers, nor is their role merely to hold decision makers accountable after the fact. Instead, they are direct participants in organized dialogues about environmental planning, police procedures, budget processes, or the quality of health-care delivery. Scholars, such as Archon Fung, David Booher, John Gaventa, Eric Wright, John Forrester, and Bronwyn Hayward, have documented citizen participation in dialogue processes, usually involving the development and implementation of local government processes.[5] A number of civic organizations in the United States have adopted a mission to organize or encourage participatory dialogue processes in public issues, either within government or in civil society. These include Demos, the Kettering Foundation, America-*Speaks*, the National Issues Forums, the National Civil League, and others.[6]

James Fishkin's method of the deliberative opinion poll has been used at least as much for discussion of national as for local issues, both in the United States, the United Kingdom, and New Zealand, among other places.[7] This process follows more of a representative than a participatory approach to discussion. The poll randomly selects persons to participate in a dialogue weekend; the characteristics of the participants are thus supposed roughly to mirror the characteristics of the general population in respect to gender, age, race, income, education, religions, and political ideology; and the deliberative poll aims to test the extent to which people's opinions about issues and proposals change as a result of discussing them with experts and fellow citizens over a few days. Though there are thus many differences between Fishkin's model of deliberation and deliberative consultative practices in local government, they share features that correspond to a centered conception of deliberation. Both conceive deliberation as a give and take process of discussion aimed at persuasion within a single group that meets face to face and arrives at deliberative outcomes in a determinate period of time.

Some theorists of deliberative democracy consider legislatures as sites of deliberation. While they would not claim that parliamentary bodies are the only sites of deliberative discussion and decision making, Amy Gutmann and Dennis Thompson draw many of their examples of political exchange that either meets or falls short of their criteria of good deliberative process from congressional debates.[8] To the extent that, for some theorists, legislatures appear as paradigms of potentially deliberative process, then they too operate with a centered conception of deliberation. The setting is face to face, the group bounded, and the time span for relevant discussion relatively short, though not reduced to a single meeting.

Habermas criticizes a view of deliberative democracy that imagines political decision making in a society as *like* what occurs in bounded forums with identifiable participants who, within the time they have, try to arrive at a general will. Most deliberative theorists are less Rousseauian and more realistic than this. But they, too, look for, or aim to design, *actual* processes of discussion, exchange, and persuasion leading to an agreed upon conclusion. All these are *centered* conceptions of deliberation, because they assume that deliberation takes place in a single forum within a bounded group within a delimited time.

We can note a few problematic aspects of such a conception. First, to reiterate and expand on Habermas' objection, this centered conception assumes that there is a body politic whose discussion process should issue in a "will of the people," whether the sovereign people of a whole society or the participants in a face-to-face forum. Second, when processes of deliberative decision making are understood as enacted by representatives, whether in legislatures or citizens juries or deliberative-opinion polls, it is still the representative body that is considered the site of deliberation, rather than a process that relates the representatives to those whom they might be said to represent.

To the extent that efforts to put the values of deliberative democracy into practice lead to a focus on designing participatory forums in local decision-making processes, the significance of deliberative ideas for evaluating and enhancing modern democracies becomes diluted. To be sure, local face-to-face meetings in which citizens debate with national, state, and local officials and with each other are generally a good thing. If we assume that deliberative democracy means primarily that citizens should have opportunities to participate in the decisions made close to them, however, we risk marginalizing deliberative process and failing to use its critical potential. In large democracies, what happens locally is complexly conditioned by actions and decisions that are global, national, or regional in reach. A theory of deliberative democracy must be able to conceive how political decision-making processes with this complexity and reach do or can exemplify norms of deliberative democracy. That requires, I submit, theorizing the deliberative process and the application of its criteria of evaluation as de-centered.

De-centered Deliberation

To be useful for theory and practice of democracy today, experiments with deliberative participation in citizens juries, deliberative opinion polls, study circles, and face-to-face consultation should be understood as a *part* of a democratic process between tens of millions of strangers in multiple locales over a period of months or years. Concepts of deliberative democracy should be applied to this de-centered process in which social problems and policy issues are discussed and contested in public media, various forums organized by state agencies, businesses, or universities, as well as in more informal activities of civic associations.

Habermas' conception of de-centered deliberative democracy provides a valuable starting point for such an account. He describes contemporary democratic decision making as embedded in complex social relations, rather than able to direct them; and as involving complexly mediated relationships of communication and interdependence.[9] The theory does not simply describe these democracies as they are, however, but as they *ought* to be if their policy outcomes are to be considered normatively legitimate. Let me summarize my understanding of this model.

In large highly differentiated societies, democracy is, among other things, a method of addressing social problems. However powerful and well-functioning government institutions be, they cannot know about, anticipate, and control the activities of all of society and the conflicts or deprivations these may generate. Problems need to be communicated from their socially felt sites to political institutions whose missions are to respond to problems through systems of law, regulation, and public administration. In Habermas' view, organizations and group activity in the civil society outside state institutions serve to locate problems widely felt in society, formulate an account of the experience of them, and communicate the problems to public officials.

In Habermas' model of de-centered deliberative democracy, those concerned with social problems help constitute and have access to a public sphere in which to express the problems. A public sphere is a linked set of discussion arenas through which strangers relate to one another, in principle open to anyone in the society for expressing themselves and to which everyone in principle can be witness and auditor. When the public sphere takes up expression of a problem or issue, its discussion travels to numerous sites and forums that influence one another, and thereby the voicing of the problem becomes refined and generalized to involve the experience of more people. Its expression also becomes amplified to the extent that it is difficult for political officials to ignore the problem. In the media of this public sphere, citizens, officials, and experts discuss alternative approaches for responding to social problems, awareness of which has percolated from civic locales. Because the public sphere is open and inclusive, participants in these debates need to be careful about how they express their opinions; they should be speaking with the knowledge that unknown strangers are likely to hear them; and for their opinions persuasively to move the debate, they must be put in terms that they believe everyone can understand and accept. Public spheres therefore encourage appeal to reason and openness to the point of view of others. After a time, public opinion ideally congeals around a preferred policy approach, which participants in state institutions take up and craft into law. Democratically legitimate legislation, as well as legitimate administrative and court decisions, thus have the function of converting expression of social needs and wants into enforceable power.

Habermas' normative ideal of de-centered deliberative democracy, then, conceptualizes a process spread across space and time, through which policymaking institutions are open to and pick up communication from the broad mass of differentiated social segments and relationships. Some of the key elements of democratic process across society in this model are publicity, communicative reasons, and, as I shall discuss below, linkage among elements of the process.

Habermas is clear that "the normal business of politics in Western democracies cannot satisfy these strong conditions" (p. 356). The purpose of a theory of de-centered deliberative democracy, then, is primarily critical: to provide norms and criteria through which the normative legitimacy of the process and many of its policy outcomes can be questioned and improved. Aside from providing some guidelines for journalistic ethics (p. 378), however, in *Between Facts and Norms*, Habermas offers little in the way of criteria for evaluating the quality of political processes in modern mass democracies, or guidance for applying them.

Evaluating De-centered Politics with Criteria of Deliberative Democracy

Most theories of deliberative democracy articulate criteria for evaluating the quality of political interaction from the point of view of norms of deliberateness and democracy. Thomas Christiano offers criteria of political equality, rationality, persuasion, openness, variety, transparency, and reason-guidedness.[10] Amy Gutmann and Dennis Thompson offer three major criteria for evaluating the quality of democratic political processes: reciprocity, publicity, and accountability.[11] James Bohman also offers three criteria: nontyranny, equality, and publicity.[12]

In my own work related to deliberative democracy, I have specified four criteria of good democratic process: political equality, reasonableness, publicity, and inclusion.[13] My understanding of political equality is similar to Bohman's and Christiano's, as well as that of Charles Beitz.[14] Political and social institutions should be structured to afford members of the polity access to information relevant to democratic decision making and the views of each ought to have equal weight in deliberations.

In articulating the second criterion, reasonableness, I take some issue with theorists who follow Rawls in taking the object of reasonableness to be the content of contributions to a deliberative dialogue. On this understanding, we distinguish between claims that are reasonable or unreasonable, according to whether they are put in terms that are generally shared. This is too restrictive an understanding of reasonableness, I argue, and misses some important issues. Reasonableness refers more to certain dispositions of dialogue participants, I suggest, than to something about the content of their contributions. Participants in a deliberative process are reasonable to the extent that they are willing to listen to others, revise their opinions, reserve judgment, and treat others with respect. They understand that dissent often produces insight, and that only by trying to reach agreement can dialogue continue.

My understanding of the third criterion, publicity, resonates with those of Gutmann and Thompson and of Bohman. Perhaps more explicitly than they, however, I understand the publicity of contributions to dialogue as a reflexive consequence of the dialogue situation. A major difference between speaking publicly and speaking privately is that in a public situation one does not know some of those able to hear one's statements and should assume that many of them have differing understandings, experiences, and perspectives. That awareness induces a form to one's statements that aims toward generality and in which participants move between positions of speaker and listener and thus acknowledge the multiple statements within the discussion.[15]

I consider, however, that the most significant contribution of my own account of deliberative criteria consists in its elaboration of the concept of inclusion. All deliberative theorists specify that a process of political communication is not properly democratic unless it includes all persons likely to be affected by a decision; but I think that the meaning and conditions of this requirement are richer than most theorists acknowledge. The formal opportunity to contribute and be witness to the contribution of others is not sufficient for effective inclusion. A process of political communication should also be inclusive of diverse communication styles and enable informative contributions that do not take the form of argument. In large-scale democracies characterized by massive social differentiation and inequality, we should think of inclusion not only in terms of individuals, but in terms of structural social groups who stand in unequal relations to one another. Inclusion thus requires compensating for the potential marginalization of some groups through mechanisms of special representation. This form of inclusion is important not only as a form of giving respect to everyone, but also as a means of trying to ensure that major social perspectives on problems will contribute their situated knowledges towards solutions.[16]

While they vary in label and nuance, the criteria that theorists of deliberative democracy have articulated for evaluating the quality of political communication and decision making overlap and express similar values. With them, much about actual political processes in democracies can be criticized—for example, for allowing persons and groups with greater power to dominate discussion, or coerce and threaten others; for effectively excluding some persons and groups from participation; for allowing appeals to fear or selfishness to guide people's opinions. The sort of criteria that deliberative theorists use, however, appears at least implicitly to be derived from experiences of good discussion in face-to-face meetings. They seem easiest to apply, moreover, to evaluate centered deliberative democratic processes— i.e., to a single face-to-face meeting, or a time-bound series of such meetings, with identifiable participants. To apply a standard of inclusion, we can observe who is present at such meetings. We can see whether participants behave with openness to the expression of others or act in dismissive or hostile ways. We can analyze the content of their utterances to determine to what extent they understand themselves and are understood by others to be offering as reasons considerations that anyone should be able to understand. In principle, we can find out to what extent the decisions reached result from discussion to which everyone in the forum is party, rather than the result of behind door threats, offers, and bargaining.

Each of the criteria can and should also be applied to evaluate decentered political communication across a wide mass of persons and organizations that deal with problems and make decisions to address them. It is less obvious, however, what applying the criteria to de-centered deliberation means or how to do it. I want to begin to address this question. In it emerges a large research agenda whose elements I can only begin to identify.

If we take Habermas' account as having described the sort of process we aim to evaluate, a problem with applying criteria surfaces immediately. The process to be evaluated seems hugely complex and to have no bounds that would allow one to pick out a unit to be evaluated. Politics in contemporary mass democracies certainly is a process in which local discussion at many sites sometimes breaks into and helps constitute public processes of uptake and transsocietal influence that shift what the guardians of public media regard as important, change legislative agendas, and sometimes produce new policies and programs. The problem for evaluating the quality of such processes, using deliberative criteria, is that there are always many issues under consideration, often in rather inchoate form, and public processes often fluidly move among them. It seems to me that, in order to apply criteria of good deliberation to a de-centered political process, it is necessary to abstract somewhat from this complexity and fluidity to focus on an artificially bounded unit. Because we do not want this to be a centered unit like a single forum or discussion space, I suggest that a useful way to abstract such a unit is to construct an account of a process of political communication and its outcome as focused on a single issue area.

I'll give one example, Joan Scott has given us an excellent study of the movement of the discussion in France through the 1990s about representation of women in parliament, a discussion that eventually issued in the law of *parité*, which mandates that 50 percent of candidates for parliament be women. She treats the discussion over a significant period of time, in many forums, and considers the relationships among its moments. Her focus is on this specific issue, even though it is embedded in and flowed among a wide array of political discussions in France.[17]

Thus let us assume that we identify a de-centered political process, delimited by issue area, to which criteria of deliberative democracy can be applied to evaluate normatively its quality. Before considering how the criteria offered by deliberative theorists might be applied specifically to de-centered processes, I suggest that we must add another criterion, which I call "linkage." With a criterion of linkage, we ask for evidence that various mediated sites and occasions for discussion across diverse social spaces and over an extended time are connected to one another. Recalling Habermas' model of the movement of an issue discussion from inchoate problem expression in multiple grassroots sites, to its amplification and refinement in a public sphere, to discussion of alternative approaches that influence public officials, we can ask whether and how activities in civil society are linked to the content of mass media, and whether and how these are linked to the agenda and responsiveness of actors within state institutions.

We do not need such a criterion of linkage for evaluating centered processes of political communication and decision making. Usually the records of a forum and the memory of participants and observers will be sufficient to preserve continuity between one occasion and another, one contribution to discussion and another, and to give participants confidence that a discussion process is connected to a decision, when there is one.

We generate criteria for evaluating the quality of a democratic process partly from our negative experiences. A particular danger of de-centered processes of political discussion is that their elements become disengaged from one another. Perhaps the most important of these possibilities is that sites of official decision making are not linked to mediated processes of civic discussion and the public sphere they generate. The *ideal* of de-centered deliberative democracy requires that sites of the deliberation and decision making of legislatures, for example, should be open to and influenced by public discussion taking place outside them. It is often in the interests of legislators and their staff, however, to distance themselves from these wider social processes; it makes their own discussion process simpler, and it allows them to form alliances and broker with one another according to interests and power dynamics internal to the legislature.

Sites and occasions of the discussion of a social problem should also be linked with each other for mediated communication to be politically efficacious and for the outcome it generates to be normatively legitimate. Often they are not. If various groups and organizations are discussing an issue in ways that are not in mediated communication with one another, the terms and arguments in one site are not likely to influence others, and thus a space of public opinion will not consolidate. Thus in order to assess the quality of a de-centered deliberative process across mass democracy—whether at local, regional, national, or global levels—it is useful to consider whether and how sites and occasions that are part of the process appear to influence or refer to one another.

Application of criteria of the sort that have been offered by deliberative democratic theory so far are more and less straightforward, depending on the criteria. Application of criteria of reasonableness and publicity, for example, seem to me to present few problems when extended to de-centered processes. We can ask questions about the form and content of contributions to discussion in an extended mediated process among strangers across distance in more or less the same way as when the contributions occur in a single forum. Do people speak in the mass media, for example, in ways that exhibit openness to the point of view of others, and do they speak in ways that acknowledge that anyone in principle might be listening? Do people communicate in ways designed to persuade others by trying to express themselves in ways that the others can understand? And so on.

It is more difficult perhaps to evaluate the extent to which a public discussing issues does so on terms of political equality. It is fairly easy to discern when some agents or interests dominate a discussion, whether because they use a lot of money to buy media time and space, or because they otherwise have the power to command public attention. It is more difficult to evaluate degrees of political equality in a diffuse mass public wrestling with a set of issues over a significant period of time. If the majority of people who make widely disseminated contributions to public discussion have a certain limited profile—for example, if they are male, white, and middle class—this can be a sign of political inequality.

Application of a criterion of inclusion or representativeness follows on this point, and may appear somewhat paradoxical. In a de-centered deliberative democratic process, it is not necessary that each and every forum for discussion include representatives from all major affected social groups. Indeed, in a de-centered process it sometimes enhances the quality of the large-scale discussion if some discussion forums are relatively homogeneous. If members of structurally differentiated groups do indeed tend to have specific and different perspectives on how the society works, its problems, other groups in the society, and possible solutions to the problems, then a larger discussion can benefit when those who have these perspectives articulate them with one another first, before offering them to a larger public.

The existence of such segmented discussion situations are problematic when their fails to be linkage among them, or when they produce de-centered discussion that in the main tends to express the point of view of only some segments of affected people. This point raises the question of whether linkage is a phenomenon distinct from those that the other criteria evaluate. It may be that linkage is a necessary condition for or usual consequence of processes of political communication and decision making that approximate already articulated ideals of deliberative democracy when we consider those processes as de-centered.

EDITORS' NOTE

This chapter was originally published as Iris Marion Young, "De-centering Deliberative Democracy," *Kettering Review* 24:3 (2006). We have restored the footnotes from a previously unpublished version, Iris Marion Young, "De-centering Deliberative Democracy" (paper presented at the annual meeting of the American Philosophical Association, Central Division, Chicago, IL, 2006).

NOTES

1. Jürgen Habermas, *Between Facts and Norms* (Cambridge, MA: MIT Press, 1996).

2. Ibid., 296-301.

3. Ibid., 301.

4. Joshua Cohen and Charles Sabel, "Directly-Deliberative Polyarchy," *European Law Journal* 3:4 (1997): 313-342.

5. Archon Fung, *Empowered Participation: Reinventing Urban Democracy* (Princeton, NJ: Princeton University Press, 2004); John Forester, *The Deliberative Practitioner: Encouraging Participatory Planning Processes* (Cambridge, MA: MIT Press, 1999); John Gaventa, "Strengthening Participatory Approaches to Local Governance," *National Civic Review* 93:4 (2004): 16-27; David E. Booher, "Collaborative Governance Practices and Democracy," *National Civic Review* 93:4 (2004): 32-46; Bronwyn Hayward, "Effective Citizen Engagement and Social Learning in Environmental Policy: The New Zealand Experience" (paper presented at annual meeting of the American Political Science Association, Washington, DC, 2005).

6. For excellent discussions of some of the most important of these discursive designs, see John Gastil and Peter Levine, *The Deliberative Democracy Handbook: Strategies for Effective Civic Engagement in the 21st Century* (San Francisco, CA: Jossey-Bass, 2005).

7. James S. Fishkin, *The Voice of the People: Public Opinion and Democracy* (New Haven, CT: Yale University Press, 1995).

8. Amy Gutmann and Dennis Thompson, *Democracy and Disagreement* (Cambridge, MA: Harvard University Press, 1996).

9. James Bohman is one deliberative theorist who takes this complexity seriously and even argues that complexity can sometimes be good for democracy. He draws on Habermas for his own theory of public deliberation. He criticizes Habermas, however, for inappropriately disconnecting political process to state institutions from civil society. In this paper I do not have the space to examine and evaluate Bohman's interpretation of Habermas' de-centered theory; I think that Bohman may overdraw the picture he finds. See James Bohman, *Public Deliberation* (Cambridge, MA: MIT Press, 1996), especially.

10. Thomas Christiano, *The Rule of the Many* (Boulder, CO: Westview Press, 1996).

11. Gutmann and Thompson, *Democracy and Disagreement*.

12. Bohman, *Public Deliberation*.

13. Iris Marion Young, *Inclusion and Democracy* (Oxford: Oxford University Press, 2000), esp. Chapter 1.

14. Charles Beltz, *Political Equality* (Princeton, NJ: Princeton University Press, 1995).

15. Bohman, *Public Deliberation*.

16. Young, *Inclusion and Democracy*, Chapter 3. Joan Wallach Scott, *Parité: Sexual Equality and the Crisis of French Universalism* (Chicago: University of Chicago Press, 2005).

From Talk to Action:
Democratic Practice
and Public Work

Sustaining Public Engagement: Embedded Deliberation in Local Communities

by Elena Fagotto and Archon Fung

Introduction

Over the past four years, we have studied local public deliberations in nine communities across the United States. We searched for communities where it seemed that the practice of regular and organized deliberation had taken root and grown. We wanted to understand how what almost always begins as a limited effort to mobilize citizens and convene them to consider a public issue or political problem can sometimes grow into a regular practice that involves many different segments of a community and spans multiple issues that bear scant relation to one another. Such communities, we thought, would be interesting because they would be ones in which the skills, practice, and organizational wherewithal to conduct regular public deliberation had become "embedded."

Embedded Deliberation

Embeddedness is a habit of deliberation among citizens. When that habit is embedded in a community's political institutions and social practices, people frequently make public decisions and take collective actions through processes that involve discussion, reasoning, and citizen participation rather than through the exercise of authority, expertise, status, political weight, or other such forms of power.

Consider the progress that has been made in understanding the practice of public deliberation to date. First, practitioners of public deliberation, or deliberative democracy, have by now mastered the art of creating high-quality organized deliberations as one-off events that last from a day to several weeks. Though never easy and often expensive, we know how to organize and convene citizen juries, National Issues Forums, 21st-century town meetings, study circles, and deliberative polls. Second, networks like the National Issues Forums have created community institutions—such as the Public Policy Institutes—that house, host, and support public deliberations. Third, several investigators have looked at the practices and realities of informal public deliberation in communities and community institutions. These remarkable accomplishments in practice and understanding mark real progress in the state of deliberative practice.

Embedded deliberation takes the state of the art one step farther—a community that has embedded deliberation in its practices of public reflection and action: *utilizes methods of more or less formally organized deliberation, to consider a range of public issues or problems, over a period of several years.* As we shall see, it is also often the case that deliberation in these communities is linked to a range of community-based or governmental organizations in ways that affect the decisions, resources, or policies of those bodies.

The main sections of this report describe our general investigative process and the results of our analysis. We begin by outlining our methodology and offering capsule descriptions of the nine communities we investigated. The rest of the report grapples with the challenge of understanding—sometimes interpreting—what these communities have accomplished. We start by asking what challenges induced them to adopt deliberative interventions. At the most obvious level, each has used public deliberation to address a concrete local problem or issue. In a notable number of those communities, deliberations address challenges around public education, but problems like urban planning and growth management, racial tension and diversity, domestic abuse, and child welfare also appeared. We argue that deliberative projects and reforms in these communities work at a deeper level as well. Though they themselves may not recognize it, deliberative practitioners also address more fundamental shortcomings of the structures of local democratic governance through their work. We contend that local democratic governance arrangements face certain characteristic problems, or democratic deficits. These deficits may include: weak social fabric, unstable public judgment, gaps in communication and accountability between officials and communities, and insufficient governmental resources to tackle a range of social challenges. The structures of organized public deliberation can help address each of these deficits although different kinds of democratic deficits require different forms of public deliberation and deliberative action.

We attempt to understand why deliberation in our study communities has successfully spread over time by developing the concept of embedded deliberation. We explain the characteristics of embeddedness and why it is helpful to understand embeddedness on two levels: some practices embed deliberative reflection while others also embed deliberative public action. The first establishes habits of ongoing deliberation to improve community relations, clarifies the understanding of public policy problems, or provides input to policymakers, while the second translates deliberation into action by mobilizing communities and resources to solve local problems. The first level of embeddedness is a necessary condition for the second. All of the communities that have embedded public action have also developed habits of public reflection. The final sections of this report offer some tentative thoughts about the kinds of civic leadership and strategies that are likely to sustain local deliberative practices.

Methodology

The objective of these case studies was to learn about the paths and patterns that lead from deliberation to action and about the conditions under which deliberation becomes socially and politically embedded. Therefore, our selection of case studies was highly opportunistic. We singled out cases where deliberative practices had become fairly widespread and repeated over time and had led to some action around the issues. We selected these cases not only to illustrate successful examples of embedded deliberation, but also to explain the breadth of problems that can be addressed through deliberative interventions. Subsequently, we wanted to focus on the reasons that made these interventions successful, including how and why deliberation became embedded, the role of deliberative entrepreneurs, and the strategic choices they faced to promote deliberation. The advice of national experts on community-level deliberations guided us in our process of case identification.

We selected mature or relatively mature cases. Efforts to influence policymaking or mobilize communities are slow processes that require capacity building, resources, and the creation of strategic alliances. The relative maturity of our cases enables us to observe how deliberative practices evolved through time and to understand their embeddedness and impact over a period of several years. In each case, we conducted at least one field visit of several days and observed deliberative events and trainings of facilitators. These observations enabled us to better understand different deliberative models, the dynamics among participants, and the mechanisms employed to promote action. We also conducted extensive semi-structured interviews with participants, experts, facilitators, local activists, and institutions involved in the deliberations.

Our case studies drew upon different deliberative approaches. Many were informed by the study circles model, which combines public deliberation (and dialogue) with community organizing. Participants—often numbering in the hundreds—meet in both large and small gatherings. Most of the deliberations take place in smaller groups of 8 to 12 that meet in a series of sessions to explore an issue with the guidance of peer facilitators. Participants start by discussing an issue, then move on to explore concrete ways they could address the problem, and come up with specific action ideas.[1]

At National Issues Forums, a diverse group of participants (the number can vary greatly) may gather for one or more deliberations, often lasting two hours, about a public policy problem, such as reforming health care or US-international relations. A moderator invites participants to weigh different approaches, considering their pros and cons so they can deepen their understanding, appreciate the complexity of an issue, and move in the direction of making a collective decision. The Community Conversations we observed in Connecticut mobilize a large, diverse group for an evening during which participants discuss public education issues in small groups and formulate concrete action plans. The Indigenous Issues Forums, employed by Native Americans in South Dakota, are small-group dialogues where participants share personal stories and explore tribal issues. Facilitators invite participants to reflect about the characteristics of a healthy dialogue process. Finally, the Keiki Caucus (Children Caucus) in Hawaii convenes stakeholders, legislators, advocacy groups, and public agencies to focus on issues relating to children. The caucus meets monthly to discuss pressing problems, prioritize needs, and assemble a legislative package.

Most of these deliberative approaches were developed by national organizations. In every case, however, those in local communities adapted the different models to their specific circumstances and needs.

What Does Success Look Like?

We began our study by identifying communities in which efforts to create public deliberation seemed to have taken root and, in one way or another, resulted in some kind of public action. We based preliminary assessments of "success" on the suggestions of staff members at national organizations, such as Everyday Democracy (formerly Study Circles Resource Center) and the Kettering Foundation, and word of mouth in the community of deliberative practitioners. We also looked at the database Everyday Democracy uses to track its work in the communities it assists. From this list, we contacted principals in various communities to verify that substantial and ongoing deliberation did, in fact, occur there.

Ultimately, we went on to conduct detailed studies of nine communities. Readers should not regard the experiences of these communities as typical. Indeed, we selected them because their experiences seemed in their own ways extraordinary. But neither can we say that we have identified the most successful cases of local deliberation. There are almost certainly other communities in which public deliberation has been longer lived, more widespread, more inclusive, or more effective. Nevertheless, the experiences of the communities we selected were highly instructive. Each of these communities succeeds deliberatively in its own distinctive way. Between them, we believe, they constitute frontiers of deliberation that offer many lessons for those who seek to spread deliberation and deepen democracy. The brief community profiles below are intended to convey a sense of what we thought success looked like.

Since 1997, New Castle County, Delaware, has hosted widespread community deliberations about race relations, equality of opportunity, diversity, and tolerance. More than 12,000 individuals have participated in this effort, making the New Castle program the largest of its kind in the country, as far as we know. The success of this program lies in its broad inclusivity as well as in its sustained nature. Under the auspices of the YWCA but joined by several dozen local organizations, more than 600 people participated in community-based study circles on race relations in 1997. In 1998, more than 600 people in the Delaware Department of Labor and in local public schools participated in deliberations about workplace race relations. Subsequently, many area businesses, public agencies, community organizations, and churches held study circles as well. Thus, the YWCA and other community leaders managed to build a deep and pervasive network for public deliberation about race that spanned the public, private, and nonprofit sectors.

In Kuna, Idaho, an organization called Kuna ACT began to convene study circles around local controversies in 1999. Between 1999 and 2003, approximately 400 Kuna residents participated in dozens of circles on issues like quality of life in a growing population, public school finance, drug testing, and comprehensive community planning. As an instance of successful deliberation, Kuna stands out in two respects. First, study circles were convened on a wide array of topics—involving a variety of local public entities, such as the school board, the planning and zoning board, and local emergency-preparedness agencies—over a period of many years. Second, these government entities came to rely on study circles as an important two-way channel of communication and consultation. Residents improved their understanding of the reasons for various public policies and local officials gained a better grasp of public priorities and sensitivities.

Portsmouth, New Hampshire, is a town of some 20,000 people that lies near the state's southern border with Maine. Like Kuna, the community has hosted several rounds of study circles on issues like school violence, school districting, and community master planning. Approximately 850 citizens have participated in these circles. While the large majority of the town's residents are racially homogeneous, those with whom we spoke noted that the community was nevertheless divided—in this case between many new and professional residents on the one hand, and long-time residents who were less well off, on the other. Against this background, one noteworthy accomplishment of the Portsmouth study circles was to confront this class division in the context of school redistricting. After the Portsmouth school board failed to gain popular acceptance of one redistricting effort, the group sponsored a round of study circles on the issue in 2000. Over 100 residents from different parts of the city met with one another and toured neighborhood schools. They agreed on a set of principles to guide a redistricting plan that both the school board and town residents were willing to accept. Subsequently, large study circles on several other topics were held and an independent organization called Portsmouth Listens was formed to sustain these public deliberations.

With resources and staff support from the United Way of Wyandotte County, Kansas City, Kansas, has been home to community problem solving and public deliberation efforts in its schools and neighborhoods. Beginning in 1999, the United Way and the public school district initiated a study circles project designed to bridge the gap in trust and understanding between

schools and parents. Subsequently, study circle techniques spread to community problem solving around issues of public safety and local revitalization of
the city's public housing projects. Since 1999, organizers estimate that some
1,600 adults have participated in more than 100 discussion sessions, and
more than 1,800 students attended youth circles that explored diversity, tolerance, and responsibility. Some 150 adults have been trained as facilitators.
Public deliberations in Kansas City produced mentoring and after-school
programs, improved relations between schools and families, and promoted
volunteerism. Participants in public housing projects formed tenant associations and mobilized to rid their neighborhoods of crime and improve their
living conditions.

In many of our case studies, public dialogues were introduced by deliberative entrepreneurs in the civic sector. In Montgomery County, Mary-
land, however, deliberations started as an initiative of a public institution.
In 2003, the Montgomery County school district launched a study circles
program to support dialogue on race in schools and close the academic
achievement gap between primarily white students, on the one hand, and
minority and economically disadvantaged students, on the other. Organizers
viewed study circles as a potentially more appealing and inviting route to
educational engagement than traditional parent-teacher organizations. Since
2003, more than 64 circles have been held, engaging over 900 participants,
including teachers, school staff members, parents, and students. Some schools
held repeated rounds of circles, and in some high schools, students were
trained to facilitate student-only deliberations. The circles brought to light
prejudice and other challenges that minority students and parents are faced
with. Teachers and school administrators gained awareness of racial barriers and learned about ways to create a more inclusive school environment.
Actions included hiring special outreach coordinators and encouraging minority students to join more challenging classes. The dialogues also helped
build trust among participants, spurred collaboration and volunteering, and
boosted the participation of minority parents. Study circles became increasingly embedded in the school district. Initially begun as a school-sponsored
initiative managed by an independent organization, they later became fully
embedded as a school program. The circles' impact on the schools has been
so positive that some school district departments organized special circles
on race for their employees. This expansion of study circles has altered the

ways in which the school system addresses the challenge of its academic achievement gap.

Owing largely to the support of the League of Women Voters and the William Caspar Graustein Memorial Fund, Community Conversations about Education have been held in some 80 communities across the state of Connecticut.[2] According to organizers, well over 5,300 people have participated in these public deliberations since 1997. The conversations are particularly well embedded in the city of Bridgeport, which has held over 40 public deliberations thanks to the support of the local Public Education Fund. Residents of Norwalk and Hartford have held six and five conversations respectively. Conversations in various communities aim to create shared understandings and goals among educators, parents, and other community members around challenges and priorities in public education. Various communities have chosen to focus on issues like school funding, parental involvement, school choice, child care, educational standards, and family learning. Community Conversations structure local deliberations around different approaches to addressing these challenges and encourage participants to develop and implement problem-solving strategies. Community Conversations have led to coordinated social action—for example, improving the accessibility of child care, altering the structure of the school day to address student fatigue concerns, and taking steps to reduce substance abuse by students.

Established in the mid 1990s, the West Virginia Center for Civic Life is an important deliberative catalyst for promoting the use of deliberation at the local level. Hosted at the University of Charleston, it has convened dozens of forums and disseminated deliberative practices in a number of key organizations, involving over 2,000 participants. While it is not uncommon for agencies to join broad coalitions that support deliberations, the West Virginia experience is distinctive in that two organizations adopted public deliberations as a strategy to further their advocacy missions. The center has worked with organizations that seek to reduce underage drinking and domestic violence, helping them raise awareness and mobilize residents through the use of public forums. Operating now for more than a decade, the West Virginia center trains students, faculty, and staff at the university in deliberative practices. The center developed forums on important local and regional issues, such as the relationship between citizens and their public schools and the challenges facing low-income families in the state. Though the direct policy effects of these public deliberations are not as clear as in Kuna or Portsmouth, the center has developed good relationships with state legislators in order to convey and make accessible the results of deliberation.

In South Dakota we examined two institutions that promote public deliberation. The South Dakota Issues Forums convene forums using the National Issues Forums approach. The Indigenous Issues Forums developed an original model that draws from both indigenous traditions of deliberation in the Native American population and the National Issues Forums, in order to create a safe space to talk about challenging tribal issues. With an average of 25 events a year, the Indigenous Issues Forums have involved approximately 800 participants. Participants are encouraged to listen with respect and to suspend their cultural and personal assumptions. By focusing on the procedural aspects of dialogue, participants are expected to gradually improve their ability to communicate, their self-understanding, and their knowledge of their communities. Organizers of these forums aim to improve interpersonal relations and restore the social fabric of Native American communities.

The Public Policy Forums based at the University of Hawaii are distinctive because they are supported by a sitting state legislator, Senator Les Ihara, who has championed several initiatives to make policymaking more deliberative. In partnership with the Public Policy Forums, he helped convene forums that were coordinated with legislative activities. The Keiki Caucus at the Hawaii state legislature focuses on issues related to children and youth and offers a quite different example of deliberation—this time as a collaborative governance tool. Launched by two legislators, the Keiki Caucus brings together policymakers, public agencies, service providers, and NGOs to exchange information and draft annual legislative packages aimed at improving child welfare. Over 400 participants have been involved in the Keiki Caucus thus far. The caucus has been a fully embedded practice for over 15 years and legislators endorse most of the bills emerging from it because of the legitimacy and reputation of the process. The Keiki Caucus has created a distinctive forum for deliberative problem solving around social policy and program implementation that is directly and reliably linked to the state's legislative apparatus. The caucus is unlike other instances of deliberation in our study in that its participants are not drawn from the public-at-large. They are instead an array of stakeholders: professional policymakers, social service workers, and advocates for children's interests.

Solving Local Problems

In these case studies, community leaders, civic activists, and policymakers were drawn to public deliberation first and foremost because it was a promising means of addressing public problems in their communities. Communities turned to deliberative strategies of public engagement in the hope of mobilizing citizens to address some pressing tangible challenge like failing schools or a longstanding social problem like racial inequality. In some cases, policymakers turned to deliberation when faced with logjams on specific policy choices.

In the 1990s, for example, a significant communication gap caused a great deal of finger-pointing between schools and families in Connecticut. Educators believed schools had improved over time. Many parents, however, thought that school quality had declined. Some groups, especially African Americans and Hispanics, faced substantial achievement deficits. A local foundation decided to invest in an initiative called "Community Conversations" to fill this communication gap by engaging parents in dialogue with school administrators and teachers.

Kansas City faced a similar challenge. There, many parents, especially those in the African American population, thought their children were ill-served by the public schools and distrusted school staff and administrators. Many neighborhoods in the city were afflicted with rampant crime, poverty, and a pervasive sense of disenfranchisement. A coalition of schools and NGOs began looking for ways to restore trust between residents and schools. They chose the study circles model and held dozens of deliberations that resulted in increased mentoring and volunteering in schools, programs to reduce crime and clean up neighborhoods, and the formation of active tenant associations.

While crises often motivate civic engagement, the New Castle County study circles were not driven by a specific galvanizing event. The relevant problem there was a persistent lack of opportunity for African American and Latino residents. Race and ethnicity represented a substantial barrier to higher paying jobs, educational opportunities, and home ownership. This was especially true in Wilmington, a city with a predominantly African American population (57 percent) located in a county in which only 20 percent of residents are African American. A coalition led by the local YWCA wanted to give residents an opportunity to become actively engaged in discussing these issues. The study circles model, with its blend of deliberation and action, enabled participants to raise their own awareness of racial issues and encouraged them to change their own behaviors in collaboration with others.

In Kuna, community conflict catalyzed public deliberation. The school board was handed a stinging—and to them, surprising—defeat in a ballot proposal to fund new school construction. At a later time, parents and students were divided over a drug-testing policy. In the face of these social conflicts, policymakers turned to public deliberations, in the form of study circles, to give residents a venue to reflect on the issues and to offer policy guidance to the school board.

In Portsmouth, city officials used study circles to obtain citizen input on issues, such as a school redistricting plan, which faced strong opposition from parents. Parents met in deliberations that crossed class and neighborhood lines. Exposure to a variety of perspectives helped defuse opposition to the redistricting plan. In these cases, deliberative procedures reduced social conflict by giving residents opportunities to inform themselves and provide input to policymakers.

Making Democracy Work

The previous section described these cases of public deliberation as solving various kinds of community problems. At a more fundamental level, however, the most successful of these efforts also improve the quality of local democratic governance by repairing certain persistent problems in the ways that local decisions are made and public actions taken. One important lesson that emerges from this analysis is that different challenges—different democratic deficits—call for very different forms of deliberative intervention and citizen participation in order to be effective.

Democratic Deficit #1: Weak Social Fabric When trust among citizens and between citizens and government is low, citizens feel disenfranchised and fail to engage in public life. Although a weak social fabric is not strictly a deficit in the representative policymaking chain, democratic governance functions more effectively when citizens are reflective and possess a high level of mutual understanding. Hence efforts to strengthen the social fabric of communities through public dialogue build an important precondition for a healthy democracy. Through public dialogues, residents can gain awareness of specific issues, change their individual behaviors, build trust among one another, and restore positive social interactions.

Deliberative activists in two of our case studies focused on the health of relationships between individuals in their communities. The New Castle County study circles on race relations and the Indigenous Issues Forums in South Dakota were introduced (1) to address poor awareness of race relations and tribal issues and (2) to strengthen individual capacities to engage in dialogue and to collaborate with one another.

The Indigenous Issues Forums have reached numerous organizations and individuals, hoping to start a slow transformative process that enables indigenous peoples to understand themselves, their history, and each other in ways that generate the self-confidence and self-respect necessary for democratic engagement. New Castle County's study circles on race have reached thousands of participants and involved more than 140 organizations, many of which have held dialogues with their employees. Although it is too early to tell whether these initiatives transformed individual behavior and restored the social fabric in their respective communities, data for New Castle County show that participants became more aware of prejudice and increased their ability to communicate with others.

These deliberative projects were not designed to inform participants' political preferences, much less to influence the course of public policy or governmental action. Rather, they encouraged individuals to reflect more deeply about their situations in relation to others through dialogue. By transcending mistrust and misunderstanding, these initiatives aim to strengthen the social fabric that binds communities together. Transforming individuals and restoring social fabric in this way might be described as creating a form of "stored action" that may enable civic engagement and collective action in the future. In order to be successful, initiatives whose goal is to build healthy community relationships through personal change must touch a large number of people over long periods of time. The New Castle County study circles are a good example, with some 12,000 participants, about 1.4 percent of the population in Delaware, since their inception in 1997.

Democratic Deficit #2: Unstable Public Judgment Citizens often make poor judgments about public issues because they lack information, or have not taken the pains to face the trade-offs that sound judgment requires. This contributes to making poor choices at the ballot box and, ultimately, inadequate public policies. To correct this deficit, citizens need to acquire additional information and test their views against those of others. Public deliberation provides the opportunity to remedy this deficit and improve public judgment through collective reflection. Much of the work on deliberative practice aims to address the problem of unstable public judgment. Daniel Yankelovich described the problem, and solutions to it, in books such as *Coming to Public Judgment* and *The Magic of Dialogue*.[3] Before and after him, researchers and other political observers have documented the low levels of political knowledge among the general public.[4] Deliberative methods, such as those employed by the National Issues Forums, intervene in this problem area. They gather a diverse group in a structured deliberation on a public policy issue designed to help participants develop a more complete understanding of problems. Participants also learn to appreciate the reasons given to support views they would normally oppose and become more open to deliberative exchanges.

In our case studies, we have observed this type of deliberative intervention in communities in West Virginia, Hawaii, and South Dakota. Participants in those communities discussed a variety of topics, from health-care reform to immigration and public education. The West Virginia Center for Civic Life was particularly successful at involving large numbers of people in the deliberations. In Hawaii, a state legislator helped convene forums to defuse polarization on issues like gambling and euthanasia. Both were controversial topics in the state legislature, so involving legislators and stakeholders in deliberations resulted in a more balanced articulation of views.

Study circles and Community Conversations also invite participants to consider competing options to deepen their understanding of policy issues. Whether or not they ultimately have an impact on policy, all public deliberations are designed to improve the quality of judgment of those who participate by providing them with additional information and exposing them to the opinions of other citizens.

Democratic Deficit #3: Gaps in Communication and Accountability between Officials and Communities In the standard model of representative democracy, elections and campaigns provide a central channel through which politicians learn about the views and priorities of their constituents. The need to compete in elections creates incentives for politicians to hear from their constituents through public meetings, social events, focus groups, and polls. Despite these mechanisms, gaps of trust and mutual knowledge often separate policymakers from citizens.

Those gaps can occur if politicians hear only from some citizens and not from others or because new issues arise for which existing processes do not generate clear preferences. In a noxious form of this democratic deficit, politicians and policy professionals may choose to pursue their own agendas with little regard for public interests and priorities—and apparently without fear of being checked by devices of public accountability. Deliberative initiatives can improve the machinery of democratic governance by broadening the channels of communication between politicians and the public and empowering citizens to hold their representatives accountable.

In Kuna and Portsmouth, local government officials supported study circles because they faced contentious issues, and did not clearly understand what the public's views were on these topics. So they sought the public's input through deliberation. When community members in Kuna divided over a proposal to issue a school bond and on a drug-testing policy, deliberations helped articulate public preferences and provided input to decision. Whether or not they ultimately have an impact on policy, all public deliberations are designed to improve the quality of judgment of those who participate by providing them with additional information and exposing them to the opinions of other citizens. In Portsmouth, study circles were convened to clarify citizens' opinions on a controversial school redistricting plan and on the city's master plan. This two-track policy process—combining traditional chains of representation and policymaking with deliberative mechanisms to gather public input—proved effective in both communities. Policymakers have returned to it on various occasions where the traditional process has proved inadequate.

The Keiki Caucus in Hawaii was formed by two state legislators to gather input from stakeholders in order to draft more effective child-welfare legislation. In that sense, it filled a gap in policymakers' knowledge but it also strengthened the relationship between legislators and stakeholders and increased scrutiny on legislators' decisions. The mechanisms of dialogue and information sharing also served to increase accountability, both for policymakers and for the different public and nongovernmental agencies represented in the group.

The deliberative initiatives in Kuna and Portsmouth share several characteristics. First, local policymakers in both places supported and participated in a series of public deliberations. Whereas many deliberative initiatives focus on citizens and perhaps on civic organizations, these initiatives were successful because they engaged the relevant officials from planning agencies, school boards, and city hall. Repairing deficits caused by a limited understanding of constituents' preferences requires building bridges between citizens and government. If government is not involved, the bridge leads nowhere.

Second, deliberative activists in both Kuna and Portsmouth convened highly effective deliberations using variants of the study circles model. These deliberations included broadly representative sectors of their respective communities and they were well attended, well facilitated, and informative for participants.

Finally, success was made possible because the deliberations were sponsored by capable community-based organizations—Kuna ACT and Portsmouth Listens—that had the know-how and resources to organize effective events. Importantly, these organizations did not limit their efforts to one topic or controversy. Rather, they had the wherewithal to sponsor several different rounds of public deliberation as important problems and issues arose over the years.

Kuna and Portsmouth are impressive in this regard. Few small community organizations manage to catalyze sustained public deliberation in this way. But these efforts are also notable for what Kuna ACT and Portsmouth Listens did not have to do. First, they did not have to alter the perspectives and behavior of a substantial portion of their communities. It can be enough, for example, that a representative group of citizens deliberate with officials if those officials listen well. If the problem is that policies fail to address citizens' needs, this limited deliberation can remedy the situation. If the problem is public distrust of politicians, the fact that politicians actually listened, if widely known, can increase trust even among those who did not participate directly in deliberative exercises.

Second, these deliberations did not require the same individuals to participate over and over again. The deficit of poor communication between government and citizens can be remedied with an economy of civic engagement that does not require particular citizens (except perhaps those who staff organizations like Kuna ACT and Portsmouth Listens) to devote themselves intensively to ongoing deliberations. It doesn't require all the citizens to deliberate all of the time, or even some citizens to deliberate most of the time. It simply requires that some citizens engage in public deliberation some of the time.

Democratic Deficit #4: Insufficient Governmental Resources to Tackle a Range of Social Challenges Traditionally, public agencies are responsible for providing public goods and services, from functioning schools and public transportation to safe neighborhoods. Some services, however, cannot be effectively delivered without active engagement from the community. Strengthening local schools and making neighborhoods more secure, for example, often demand not only sound public policy, but also support from community members. Only residents have the knowledge to identify areas of need and suggest sustainable projects they would be willing to work on and maintain.

Through public deliberation, residents can discuss problems in their area, identify solutions, mobilize for local problem solving, and strengthen their relationships with public officials. A significant portion of the deliberation is devoted to formulating action steps and assigning responsibilities for follow-up so that participants will stay engaged after the deliberations are concluded. This type of deliberation, of course, requires more sustained, frequent, and iterative participation. And clearly, it can be successful only if local government or other institutions take engagement seriously and are willing to collaborate with, or even delegate power to, organized citizens.

Our case studies offer several examples of successful deliberative interventions of this sort. Communities in Connecticut, Kansas City, and Montgomery County were struggling with problems that could not be solved by policymakers and bureaucrats alone. In the 1990s, Kansas City's superintendent of schools embarked on a bold school reform effort. One of the strategies in his plan was to strengthen communities so they could support schools. Together with the local United Way chapter, he formed a coalition to restore trust between families and schools and to empower disenfranchised communities.

The Kansas City group adopted study circles to engage residents of public housing complexes in deliberations that led to strategies that reduced crime and improved their neighborhoods. Other study circles successfully connected schools in need of resources with churches and community members willing to help. These deliberations involved approximately 2,000 people, including hundreds of young people. Mentoring programs and numerous volunteer campaigns to support schools and communities grew out of these deliberations.

In Connecticut, a charitable foundation sponsored dialogues designed to bridge gaps between schools and families. In many areas across the state, school authorities participated in productive conversations with parents and other residents. They learned about areas of need they had previously overlooked, and adopted new strategies to improve their services. For many, especially socially isolated minorities, it was the first time they could voice their concerns to public authorities. Organizers estimate that the program reached well over 5,000 people in the state.

The Montgomery County school district realized that providing more resources to students and teachers was not enough to close the achievement gap: families and other parts of the community also needed to be involved. Study circles were adopted to open discussions of race relations and to facilitate collaborative efforts involving families, students, and school staffs to help all students achieve. The circles successfully involved about 900 people and are now spreading to reach all the schools in the district. Deliberations have created a safe space to bring up challenging issues and built trust among families and schools. As a result, parents have become more involved in school life and new initiatives have been introduced to meet the specific needs of minority students and their families.

Deliberative initiatives that succeed in shoring up insufficient capacity must mobilize citizens to contribute their labor, ideas, and material resources to solving public problems. The structure and demands of these initiatives are, therefore, quite different from those that address problems of unstable public judgment or the gap between citizens and government. In particular, these initiatives required a substantial number of citizens to invest themselves in problem-solving deliberations over substantial periods of time—months and even years. Deliberative initiatives that mobilize civic resources this way are more akin to community-organizing efforts than to the familiar "public forum" image that is commonly used to describe deliberative practices.

In the sections above, we have characterized what public deliberation at its best can achieve. It contributes to the solution of tangible local problems and, at the same time, helps to mend certain deficits in the democratic process of representative government. These achievements, however, can be short-lived and easily reversed. Thus we turn now to an examination of the conditions that sustain deliberation over time.

The Concept of Embeddedness

A central hypothesis of this research is that deliberation's impact will be sustained in a community only when deliberative practices become embedded in its institutions, organizations, and social practices. When members of a community repeatedly utilize deliberative methods to address community problems, we say that community has embedded deliberation. Embeddedness is a habit of deliberation among citizens. It requires an infrastructure of civic organizations and local government institutions prepared to act on public input and to collaborate with residents. Deliberative events can engage residents in solving local problems even without embeddedness, but unless competent institutions are ready to listen and act on the public's suggestions, deliberations are likely to have only a modest and short-lived impact.

The concept of embeddedness highlights how, in most places most of the time, self-conscious and organized public deliberation is a novel act. That is, processes of problem solving, decision making, and public action frequently occur without substantial deliberative engagement from citizens. Instead, professional politicians and organized interest groups jockey for position in shaping policies that favor their constituents by bringing to bear money, authority, or adversarial mobilization. Policy implementation occurs through the offices of professional public servants.

By way of contrast, when deliberation is embedded, political institutions and social organizations systematically include public deliberation in their repertoires of decision making and action. Embedding deliberation alters the decision-making processes of public institutions and other organizations in ways that make them adept at convening public deliberations and acting on their input. When they embed public deliberation, policymakers improve the formulation of policies and the delivery of public services. When a community embeds deliberation, it strengthens its social fabric by creating a citizenry that is open to dialogue and collaboration, improves the public judgment of its citizens, and makes them more reflective public actors. Finally, embedding deliberation may contribute to solving systemic deficits of democratic institutions.

Embedded Public Reflection When a community uses deliberation with some regularity to address problems of weak social fabric, to transform individuals, or to inform public judgment, we say they have embedded public reflection. Often, small organizations play an important role in this type of embeddedness by convening forums and training facilitators.

The deliberative entrepreneurs in our case studies have embedded public reflection primarily by creating or transforming independent, nonprofit organizations whose mission is to organize deliberative forums and mobilize community residents to participate. Organizational capacity thus seems to be an essential element for embedding public reflection. In many cases, deliberative entrepreneurs coopted existing organizations to adopt public deliberation as part of their mainline activities. For example, Betty Knighton in West Virginia established the Center for Civic Life at the University of Charleston; the YWCA catalyzes the discussions on race in the Delaware study circles; and National Issues Forums are housed at the University of Hawaii. The Indigenous Issues Forums in South Dakota, on the other hand, are an independent initiative anxious to preserve their autonomy and, although they cultivate relations with many local organizations, they are not formally housed in any of them.

In both the cooptive and the independent approaches, the organizations that facilitate public deliberation did not have specific issue orientations. They were more civic than activist. Issue neutrality may be important because the topics that merit broad deliberation in any community will vary over time.[5] Advocacy and activist organizations by their nature have particular substantive positions on issues, whereas the point of public deliberation is to develop such positions through natural discovery and reasoning.

Embedded Public Action While subjects in all of our cases tried to improve public reflection, some also tried to enhance the quality of public action. When public deliberation is connected to policymaking, policy implementation, or other collective action in a sustained way, we say that it is embedded in the routines of local public action. For deliberation to be embedded in public action and improve the character and consequences of that action, it must be intimately connected to institutions and organizations that possess the resources and authority to address the problems at issue. We therefore suggest that deliberations that provide public input to policymakers, local problem solving, or collaborative governance are more likely to be successful when deliberative practices become embedded into the procedures and practices of these organizations.

Deliberations designed to provide public input to policymakers are significantly more effective if embedded. There is no doubt that embedding deliberation comes at a cost for public institutions and other organizations: they need to dedicate time and resources to the planning process, undergo training, and overcome internal resistance. They may also need to alter some of their decision-making processes—for example, by formally creating mandates for public input and by involving other organizational layers in the deliberations to ensure that the public input not be disregarded by other departments. For organizations that invest in deliberation, acting on the public's input is simply a way to maximize their return. By listening to citizens and working collaboratively with them, institutions reap the full benefits of embedding deliberation.

Collaborative governance involves the joint determination of policies and public actions through the deliberation of citizens or their representatives. It differs from local problem solving in two main respects. First, because it often aims to establish framework decisions—for example school attendance boundaries, urban plans, and city budgets—that are less frequently revisited, it requires less frequent participation.

Second, decisions involved in collaborative governance (as the term is used here) usually involve higher levels of decision making and authority: school board members and superintendents rather than teachers and principals. Because deliberations are less frequent, and participants often less numerous, the burden on sponsoring organizations may be lighter. However, collaborative governance almost always requires elected or appointed decision makers to share their authority with others who join the deliberations.

At its lowest level, collaborative governance requires officials to take public deliberation seriously as an input into their decisions. At a higher level, as in Hawaii's Keiki Caucus, collaborative governance produces policies and public actions that are jointly forged. Because collaborative governance involves an explicit sharing of authority, it is typically more difficult to achieve than other forms of deliberation.

Although it is the product of embeddedness, collaborative governance may also be enhanced by embeddedness. For example, an institution may delegate some of its prerogatives to the public, but if other relevant functions are still carried out in nondeliberative ways, that may limit the impact of collaborative governance. The Keiki Caucus in Hawaii is a good example of deliberative practices that are well embedded because legislators who do not attend the deliberations trust the bills that emerge from this body.

Strategies for Establishing and Sustaining Deliberation

Now that we know what kinds of deliberative interventions can address the democratic deficits of the policymaking process and how embeddedness can sustain the impact of deliberations, we turn to the strategy and choices adopted by those who first introduced deliberation in their communities or organizations. How do entrepreneurs form alliances with other groups that can help spread deliberation and utilize these networks to advance the specific purposes they have? Let's start by examining the strategic choices civic entrepreneurs make when they want to achieve embedded public reflection.

Institutional support is crucial to engage residents in regular dialogues that change them as individuals, or inform their public judgment and instill the habit of public deliberation in a community. Institutional partners can provide credibility and resources. Being affiliated with a reputable institution with good connections in the community facilitates embedding deliberation and forming partnerships. In New Castle County, for example, YWCA promotion of study circles facilitated a successful outreach effort. In West Virginia, public deliberation thrived due in part to a visionary deliberative entrepreneur, but also due to the strong backing of the University of Charleston.

Institutions can also provide concrete resources, such as financial support, staff, or office space. All of these elements are critical in organizing effective deliberations over time. Another important consideration is the neutrality of the organizations. We noticed that many deliberative entrepreneurs established alliances with nonpartisan institutions, such as universities, because deliberations that are perceived as self-serving or driven by partisan agendas can undermine participation. Deliberative entrepreneurs in Hawaii, South Dakota, and West Virginia depend on institutional support to sustain deliberative practices and conduct annual facilitator trainings and public deliberations. In these cases, institutional support comes from the University of Hawaii, the Chiesman Foundation, and the University of Charleston, respectively. In New Castle County, the local YWCA has supported deliberation. The Indigenous Issues Forums have established relationships with several local institutions, such as churches and libraries, to promote deliberation.

All these study sites have embedded deliberative public reflection to some extent, but some have been more successful than others in holding frequent deliberations and increasing the number of citizens exposed to deliberation. Promoting deliberation with other institutions and harnessing their capacities and networks significantly increased the number of participants. In New Castle County, more than 12,000 people participated in study circles. Because the initiative was sponsored by the YWCA, the effort benefited from the network, reputation, and resources of its institutional sponsor, reaching out to more than 140 organizations, including not only public institutions but also large corporations like Dupont. The YWCA's sponsorship has helped the New Castle County program in several ways. First of all, because of its reputation, many organizations interested in hosting dialogues on race contacted the YWCA for assistance. Second, the YWCA has nurtured a large group of facilitators, who spread deliberation in their respective organizations. Third, the YWCA has promoted study circles as a vehicle for social change with other organizations. It even succeeded in embedding deliberation within the Department of Labor, which held study circles on race and on issues of gender and disability.

In West Virginia, several universities and two NGOs adopted deliberations to advance their missions. College students, faculty, and staff participated in deliberations, were trained as facilitators, and ended up holding additional deliberations. Two NGOs trained their staff to hold dozens of forums across the state on issues of domestic violence and underage drinking.

Entrepreneurs who seek to embed public action face additional challenges. Like entrepreneurs who promote embedded public reflection, they need to think strategically of alliances that can secure the reputation, capacity, and resources to support deliberations. However, they also need to think of ways alliances can sustain action.

Consider the Connecticut Community Conversations. The foundation that sponsors the conversations secured resources and alliance with the League of Women Voters, which manages the project, and ensured credibility, outreach, and visibility. Additionally, the organizations that intend to hold deliberations are required to form large planning committees to guarantee outreach to a diverse constituency. The organizations in the Connecticut planning committees are generally well established and have the institutional capacity necessary to continue to mobilize participants even after the deliberations. Shared leadership teams bring together organizations with different areas of expertise, spread organizing and follow-up tasks evenly, and ensure accountability among team members. Naturally, when action is desired the institutional actors that have the authority and resources to implement deliberative recommendations should be on board from the beginning.

Study circles have a similar organizing philosophy: there, too, convenors seek the support of a broad network of institutional partners to mobilize, from the beginning, the organizations and local government institutions that have the capacity to translate the deliberative input into action. Deliberations on underage drinking in Clarksburg, West Virginia, were successful because they were endorsed by the city council, the police, and other public and private agencies, which continued to work together well after the deliberations ended.

The Montgomery County Study Circles enjoy the highest level of institutional support among all our case studies, but they are an atypical example, as they were introduced by the local school district to close the achievement gap.

Conclusion

In several communities across the United States, civic and political innovators have not only sponsored successful deliberations, but they have also incorporated deliberative practices into the ways that public decisions are made and public actions are taken. In doing so, these deliberative entrepreneurs often begin with the aim of using methods of public reflection to address particular, identifiable community problems. As they work to solve those problems, we have shown that they also develop reforms and structures that improve the very process of democratic governance.

This is not easy work. Success requires mobilizing citizens to engage in deliberation and often to take action following deliberation. It requires building civic organizations that can sponsor and facilitate public deliberation over controversial issues and community problems as they arise over time. And success often requires deliberative entrepreneurs to persuade reluctant politicians and policymakers to become allies and supporters of civic engagement efforts, or at least to respond constructively.

All this is made still more complicated and challenging because there is no general recipe for embedding deliberation. Differences across contexts and communities matter, but that is always true and should go without saying. More fundamental, deliberative initiatives often aim at quite different problems with democratic governance—repairing social fabric, improving public judgment, bridging gaps between communities and government, holding government officials accountable, and mobilizing civic resources and energies. These different aims require different deliberative practices, organizational strategies, and forms of embeddedness. At the very least, we hope this report illuminates those differences and, perhaps most important, in showing how several communities have quite remarkably managed to improve the quality of local democratic governance by embedding deliberation, we hope we have provided some inspiration and guidance to others who may wish to pursue those ends.

EDITORS' NOTE

This was originally published as Elena Fagotto and Archon Fung, *Sustaining Public Engagement: Embedded Deliberation in Local Communities* (Hartford, CT: Everyday Democracy and the Kettering Foundation, 2009). Reprinted by permission of Everyday Democracy and the Kettering Foundation. The text has been edited for length and style.

NOTES

[1.] In 2008, the Study Circles Resource Center changed its name to Everyday Democracy to better communicate the nature of its mission—and also to signal its growing understanding that the term *study circles,* by connoting individual small-group meetings, paints an incomplete picture of the organization's work and that of its community partners. The authors use the old study circles language in this report because the case studies were completed before the organization changed its name and its sense of how to describe this work.

[2.] The Community Conversations are an initiative developed in collaboration with Public Agenda.

[3.] Daniel Yankelovich, *Coming to Public Judgment* (Syracuse, NY: Syracuse University Press, 1991) and *The Magic of Dialogue* (New York, NY: Simon & Schuster, 1999).

[4.] See Benjamin Page and Robert Shapiro, *The Rational Public: Fifty Years of Trends in Americans' Policy Preferences* (Chicago: University of Chicago Press, 1992).

[5.] Issue neutrality is not, however, exclusive to public reflection. Kuna ACT and Portsmouth Listens, whose focus is embedded public action, are independent organizations that, thanks to their neutrality, were called upon to convene public deliberations on a variety of issues.

Constructive Politics as Public Work: Organizing the Literature

by Harry C. Boyte

The Dutch have a long history of reclamation of marshes and fenland, resulting in some 3,000 polders nationwide. The first polders were constructed in the 11th century. Due to flooding disasters water boards . . . were set up to maintain the integrity of the water defenses around polders, maintain the water-ways inside a polder and control the various water levels. Water bodies hold separate elections, levy taxes and function independently from other government bodies. . . . They are the oldest democratic institution in the country. The necessary cooperation between all ranks in maintaining polder integrity also gave its name to the Dutch version of third way politics—the Polder Model.

"Polder," *Wikipedia* Entry[1]

It is a fine sight to see a handful of workmen . . . checked by some difficulty, [who] ponder the problem each for himself, make various suggestions for dealing with it, and then apply unanimously the method conceived by one, who may or may not have any official authority . . . at such moments, the image of a free community appears.

Simone Weil, *Oppression and Liberty*[2]

In the 1960s and 1970s social movements took up a myriad of causes—civil rights, women's liberation, independence, ending apartheid, nuclear disarmament, peace in Vietnam, environmentalism, gay rights, neighborhood power, among others. Beyond differences, all challenged modern hierarchies and depersonalizing trends. Alain Touraine's description of the French student and labor strikes in May 1968 had wider application: "The enemy is no longer a person of a social category, the monarch or the bourgeoisie. He is the totality of the depersonalized, 'rationalized,' bureaucratized modes of . . . power in modern society."[3]

Participatory democratic theory can be seen as a conceptual and programmatic response to such democratic aspirations, with wide currency. As Jeffrey Hilmer observes, "during its heyday in the 1960s and 1970s, participatory democratic theory . . . was considered a viable alternative to liberal democracy as theorized by American political scientists."[4] Northerners like Carole Pateman, Jane Mansbridge, and Benjamin Barber joined theorists of the Global South like Frantz Fanon, Paulo Freire, and Stephen Biko in considering what activist democracy requires.[5] Yet neither movements nor theorists stemmed revolutions from above—corporate-led globalization and marketization,[6] technocratic interventions[7]—that thwarted the "long march through the institutions," in the phrase of Il Manifesto,[8] needed for democratization.

By the 1990s, participatory democratic theory had declined. Hilmer's survey finds little mention of it in recent literature on democracy. Some propose that deliberative democracy is a new stage of active democracy, even a "revolutionary political ideal,"[9] but I argue that deliberation is a useful but modest attempt to create an enclave of agency in times of diminished democracy, not sufficient for strong democracy. Jürgen Habermas describes its limits: "We are concerned with finite, embodied actors who are socialized in concrete forms of life, situated in historical time and social space."[10] Deliberation, he says, "invests the democratic process with normative connotations stronger than those found in the liberal model but weaker than those found in the republican model." In his view, "The success of deliberative politics depends not on a collectively acting citizenry but on the institutionalization of the corresponding procedures and conditions of communication, as well as on the interplay of institutionalized deliberative processes with informally developed public opinions."[11]

Hilmer also describes stirrings of participatory democracy in the Global South which are producing much more change than is suggested by deliberative democracy.[12] The first section of this essay examines deliberative democracy from the vantage of participatory democracy in order to clarify deliberation's strengths and limits. I build on the concept of maximum participation of people in governance across diverse settings (not only formal politics but also family, workplace, education, etc). This is Hilmer's definition, widely shared.[13] I also argue that for participatory democratic theory to realize its promise, citizens need ways to *reconstruct* the world, not simply to improve its decision-making processes. *Civic agency*, people's capacities to work collectively across differences to build and sustain a democratic life together, addresses this challenge. Civic agency accents the *productive*, not simply distributive, side of politics, including creating the commons, shared resources of a common life. It illuminates immense histories of popular struggle whose memories are threatened with obliteration.[14] Civic agency puts citizens as *co-creators* of the world, not only deliberators or decision makers *about* the world. The concept of public work, taken up in a later section, embodies co-creation. I locate *public work* in relation to other views of active citizenship, particularly deliberation and associative democracy.

Public work is a normative, democratizing ideal of citizenship generalized from communal labors of making and tending the commons, with roots in diverse cultures. Constituting elements of the ideal are present in "poldering," from the introductory Dutch case. Public work involves cooperative, egalitarian, practical labors "across ranks" on public projects, with self-organized governance. Such work accents co-creation ("God created the world, the Dutch created Holland" is the quip). Shaped through contention with forces which threaten shared ways of life, from the sea to markets and states, grounded in an understanding of human plurality, public work has *political* qualities which unmask sentimentalized elite discourses of citizenship. Generalizing beyond specific contexts, I define public work as self-organized efforts by a mix of people who solve common problems and create things, material or symbolic, of lasting civic value.

Public work, expressing civic agency, can be usefully compared and contrasted with *civic capacity*, a concept developed by Xavier de Souza Briggs and others to convey the idea of efficacious collective action on public problems under conditions of great diversity. Civic capacity draws on both the liberal "contest" view of democracy, stressing conflicts of interest, and on the "deliberative" view, which asks how decisions can be more attentive to the interplay of different vantages and how people can learn in the process. It also differs from both. Civic capacity stresses flexible, ever-changing learning processes and actions across sectors of government, business, and civil society to increase capacities to effectively address public problems. It goes beyond the governance focus on decision making, focusing on how publics can best tackle real-world challenges, from education and land use to economic development, in a way that reconciles often competing logics of "empowerment," changing political and social relationships to enhance access to influence, and "efficiency," stressing public results. Civic capacity has kinship with public work in its emphasis on changing the "state of the world" itself, but public work has a broader view of politics, making a shared life as the context for problem solving, and of the citizen, as co-creator. Public work's concepts of politics and the citizen illuminate dysfunctions of consumer culture which civic capacity theorists neglect. Thus the new public management, which Briggs celebrates for its shift from rules compliance to behavior which produces public results, is partly constituted by consumerism, appearing in its metaphor of "citizen as customer." Similarly, Briggs' treatment of accountability slights mutual responsibility for the whole, essential to a shared life.[15] Today it is as if people decorate their own apartments and attend to their own issues while the building collapses. Without a civic counterweight to the ravages of privatization, government is the singular bulwark against growing public squalor.

I argue that public work is necessary to achieve strong democracy and to reinvigorate the commonwealth. There are large obstacles. The third section details these in societies where "work" is largely an instrumental means to consumerist ends. As daunting as these are, the fourth section points to four resources for making work public: historical traditions, lessons from broad-based organizing, pressures on governments to enlist civic energies, and citizen professionalism. Public work is a politics of productive action by diverse agents to create a democratic way of life. It makes citizens, not markets or states, the agents and architects of democracy, suggesting reintegration of states and markets into civic life. It opens a path beyond the political crisis.

The Limits of Deliberative Politics

Deliberative democracy has the virtue of conceiving of human actors in an open-ended process of listening, presenting arguments, and exchanging views in ways that can produce better judgments and deepen collective learning. Most accounts also take governance structures, especially the state system, as a given, impervious to deep change. Citizens' deliberative role is to enrich and inform, not to reshape or reconstruct. John Dryzek, who seeks partially to de-link deliberation from the state, nonetheless reproduces a two-tier system in which state actors are the main architects and agents of crucial experiences like ending apartheid.[16] Others in the deliberative camp like John Forester, with a more co-creative view of the citizen, show the insufficiency of deliberative politics when they reach for language to describe what is at work in making substantial change. I argue that deliberation in all these cases is too limited to convey the idea of citizens as co-creators of the world.

Contemporary theory of deliberative politics originated in a distinction Habermas makes between Greek democracy and contemporary conditions. For the Greeks, public judgment was conveyed by the concept of *phronesis*, practical wisdom developed through public action around common issues in the space of the *polis*. For Habermas, the public sphere in the modern world is qualitatively different. "The theme of the modern (in contrast to the ancient) public sphere shifted from the properly political tasks of a citizenry acting in common . . . to the more properly civic tasks of a society engaged in critical public debate."[17] This distinction signals insights into new spaces of civic freedom as well as his adjustments to modern conditions. Habermas describes civic life in such spaces during the late 18th and 19th centuries, as the language of public opinion became connected to a vibrant urban public sphere of debate and discussion rooted in lecture halls, museums, public parks, theaters, meeting houses, opera houses, coffee shops, and more. These were supported by an information infrastructure of the press, publishing houses, lending libraries, and literary societies. In the deliberative public sphere, older hierarchical principles of deference and ascribed social status gave way to principles of rational discourse. Emergent professional and business groups asserted claims to a more general social and political leadership. In public spaces, patterns of communication emerged, which were characterized by norms of inclusivity, the give and take of argument, and a relatively horizontal experience of interaction. Arguments were judged by their fit, by pragmatic considerations of anticipated consequences, by excellence of logic and so forth, not mainly by the social status of the speaker.[18]

Habermas develops his theory to dispute schools of thought, from functionalism to structuralism and post-structuralism, which hold citizens to be pawns of forces beyond their control. He charges that in such theories "subjects who constitute their own worlds or, at a higher level, intersubjectively share common lifeworlds, drop out."[19] Habermas' effort to maintain a sense of human agency is clear, but its limits are also noteworthy. Critics have pointed out the detachment of citizens from democratic empowerment in Habermasian theory. For Ian Budge, Habermasian deliberative theory is a communicative rationality "free from domination, coercion, manipulation and strategizing." Such deliberation threatens "to take the politics out of politics." Budge (tongue-in-cheek?) says that this is a "university seminar" model of deliberation.[20] Aviezer Tucker sees oligarchic tendencies in both the theory and practice descending from Habermas, in which "an educated intellectual *avant-garde* is in charge both of identifying the common will [produced by deliberation] and of homogenizing and re-educating the deliberating public" to conform to principles of rational discourse.[21]

Such limited agency stems from Habermas' assumption that the state is largely impervious to change. Thus he criticizes Hannah Arendt as unrealistic for imagining that "the political public sphere should be revitalized to the point where a regenerated citizenry can, in the forms of a decentralized self-governance, (once again) appropriate bureaucratically alienated state power."[22] Habermas sees deliberation as a communicative practice with little involvement of citizens in public problem solving, which occurs through the state. In *Between Facts and Norms*, he argues that the capacity of civil society "to solve problems on its own is limited." The basic function of the public sphere is to move problems to the formal system. He proposes that "the communicative structures of the public sphere *relieve* the public *of the burden of decision making*." Citizens should be "communicatively-oriented" rather than "success-oriented," and in deliberation the goal should be "influence," not "power." Thus, "political *influence* supported by public opinion is converted into political *power* only when it affects the beliefs and decisions of *authorized* members of the political system (politicians, voters, etc.)." Without translation into formal structures, citizen efforts amount to little. "The public opinion that is worked up via democratic procedures into communicative power cannot 'rule' of itself but can only point the use of administration power in specific directions."[23]

Actual deliberative practices studied and promoted by theorists such as David Mathews, John Dedrick, Laura Grattan, Archon Fung, Matt Leighninger, Lawrence Jacobs and others make few such distinctions. They mix practical problem solving with communicative interests.[24] Drawing on these, Noëlle McAfee distinguishes practically oriented deliberation in everyday experience and groups like the Kettering Foundation and Everyday Democracy from the "preference-based model" of social scientists, and the "rational proceduralist" model of Rawls and Habermas.[25] Forester is a deliberative theorist in the practice tradition. His book *The Deliberative Practitioner* generates powerful insights about deliberative practices in the messy, real-world political environments in which planners practice their craft. Forester argues that there is a tension in Habermas between "the critical pragmatist" and "the theorist of justice." While the latter is "ahistorical and overidealized," Forester sees Habermas' "sociology of action [as] far more useful than many believe."[26] Forester calls for "removing the blinkers and emotional tone-deafness of much of conventional social science," identifying challenges like "traditions of thought that reduce politics to exchange, objectivity to quantification, representation to abstraction, and ethics to mere prescription."[27] He calls for theory with a "bias toward practice." Planning should "focus on political agency, staged by political-economic structure and culture" and be understood as "deliberative action that shapes others' understandings of their cities, their selves, and crucially their possibilities of action, for better or worse."[28] Grounding deliberative theory in practice stories, Forester contrasts his approach with what he calls the "Deweyan model," after John Dewey, and "the Freirean model," after Freire, with whom he associates Habermas' critical pragmatism. The former is focused "on the ways we learn in dialogical action together by testing our hunches, assumptions, and suggestions of action" in a "trial-and-error reflection in action on practical experience."[29] The latter, informing critical theory, "focuses on the ways we learn in dialogue by probing our political possibilities. . . . Whose definitions of problems and solutions, of expertise and status, of power and powerlessness perpetuate relations of dependency and hopelessness?"[30]

Drawing from both, Forester proposes a third model, a "transformative theory of social learning that explores not only how our arguments change in dialogues and negotiations but how we change as well." This model "leads us to stand the traditional fact-value hierarchy on its head. If value-free facts would be, by definition, without value . . . we can come to see that a claim about a 'fact' is simultaneously a claim that something is important." Storytelling is thus central to transformative learning. Stories "can produce or reproduce, strengthen or weaken, the public sense of self." They can help generate "new groups, organizations, or networks, not just arguments." They can "provide a source of creativity and improvisation . . . engendering new social, cultural, and political forms." And they can transform ends, as well as relationships, identities, and agendas. "Listening together, we recognize as important not only words but issues, details, relationships, even people we may have ignored or not appreciate."[31] Forester stresses the importance of inclusion of marginalized voices. He argues that critical pragmatism "leads us directly to questions of power and hegemony, agenda setting, and the contestable reproduction of citizens' knowledge, consent, and social relationships . . . in which parties not only protect their autonomy but learn with one another, and learn how they can act together as well."[32] An insight from Forester here is the way planners can give "diplomatic recognition" to others' efforts. Baruch Hirschberg explained his use of the term. Diplomatic recognition is "making people feel that you take seriously what they have to say to you . . . when you give other people 'diplomatic recognition,' even as a tactic, it changes them. [And] *you* end up changing too . . . you, having recognized them, have to take them more seriously."[33]

Forester's approach illustrates the "cultural turn" that I detail later, conveying a political understanding of humans as unique meaning-makers and storytellers, each capable of "new beginnings," and of co-creating a common world. Forester shows the insufficiency of deliberation to convey co-creation when he seeks to describe what is going on in significant change. Thus he warns of the dangers of excessive focus on language: "We always face the danger that we will listen to what is said and hear words, not power; words, not judgment; words, not inclusion and exclusion; 'mere words' and not problem-framing and . . . strategies of practice."[34] He uses the phrase *city building in practice* to describe "the politically astute work of these practitioners and the planners and designers like them."[35] He employs *participatory action research* to convey the richness of bottom-up stories, describing changes that take place: "Transformation of done-to into doers, spectators and victims into activists, fragmented groups into renewed bodies." He calls this "the ability to act together," arguing that "if we overemphasize the talk and the dialogue . . . we risk missing what is truly transformative about such work."[36] Forester's analyses clearly show limits of "deliberation" pointing toward the need for a framework that describes how people build a common life through their everyday efforts.

The Communal Roots of Public Work

A focus on co-creation of a common life draws attention to communal labor practices across the world.[37] Despite immense variety, certain elements recur regularly which allow generalization of a civic ideal beyond particular communities. These include self-organized governance; relatively egalitarian and cooperative effort across divisions; practical concerns for creating shared collective resources; adaptability, entailing a certain political savvy; and incentives based on appeal to immediate interests combined with cultivation of concern for long-term community well-being. Elements of communal labor practices sometimes combine in languages and frames of larger, cross-community popular movements that seek democratization of power. These elements create foundations for a civic ideal different than either state-centered or market-centered approaches to public questions and democracy itself. I use the concept of public work to describe democratizing practices either within communities or across them, and contrast public work as a democratizing practice with communal labor themes manipulated by elites.

An early collection edited by the Norwegian anthropologist Leif O. Manger, *Communal Labor in the Sudan*, found that despite "many prophecies about expected disintegration and decline" as rural economies become increasingly involved in markets and state structures, communal labor showed signs of "adapting to new circumstances and developing new ways of survival."[38] Manger defines communal labor as "formal reciprocal groups that are employed to solve tasks that the basic economic units cannot solve alone," noting that such tasks are common in agricultural production, animal husbandry, or hunting. They include reciprocal efforts to help families such as house-building, and also creation of public goods that contribute to the well-being of the whole community, such as well-digging. They also include supplemental activities surrounding production, such as magical rites and prayers.[39] Communal labor practices like this combine practical calculation and bargaining with attentiveness to the reciprocities of a shared life built over time. Manger details the careful measuring of quantities of food, drink, and other payments in parties after communal labor practices. In *Mayordomo*, Stanley Crawford recounts how he and his wife settled in the 1970s in a Mexican community in New Mexico. He was elected leader (*mayordomo*) of the communal labor crew on his irrigation ditch, *acequia*, one of about 1,000 in the region, the heart of community life. Crawford describes the combination of contentious bargaining with calls for attention to community welfare in a meeting about water rights: "The sky rumbled and growled as we argued with each other into the night and heard accusations of cheating and hogging, waiting for the peacemakers to come forth . . . to remind us again of the one community of which we all formed part, whatever our many differences."[40] Such practical, gritty, political qualities of communal labors are often absent in today's sentimentalized, hortatory discourses of "voluntarism" and "service."[41]

Prophecies of the disappearance of communal labors are paralleled by predictions that the "commons," symbolic and material foundations for a shared life, are doomed. Commons is defined by Charlotte Hess and Elinor Ostrom as "a resource shared by a group of people that is subject to social dilemmas."[42] *Social dilemmas* means "threats to their survival." Garrett Hardin shows the fatalistic cast of mind with his 1968 article "The Tragedy of the Commons." Hardin defines *commons* as a "free resource" open to all that erodes as each pursues his own interest. "Ruin is the destination toward which all men rush, each pursuing his own best interest in a society that believes in the freedom of the commons."[43] Researchers counter Hardin by looking at actual cases of commons. While agreeing that threats to the commons exist—free riding, overuse, competition, and enclosure, among others—they find several of Hardin's arguments to be simply mistaken: that the commons is by definition open to all, rather than a managed collective resource; that little or no communication exists among users; that users act only in their immediate and narrow self-interests, failing to take into account any long-term collective benefits; and that there are only two outcomes— privatization or government control.[44] Studying forest management, irrigation, inshore fishery, and more recently the Internet, they discover that decentralized governance with higher popular participation has advantages in terms of efficiency, sustainability, and equity. These include incorporation of local knowledge; greater involvement of those who are trustworthy and respect principles of reciprocity; feedback on subtle changes in the resource; better adapted rules; lower enforcement costs; and redundancy, which decreases the likelihood of a system-wide failure. Decentralized systems also have disadvantages, such as uneven involvement by local users; possibilities for "local tyrannies" and discrimination; lack of innovation and access to scientific knowledge; and inability to cope with large common pool resources. Ostrom argues for a mix of decentralized and general governance, what she calls "polycentric governance systems . . . where citizens are able to organize not just one but multiple governing authorities at different scales."

Such mixed systems may be messy, but in studies of local economies, "messy polycentric systems significantly outperformed metropolitan areas served by a limited number of large-scale, unified governments."[45]

Work on governance highlights elements in *sustaining* the commons. In *Understanding Knowledge as a Commons*, edited by Hess and Ostrom, Peter Levine emphasizes another dimension, the public work involved in *making* it. "Such work," he argues, "builds social capital, strengthens communities, and gives people the skills they need for collective citizenship."[46] I argue that public work more broadly shifts the emphasis from *users* to *producers*.

Modern intellectual history includes a narrative of enclosure, the story of "the haves versus the have-nots, the elites versus the masses."[47] Recent studies of communal labor, replete with examples of collective activities with public and political qualities, add to our understanding of the struggles around the commons by incorporating a politicized *cultural turn* that draws attention to humans as meaning-makers and storytellers involved in a continuing, power-laden process of contesting, negotiating, and integrating interpretations of experience. People's identity is shaped over a life course by the narrative sense they make of their experiences, individually and collectively, by relationships with core reference groups, and by the public meaning of their stories, the way individual and communal life narratives are infused with evaluative systems. Collective public narratives often sharply clash with those of other groups.[48] The cultural turn includes interrogation of the particular understanding of the self associated with positivist science, connected to the rise of modern states and markets, the drive to make legible societies in pursuit of rationalization and control, and a constellation of mentalities associated with the term *mass*, implying a one-directional process of homogenization and deracination.[49]

The cultural turn deepens understanding of the symbolic dimensions of politics. Cultural politics, recognizing science's uses, challenges the claims of those who maintain its sufficiency in grasping the human condition.[50] An awareness of the limits of science has been growing among scientists themselves. Thus John Holland, a leading figure in the science of complex adaptive systems, points out that the scientific aim is to develop a theory which can apply across radically different contexts for predictive purposes. As Holland says, "Model-building in science depends upon shearing away detail. . . . Numbers go about as far as we can go in shearing away detail.

When we talk of numbers, nothing is left of shape, or color, or mass, or identities of an object, except the very fact of its existence. . . . Three buses, three storks, and three mountains are equivalent 'realizations' of the number three."[51] In contrast, a "poem aims at obliqueness and ambiguity to engage the reader at multiple levels." The result, in Holland's view, is that "the insights of poetry far surpass those of science in these domains . . . characterized by words like *beauty, justice, purpose, and meaning*."[52] Politics, like poetry, is partly about complex interpretative acts, concerned with meaning, purpose, justice, and even beauty. In terms suggested by Forester, politics is the way to construct the *meaning* of "facts." Politics adds practical concerns for getting things done in a world of plurality. In the sense of politics dating from the Greeks, it engages the unique stories and interests of every person.[53]

Studies of communal labors attentive to cultural politics detail a wide repertoire of resistances to centralizing authorities. Cultural politics in this vein was pioneered by James C. Scott, whose studies of peasant resistance in Southeast Asia in the 1960s and 1970s led him to see parallels between "the struggle of state-making in early modern Europe . . . to create a legible society that could be understood before it was possible to intervene" and "the way the World Bank is changing the Third World nowadays."[54] Tad Mutersbaugh employs cultural politics to show the importance of communal labors in an indigenous Oaxacan village in Mexico facing dilemmas of labor migration. He emphasizes power "that is not exercised mechanically but within a political culture that includes negotiation, cooperation, contestation, and resistance as multiple modes by which collective tensions may be resolved," detailing how communal labor practices are associated with wide participation in governance. He also demonstrates how villagers develop communal agency in the face of threats like migration.[55] "Villagers protect local institutional integrity by managing migration timing via sanctions, by producing a sense of community belonging, and by constructing community identification through social practices such as communal labor."[56]

Communal labors take on added public dimensions when employed by larger social and political movements. Thus, Tanya Korovkin shows how norms of communal labor called minga have been used by indigenous Otavalo communities as political resources in struggles against centralizing powers in the Ecuadorian Andes. These communities combined traditional and modern elements in adaptive ways, what she calls "strategic essentialism."[57]

Minga, unpaid communal work that effected communitywide improvements like water systems and schools, proved central to this process, embodying egalitarian norms of exchange and reciprocity and decentralized governance. Such norms are "evoked repeatedly at communal assemblies and province-wide meetings by the new indigenous leaders as part of their campaign to build a new ethnic identity."[58] *Minga* is a rallying cry of indigenous communities across the region.[59] Elsewhere, generalized themes of communal labor informed movements for independence, such as the famous use of *harambee* by the anticolonial movement in Kenya. After the genocide in Rwanda, the communal labor concept of *umuganda* has been used in a successful, if still fragile, effort to bridge the divisions between Hutu and Tutsi.[60] Public work themes are also used explicitly to champion "citizen-centered democracy" against statist approaches. In 2006, Omano Edigheji, an African theorist, challenged South African leaders in a high-level presidential seminar to return to a view of democracy in which citizens, not the state, are foundational agents. He drew on "cooperative work and deliberative traditions bringing people together [across differences]," building on a nationwide discussion organized by Idasa in 2004, ten years after the 1994 election, which raised civic agency and public work and resurfaced the immense popular struggle of the 1980s.[61]

In contrast to democratic usages, there are many cases of elites' appropriating themes of communal labor to serve their own ends. Otavalo communities explicitly contrast *minga* with *faena*, conscripted collective labor on public projects organized by colonial elites. Jacqueline Nzisabira, a Burundian with Idasa, the African democracy institute, describes how *harambee* radically changed meaning when it became a top-down practice invoked by politicians after independence, often associated with bribery and payoffs. Similarly, in her native Burundi, communal labors, known as *ibikorwa rusangi*, underwent change. "When I was growing up collective work was used to cultivate land in Burundi," Nzisabira describes. "Such labors empowered people and created a stronger sense of community." In recent years, she observes, "There has been a tendency for the government to control the process. The work shifts meaning when it is state directed, rather than coming from the community."[62] There are echoes of such dynamics in societies of the North Atlantic arc, where elites employ sentimental discourses of citizenship to mask other political agendas. The term *voluntarism* acquired general uses associated with budget cutbacks of Richard Nixon.[63] George Bush built his first inaugural address around citizenship, which he equated with service. David Cameron in Britain combines calls for volunteerism with sharp government reductions.[64]

Who owns and controls the symbols and practices of generalized communal labor appears as a central question in such cases. The question highlights the importance of the theory building of the Workshop on Political Theory and Public Policy on polycentric governance which focuses on questions of power, authority, and collective accountability.[65] Its design principles for governing the commons include rules well matched to local needs, capacities of people affected to participate in changing rules, respect by external powers for local community decision making, and locally imposed sanctions for breaking the rules. Such principles are useful in analyzing the obstacles to public work in modern societies.

Contemporary Obstacles to Public Work

Public work as a normative ideal of citizenship, combining self-organized governance and cooperative labors across differences to solve problems and create collective resources, prompts imaginings of democracy in which citizens take center stage. I propose that by understanding humans as meaning makers and storytellers, public work also suggests pathways toward the reintegration of corporate and governmental institutions into civic life. Bureaucracies of every sort can be reimagined differently than Habermas' system world, structures beyond change. They can be reconceived as complex human communities, products of human labors which can be reconstructed in more democratic ways by public work. Yet daunting obstacles arise from the evisceration of work's public dimensions. Susan Faludi dramatized work's public decline in *Stiffed*, exploring changing identities of men, from African American shipyard workers to television executives and athletes. Men at century's end were "in an unfamiliar world where male worth is measured only by participation in a celebrity-driven consumer culture." With productive measures of success—supporting a family, contributing to the community, helping to build the nation—in shards, men resembled Betty Friedan's "trapped housewives" of the 1960s, without words to name discontents of a culture "drained of context, saturated with a competitive individualism that has been robbed of craft or utility and ruled by commercial values that revolve around who has the most, the best, the biggest, the fastest."[66]

Arriving at such a condition took decades. Matthew Crawford, in *Shop Class as Soul Craft*, champions "attentiveness," the importance of "seeing oneself in the world" through one's products, and engaging in "work that is genuinely useful."[67] Skilled labor, in his view, cultivates intellectual and manual dexterity, "a systematic encounter with the material world that requires thought."[68] Such qualities—engagement with the world, intellectual and manual capacities developed through self-directed effort, and a sense of the consequentiality of one's effort—all are associated with the ideal of public work, but they have radically eroded.

Using useful, skilled work as his standard, Crawford traces the *process* through which consequentiality of work became hollowed out as work became increasingly degraded, detaching "manual" from "mental" labor, eroding the agency of workers of all kinds. Scientific management replaced skilled labor with centralized processes. Self-directed activities were "dissolved or abstracted into parts and then reconstituted as a *process*." As Frederick Winslow Taylor, scientific management guru, put it, "All possible brain work should be removed from the shop and centered in the planning or laying out department."[69] Spiced with his own experiences in mind-numbing "intellectual work," Crawford shows how white collar and intellectual labor, celebrated as the "new knowledge economy," has become subjected to the same logic. "The time-and-motion study [of Taylor] has become a time-and-thought study," he writes. "To build an expert system, a living expert is debriefed and then cloned by a knowledge engineer. . . . Eventually hundreds or thousands of rules of thumb are fed into the computer. The result is a program that can 'make decisions' or 'draw conclusions' heuristically."[70] Consumerism formed a key strategy to get workers to go along with the degradation of work. "It was learned that the only way to get [workers] to work harder was to play upon the imagination, stimulating new needs and wants." For this purpose, "consumption, no less than production, needed to be brought under scientific management—the management of desire."[71] Parallel erosion of self-governance occurred in public institutions, where centralizing dynamics were fed not by profit-seeking but by goals of distributive justice, equity, and protection of rights, implemented through rules which substitute for local discretion. For instance, Sara M. Evans and Barbara Nelson, in *Wage Justice: Comparable Worth and the Paradox of Technocratic Reform*, studied implementation of legislation in Minnesota to redress wage inequities between men and women. They find that equalizing wages was accomplished through centralizing processes which had the unintended effects of making workers increasingly powerless.[72] The endpoint of such processes is a focus on "outcome measures" accompanied by redefining citizens as customers and government agencies as service providers.[73]

Associational life has similarly been subject to instrumentalization in ways which greatly complicate hopes for civil society as "a place for us," a site of self-directed civic activity.[74] Civic practices and identities of the citizen-doctor or citizen-teacher or citizen-pastor once lent public meanings to community life, rooting professional work in local cultures, creating relatively horizontal relations between professionals and other citizens. These roots radically eroded, as Thomas Bender has detailed, as professional education lost connections to the life, history, and cultures of places.[75] Unions, nonprofits, schools, and congregations turned from civic centers to service providers. As Craig Dykstra observes about congregational life, quoting Eugene Petersen, "[Pastors] are preoccupied with ... how to keep the customers happy, how to lure customers away from competitors down the street, how to package the goods."[76]

Most strands of progressive politics both reflect and exacerbate such dynamics. A century of "mass politics" stressing universal claims, distributive justice, individual rights, and an existentially uprooted view of the citizen has come to shape progressive approaches to change.[77] Mass politics is based on a consumer conception of the person as concerned with individual appetites and needs. As Michael Sandel puts it, "A politics based on consumer identities ... asks how best—most fully, or fairly, or efficiently to satisfy [needs and wants]."[78] It is closely tied to top-down mobilizing techniques like the door-to-door canvass and Internet mobilizations, using a simplified script of good versus evil to rally large numbers of people, in which experts design both message and method.[79] In electoral politics, liberal Democrats, following consultants such as Mark Penn, frame elections as marketing to groups of voters defined by consumer niches.[80]

All these dynamics erode the public dimensions of work— self-organized governance, connections to communities, understandings of persons as co-creators of their environments. More, there is scant theoretical literature with which to challenge the erosion of work's public dimensions. As Judith Shklar observes, "The philosophers of antiquity regarded productive and commercial work as so deeply degrading that it made a man unfit for citizenship."[81] With exceptions like Dewey, Weil, and Miroslav Volf,[82] most political theorists continue to separate active citizenship from work.

Yet theoretical resources do exist. Here, despite her consignment of labor to realm of necessity, not freedom, Arendt provides the valuable concept of world-building. In particular, as Linda Zerilli emphasizes, "Foregrounded in Arendt's account of action is something less about the *subject* than about the *world*. . . . What Arendt calls the 'world' is not nature or the earth as such but is related to . . . the human artifact, the fabrication of human hands, as well as to affairs which go on among those who inhabit the man-made world together."[83] The challenge, as Zerilli suggests, is to shift the concept of Arendtian world-building from fleeting moments found in revolutionary times to everyday, quotidian labors that build a common world. There are other resources for this task, for all its obstacles.

Making Work More Public

I emphasize four resources for spreading public work in contemporary society. These include powerful histories of the democratic meanings of work; approaches to organizing which educate for citizenship; growing imperatives in government to produce public results that enlist public energies in new ways; and practice and theory of citizen professionalism that reintegrate experts and expertise with other ways of knowing and with other citizens.

1. **In English history**, village collective labors that sustained common lands, footpaths, forests, and fishing areas, as well as maintenance of common buildings like the village church, gave to peasantry a regular daily schooling in rough, grassroots democracy, even under feudalism. Immigrants to America brought such traditions with them, infusing concepts of the commonwealth and collective labors which build it with political vitality.[84] Work generally took on public and civic meanings. As Shklar put it, "a vision of economic independence . . . as the ethical basis of democratic citizenship took the place of an outmoded notion of public virtue."[85] Conceptions of the civic and democratic meanings of work continued well into the 20th century. Thus the late Vice President Hubert Humphrey, shaped by the populist movements of the 1930s, championed a decentralized economy in a Senate debate in 1952. Humphrey declared that the purpose of small busi-

ness was not cheap prices but survival of independent producers who were the foundation of democracy. As he said, "Do we want an America where the economic market place is filled with a few Frankensteins and giants? Or do we want an America where there are thousands upon thousands of small entrepreneurs, independent businesses, and landholders who can stand on their own feet and talk aback to their Government or anyone else?" For Humphrey, this concept of property was tied to citizens as the foundational agents of democracy, embodied in the Preamble to the Constitution with its focus on "we the people."[86] Humphrey's view of a decentralized economy represented the revival, not simply survival, of the civic meanings of work. Studies such as Michael Denning's *Cultural Front* and Lary May's *The Big Tomorrow* have shown how "cultural workers," journalists, screen-writers and artists, scholars, educators, and others, complemented union and community organizing efforts.[87] United by goals including the defeat of fascism, the pursuit of economic and racial justice, and the defense of democracy, they sought with some success to change the symbols and narratives of the American dream from the individualist, WASP-oriented, consumerist ideal of the 1920s to a more cooperative, racially pluralist and egalitarian vision of democracy that emphasized productive work with public meaning. In parallel fashion, the intellectual historian Scott Peters unearthed a "prophetic counternarrative" in higher education, with roots in land-grant colleges and universities, in which faculty, staff, and students worked in sustained, egalitarian partnerships with communities, using the language of public work to describe their efforts.[88]

2. **Practices and methods of "broad-based organizing"** counter mass politics with an understanding that each person is a unique and free political agent. They cultivate a sense of "the public person" akin to what Margaret Canovan has called political sobriety, "an exceptional degree of political realism and common sense, together with a remarkable capacity to exercise self-restraint and put shared long-term interests above private interests and short-term impulses."[89] Broad-based community organizations pursue social, racial, and economic justice in ways highly attentive to political and civic education.[90] Organizers often use the concept of citizens as co-creators and sometimes refer to their efforts across communities as "public work." As Gerald Taylor, an architect of this kind of organizing, put it, "thinking about organizing as public work helps people to understand themselves as builders of cities."[91]

Drawing out the different meanings of *public* in "public work," one can detail work *of* publics, work *in* public, and work *for* public purposes. I describe broad-based organizing efforts as vivid illustrations of the first two dimensions. It involves work of a public, a diverse people who learn to work together. These groups teach members to understand the motivations and stories of others of different income, religious, cultural, or partisan backgrounds through what are called "one-on-ones." Their efforts also generate work *in* public, making visible different, sometimes conflicting, interests, teaching how to use these conflicts for public purposes. Arendt is widely read in these groups partly because their action is informed by the concept of a public arena based on difference, akin to her public space of plurality. In a public arena, people operate on principles such as respect, recognition, and mutual accountability, not on the basis of "private principles" like loyalty, intimacy, and hope for nurturance. Citizens learn to work together on public issues out of diverse "self-interests" (not narrow selfishness but core passions and relationships). They solve problems, win victories for disadvantaged groups, and create public things with those with whom they may disagree, or whom they may even dislike. Such activity often broadens people's interests toward "standing for the whole."[92]

In organizing, people experience power similar to Arendt's concept, which she contrasts with strength, an individual property; with force, which she saw as a natural phenomenon; and with violence, based on coercion. Power, for Arendt, emerges from humans acting in concert on some political project. It is always "a power potential and not an unchangeable, measurable and reliable entity like force or strength . . . [it] springs up between men when they act together and vanishes the moment they disperse."[93] Arendt's concept of power also emphasizes its rare performative moments, neglecting everyday politics.[94] As Mary Dietz observes, Arendt's horror of modern instrumentalization, with its "distortion of all things into means for the pursuit of allegedly higher ends," led her to weaken the resources of her public realm theory for "carrying out . . . purposes in the very world it strives to vitalize."[95] In broad-based organizing, participants add purposeful, everyday activity to Arendtian power. They seek to avoid instrumentalization by holding in balance "the world as it is" and "the world as it should be," combining a focus on political education with efforts to achieve benefits for disadvantaged groups. The agent in organizing combines a strategic assessment of social and political power with attention to building public relationships across differences.[96] Taylor calls this a shift from "protest to governance." Governance, in these terms, "means learning how to be accountable," he says. "It means being able to negotiate and compromise. It means understanding that people are not necessarily evil because they have different interests or ways of looking at the world."[97] Similarly, Rom Coles, a political theorist long active in such organizations, argues that organizing "inflects [diverse] traditions in light of a radical democratic ethos that accents inclusion, dialogue, receptivity, equality, difference, a taste for ambiguity, patient discernment, and an affirmation that political relationships centrally involve ongoing tension, some compromise, and humility in the face of disagreement."[98]

Broad-based community groups fit with Piotr Perczynski's model of "associative democracy." This "focuses on the *process* of societal change rather than aiming towards a predefined goal." Perczynski calls for active citizenship "realized by actually *practicing* it."[99] He emphasizes groups with participatory democratic qualities and also with some "social element" that cultivates concern for the welfare of the larger society beyond their ranks. Such groups are "schools for citizenship."[100] The limit of such groups from the vantage of participatory democracy is that their goals, achieving justice and developing citizens, while important, do not include a general democratization of society. They here reflect the fatalism of the late Saul Alinsky, often seen as the architect of broad-based organizing. Alinsky, part of the populist movement of the 1930s, conveyed its expansive hopes for democratic change in his first book, *Reveille for Radicals*. By the end of his life, he was far more cynical.[101] Organizers saw themselves going far beyond his cynicism about human motivations after his death in 1972, but they accepted his view that the larger society could not be changed.[102] The challenge for broader democratization is to integrate organizing themes of action by publics and action *in* public with multiple kinds of work infused with democratic purpose.

3. **A third resource for public work's translation** across contexts is pressure from the increasing complexity and scale of problems in modern societies to tap new sources of civic energy and talent. Current government initiatives like "empowered participatory government" and "catalytic governance" show countertrends to the customer-service paradigm, while differing also from sentimentalized citizenship. They seek to develop more

reciprocal, egalitarian, cooperative partnerships between civil servants and citizens outside of government to accomplish public tasks. Al Dzur observes that these are spurred by the failure of conventional bureaucratic and professional practices. Thus, an administrator for a New England state department of corrections argued that he was "building inefficiency into the system" by involving extensive lay citizen participation. Dzur points to the value of such "inefficiency": lay citizens, less attentive to rules and procedures, may counter flaws such as "rigidity in the face of rule obsolescence and inattentiveness to individual case complexity." In the case of juries, citizen "irrationality" may "foster reflexivity that balances courts and judges' bias toward procedural rationality with a concern for substantive rationality."[103] Carmen Sirianni details initiatives within government, from local levels to federal agencies, which integrate themes of broad-based organizing in order to generate more productive, collaborative work with citizens.[104]

4. **Finally, addressing public problems** effectively prompts attention to the civic dimensions of professions, where professionals learn to work *with* other citizens, rather than *on* them or *for* them. Theoretical foundations of civic professionalism found early expression in the work of Dewey, who stressed the educative dimensions of "all callings [and] occupations."[105] William Sullivan and Dzur have further developed theory of civic professionalism. Sullivan identifies a central tension in professionalism in the United States since the colonial period, "between a technical emphasis which stresses specialization—broadly linked to a utilitarian conception of society as a project for enhancing efficiency and individual satisfaction—and a sense of professional mission which has insisted upon the prominence of the ethical and civic dimension of the enterprise."[106] Dzur details ways in which professionals' work can be catalytic and energizing when they "step back" and practice what Forester called diplomatic recognition. He chronicles democratic trends in the areas of medicine, law, the movement against domestic violence, and elsewhere that enhance the authority and efficacy of lay citizens, adding multiple cases of what I call "public work."[107] William Doherty and his colleagues at the Citizen Professional Center have pioneered in the practices and theory of such citizen professionalism. Adapting broad-based organizing practices and public work concepts to family and health professions, their citizen-professional model begins with the premise that solving complex problems requires many sources of

knowledge, and "the greatest untapped resource for improving health and social well-being is the knowledge, wisdom, and energy of individuals, families, and communities who face challenging issues in their everyday lives." The Citizen Professional Center has generated multiple partnerships including suburban movements of families working to tame overscheduled, consumerist lives; an African American Citizen Fathers Project seeking to foster positive fathering models and practices; a new project with Hennepin County to change civil service practices into public work; and a pilot with Health Partners Como Clinic, called the Citizen Health Care Home, which stresses personal and family responsibility for one's own health and opportunities for patient leadership development and co-responsibility for health.[108] A fledgling higher education movement for engagement with communities and the larger democracy offers an expanding terrain for concepts of public work.[109] The movement draws on organizing experiences like the pioneering efforts at the College of St. Catherine by Nan Kari and her colleagues, who conceived of the college as a community and organized to "make its work more public." Civic engagement is proving a fertile ground for initiatives based on public work, such as Public Achievement, a young people's citizenship education effort now in hundreds of communities in more than a dozen countries. Public Achievement is taking root in a number of colleges, universities, and community colleges through a partnership called the American Democracy Project.[110]

Conclusion: A Return to "We the People"

In a time of concern on the left about the public squalor of a marketplace culture and on the right about the overreach of government technocrats, public work holds potential to break the impasse. It returns to "we the people" as co-creators of a democratic society. This is not simply a normative idea; it also is descriptive—civic agency is emerging across the world.[111] But there is nothing simple about this return. The effort contends not only with formidable structural impediments but also intellectual ones. The question posed in 1906 by the German socialist Werner Sombart, "why is there no socialism in the United States?" preoccupying scholars and political progressives through the 20th century, reappeared in mainstream discussion in 2009 when the late Tony Judt used it in a lecture at New York University to launch a discussion about growing inequality and public squalor.[112] He argued that social democracy is the only alternative to public degradation.

From the vantage of public work, focusing on what is "missing" in American politics eclipses the alternative based on citizen agency. This approach has been associated with populist themes now caricatured in the mainstream as a politics of grievance. In populism with a democratic cast, by way of contrast, people care about the commons when they help make and sustain it through their public labors, and the development of popular agency is a constituting theme.[113]

The gap between citizen- and state-centered politics was dramatized by the reception mainstream progressive opinion leaders gave to the populist elements of the Obama campaign, with its civic agency message of "yes we can," accompanied by the organizing dimensions of the field operation.[114] Progressive opinion either ignored these or decried them as sentimental nonsense. A recent volume of essays coordinated by Theda Skocpol and Lawrence Jacobs on the first two years of the Obama presidency, *Reaching for a New Deal*, illustrates the former. Sophisticated about the policy process, the Washington political environment, challenges of a fragmented, 24/7 news cycle, and daunting opposition, the scholars nonetheless write as if the only significant agents of politics are politicians, media, and government instrumentalities. The extended introduction by Skocpol and Jacobs has no reference to civic agency ideas and practices of the 2008 campaign and dramatically neglects the movements of the 1930s which shaped the New Deal.[115] Writing after the election in the *New Yorker*, George Packer was simply contemptuous. Packer saw "yes we can" as disingenuous. "Throughout the campaign, Obama spoke of change coming from the bottom up rather than from the top down," said Packer. "But every time I heard him tell a crowd, 'This has never been about me; it's about you' he seemed to be saying just the opposite." In Packer's view what people voted for in the election was the "ground on which the majority of Americans—looking to government for solutions—now stand."[116]

Many progressives caricature conservatives as simply selfish individualists—a "libertarian mob" in the words of Mark Lilla.[117] In fact they hold a more complex set of beliefs, including reaction against technocratic politics, which they see as devaluing diverse kinds of knowledge and suppressing human agency.[118] To counter this, conservative intellectuals have appropriated "work," once at the center of populist movements, in their assertions that government is undermining people's self-directed action. Thus Arthur Brooks, president of the American Enterprise Institute, portrays "not a fight over guns, gays, or abortion" but rather "a new struggle between two competing visions of the country's future. In one, America will continue to be an exceptional nation organized around the principles of free enterprise—limited government, a reliance on entrepreneurship and rewards determined by market forces." Brooks argues that this vision is not about getting rich but about what he calls the pursuit of happiness through earned success. "Earned success is the creation of value in our lives or in the lives of others. Earned success is the stuff of entrepreneurs who seek value through innovation, hard work, and passion. Earned success is what parents feel when their children do wonderful things, what social innovators feel when they change lives, what artists feel when they create something of beauty."[119] The other is state-centered. Such themes translate into Tea Party slogans, which depict America in an epic struggle between "makers" and "takers."

For those alarmed about the prospect of dismantling government in a time of growing inequalities and selling-off of the commonwealth, Brooks' arguments, like anti-government frenzy generally, threaten to make things worse. But progressive politics which accuses citizens of being fearful, prejudiced, and myopic and demands in ever more strident terms social democratic-style state intervention offers no effective alternative. The times call for a politics which takes back "work" from those who would dismantle government and privatize the commonwealth. This is a politics which democratizes governance while it recognizes the essential and vital roles of government, values the public conditions and purposes of work, and develops civic agency. It is the constructive politics of public work.

EDITORS' NOTE

This chapter was originally published as Harry C. Boyte, "Constructive Politics as Public Work: Organizing the Literature," *Political Theory* 39 (October 2011): 630-660. Reprinted by permission of Sage Publications, Inc. We have made minor edits for style and formatting.

ACKNOWLEDGMENT

I thank Mary Dietz and Marie Ström for splendid editorial help, and the comments of two anonymous reviewers. I am also grateful for discussions of civic agency, public work, and citizens as co-creators in the "Civic Driven Change" initiative of the Institute of Social Studies in the Hague in 2008 and 2010; and feedback on my presentations of these themes at the 2010 conference of the American Democracy Project; the 2010 Idasa annual retreat in South Africa; and the Kettering Foundation 2010 workshop on "democratizing deliberation." I want to thank especially Elinor Ostrom, William Schambra, Gerald Taylor, Albert Dzur, Peter Vale, Paul Graham, Derek Barker, Rom Coles, Peter Levine, Brian Murphy, David Thelen, Maria Avila, Matthew Leighninger, Roudy Hildreth, and Michael Lansing for their feedback. Finally, I appreciate collaboration with my colleagues at the Kettering Foundation in research on these topics.

NOTES

[1.] "Polder," *Wikipedia*, (accessed June 28, 2010) http://en.wikipedia.org/wiki/Polder. Jos Leenhouts, a Dutch educational leader, uses "poldering" to counter marketizing trends. Boyte interview with Leenhouts, May 16, 2010, Amsterdam.

[2.] Simone Weil, *Oppression and Liberty* (Amherst: University of Massachusetts, 1973), 101.

[3.] Alaine Touraine in Eric Hobsbawm, *Revolutionaries* (London: Abacus, 2007 edition), 316.

[4.] Jeffrey D. Hilmer, "The State of *Participatory* Democratic Theory," *New Political Science* 32 (March 2010): 43-63, at 43.

[5.] Carole Pateman, *Participation and Democratic Theory* (Cambridge: Cambridge University Press, 1970); Jane J. Mansbridge, *Beyond Adversary Democracy* (New York: Basic Books, 1980); Benjamin R. Barber, *Strong Democracy: Participatory Politics for a New Age* (Berkeley, CA: University of California Press, 1984); Frantz Fanon, *Wretched of the Earth* (New York: Grove Press, 1961); Paulo Freire, *Pedagogy of the Oppressed* (New York: Continuum, 1977); Stephen Biko, *I Write What I Like* (New York: Harper and Row, 1986).

[6.] Benjamin Barber, *Jihad versus McWorld: How Globalism and Tribalism Are Reshaping the World* (New York: Random House, 1995).

7. James C. Scott, *Seeing Like a State: How Certain Schemes to Improve the Human Condition Have Failed* (New Haven, CT: Yale University Press, 1998).

8. The Il Manifesto included the need to democratize the left as well as the society. See Douglas Johnson, "Althusser's Fate," *London Review of Books* 3, no. 7 (1981): 13-15.

9. Archon Fung, "Deliberation before the Revolution: Toward an Ethics of Deliberative Democracy in an Unjust World," *Political Theory* 33, no. 3 (2005): 397-419.

10. Jürgen Habermas, *Between Facts and Norms: Contributions to a Discourse Theory of Law and Democracy* (Cambridge, MA: MIT Press, 1998), 324.

11. Ibid., 298.

12. Hilmer, "State of *Participatory* Democratic Theory," 55-63. On civic agency, see Harry C. Boyte, *Civic Agency and the Cult of the Expert* (Dayton, OH: Kettering Foundation Press, 2009).

13. See John Keane, *The Life and Death of Democracy* (London: Simon & Schuster UK, 2009).

14. On agency, see Mustafa Emirbayer and Ann Mische, "What Is Agency," *American Journal of Sociology* 103, no. 4 (1998): 962-1023. Theoretical neglect of agency, described in their essay, finds counterparts in amnesia about popular agency in crucial histories. For a kindred politics of agency, see Luke Bretherton, *Christianity and Contemporary Politics* (London: Wiley-Blackwell, 2010), see footnotes 16, 61, 77, 115.

15. Xavier de Sousa Briggs, *Democracy as Problem Solving: Civic Capacity in Communities around the World* (Cambridge, MA: MIT Press, 2009); on new public management, 36-37; on accountability, 306-307.

16. John S. Dryzek, "Deliberative Democracy in Divided Societies: Alternatives to Agonism and Analgesia," *Political Theory* 33, no. 2 (2005): 218-242.

17. Jürgen Habermas, *Transformation of the Public Sphere* (Cambridge, MA: MIT Press, 1989), 52.

18. Ibid., 25-26.

19. Habermas, *Between Facts and Norms*, 47.

20. Ian Budge, "Deliberative democracy versus direct democracy—plus political parties!" in *Democratic Innovation: Deliberation, representation and association*, ed. Michael Saward (London: Routledge, 2000), 200.

21. Aviezer Tucker, "Pre-emptive Democracy: Oligarchic Tendencies in Deliberative Democracy," *Political Studies* 56 (2008): 127-147, at 127.

22. Habermas, *Between Facts and Norms*, 297.

23. Ibid., 359, 362, 363, 371, 300.

24. David Mathews, *Politics for People: Finding a Responsible Public Voice* (Champaign, IL: University of Illinois Press, 1999); John Dedrick, Laura Grattan, and Harold Dientsfrey, *Deliberation and the Work of Higher Education: Innovations for the Classroom, the Campus, and the Community* (Dayton, OH: Kettering Foundation Press, 2008).

25. Noëlle McAfee, "Three Models of Democratic Deliberation," *Journal of Speculative Philosophy* 18, no. 1 (2004): 44-59.

26. John Forester, *Deliberative Practitioner: Encouraging Participatory Planning Processes* (Cambridge, MA: MIT Press, 1999), 203-204.

27. John Forester, "Exploring Urban Practice in a Democratising Society: Opportunities, Techniques, and Challenges," *Development Southern Africa* 23, no. 5 (2006): 569-586, at 572.

28. Forester, *Deliberative Practitioner*, 6.

29. Ibid., 129-130.

30. Ibid., 130.

31. Ibid., 130, 133, 137, 138, 139, 143.

32. Ibid., 207.

33. Ibid., 108-109.

34. Ibid., 37.

35. Ibid., 111.

36. Ibid., 115, 116, 123.

37. Here are several communal labor terms: in South Africa in Sesotho, *letsema*; in isiZulu, *ilimo*; in Afrikaans, *gemeenskapswerk*; in Xhosa, *dibanisani*; in the Sudan, *naffir*; along the East African coast, in Swahili, *kidole kimoja chawa*; in Europe, *meitheal* (Ireland), *dugnad* (Norway), *talkoot* (Finland); in Asia, *huan gong* (China), *ture* (Korea), *gotong-royoung* (Indonesia and Malaysia); in North America *ga-du-gi* (Cherokee); barn-raising (English); Stephanie Conduff, policy advisor to Chief Smith of the Cherokee, argued that *ga-du-gi* has been a powerful symbol of pride and self-sufficiency, e-mail correspondence, July 16, 2010; Peter Vale argues that communal labors may be the experiential ground of the widely used African term *ubuntu*, meaning "common humanity." Boyte interview with Vale, Grahamstown, South Africa, July 19, 2010.

38. Leif O. Manger, ed., *Communal Labor in the Sudan* (Bergen: University of Bergen, 1987), 1.

39. Ibid., 2-3.

40. Stanley Crawford, *Mayordomo: Chronicle of an Acequia in Northern New Mexico* (Albuquerque: University of New Mexico Press, 1998), 168.

41. Paul Dekker and Loek Halman, eds., *The Values of Volunteering: Cross-Cultural Perspectives* (New York: Springer, 2003), illustrate depoliticized citizenship; for a critique, see Harry C. Boyte, "Civic Populism," *Perspectives on Politics* 1, no. 4 (2003): 737-742. "Voluntarism" substitutes for what once was "work." Thus Francis Willard, leader of the largest 19th-century US association of women, subtitled her book *Woman and Temperance, The Work and Workers of the Women's Christian Temperance Union* (Hartford, CT: Park Publishing, 1883) to convey unpaid civic labors and to challenge their devaluation.

42. Charlotte Hess and Elinor Ostrom, *Understanding Knowledge as a Commons: From Theory to Practice* (Boston: MIT Press, 2006), 3.

43. Garret Hardin, "Tragedy of the Commons," *Science* 162 (1968): 1243-1248, at 1244.

44. Hess and Ostrom, *Understanding Knowledge as a Commons*, 10-11; also Elinor Ostrom, *Governing the Commons: The Evolution of Institutions for Collective Action* (Cambridge: Cambridge University Press, 1990).

45. Elinor Ostrom, "Polycentricity, Complexity, and the Commons," *The Good Society* 9, no. 2 (1999): 37-41, at 39, 40.

46. Peter Levine, "Collective Action, Civic Engagement, and the Knowledge Commons," in Hess and Ostrom, *Knowledge as a Commons*, 247.

47. Hess and Ostrom, *Knowledge as a Commons*, 12.

48. On the clash between Jewish and Palestinian narratives, Phillip L. Hammack, "Narrative and the Cultural Psychology of Identity," *Personality and Social Psychological Review* 12 (May 2008): 222-247.

49. On the cultural turn in development, Amartya Sen, "How Does Culture Matter," in *Culture and Public Action*, eds. Vijayendra Rao and Michael Walton (Palo Alto, CA: Stanford University Press, 2004), 37-58; in democratic theory Nick Bromell, "Freedom Reigns," *Boston Review* (March/April 2006); on the modern self, Charles Taylor, *Sources of the Self: The Making of Modern Identity* (Cambridge: Cambridge University Press, 1989).

50. On Arendt's horror of the privileging of scientific rationalism, Mary G. Dietz, "The Slow Boring of Hard Boards: Methodical Thinking and the Work of Politics," *The American Political Science Review* 88, no. 4 (1994): 873-886, at 875.

51. John H. Holland, *Emergence: From Chaos to Order* (Cambridge, MA: Perseus Books, 1998); 23-24.

52. Ibid., 219-220.

53. Hannah Arendt, *The Human Condition* (Chicago: University of Chicago Press, 1958); Harry C. Boyte, "A Different Kind of Politics: John Dewey and the Meaning of Citizenship in the 21st Century," *The Good Society* 12, no. 2 (2003): 1-15.

54. Interview by Erik Gerritsen with James C. Scott, December 17, 2009 (accessed July 2, 2010) http://voidmanufacturing.wordpress.com/2009/12/17/interview-with-james-c-scott/.

55. Tad Mutersbaugh, "Migration, Common Property, and Communal Labor: Cultural Politics and Agency in a Mexican Village," *Political Geography* 21 (2002): 473-494, at 475.

56. Ibid., 481.

57. Tanya Korovkin, "Reinventing the Communal Tradition: Indigenous Peoples, Civil Society, and Democratization in Andean Ecuador," *Latin American Research Review* 36, no. 3 (2001): 37-67, at 42.

58. Ibid., 49, 54.

59. See Mark Becker, June 21, "Reencounter of the Original Peoples" (accessed July 2, 2010) http://upsidedownworld.org/main/ecuador-archives-49/2554-reencounter-of-the-original-peoples-and-nationalities-of-abya-yala-in-ecuador.

60. "Umuganda Has Earned Country International Acclaim" (accessed July 2, 2010) http://sigriirwanda.wordpress.com/2010/04/07/umuganda-community-service/.

61. Omano Edigheji, *The Emerging South African Democratic Developmental State and the People's Contract* (Johannesburg: Centre for Policy Studies, 2007), 47; on Idasa discussions, "Lessons from the Field," Special Supplement, *Mail and Guardian*, November 26, 2004. These resurfaced the movement in the 1980s, the United Democratic Front, which largely brought the end to apartheid, now neglected in official public renderings of the anti-apartheid movement which emphasize formal party and state negotiations, and also in Dryzek's account in "Deliberative Democracy in Divided Societies." On this history, see Allan Boesak, *Running with Horses: Reflections of an Accidental Politician* (Cape Town: Joho Press, 2009).

62. Boyte interview with Jacqualine Nzisabira, in Pretoria, June 30, 2010.

63. In 1969, the *Wall Street Journal* labeled as voluntarism "Nixon's program to enlist the help of private groups in solving social problems"; Harry Boyte, "Off the Playground of Civil Society," *The Good Society* 9, no. 2 (1999): 1-7, at 6.

64. On Bush, Harry C. Boyte, *Everyday Politics: Reconnecting Citizens and Public Life* (Philadelphia: Penn Press, 2004), chap. 1; on Cameron Nicholas Watt, "David Cameron Reveals 'Big Society' Vision—and Denies It Is Just Cost Cutting," *Guardian*.co.uk, July 19, 2010.

65. Ostrom, *Governing the Commons*, 91-102.

66. Susan Faludi, *Stiffed: The Betrayal of the American Man* (New York: William Morrow and Co., 1999), 39, 23, 599.

67. Matthew B. Crawford, *Shop Class as Soulcraft: An Inquiry into the Value of Work* (New York: Penguin Press, 2009), 82, 14, 6.

68. Ibid., 21.

69. Ibid., 40, 39.

70. Ibid., 46.

71. Ibid., 43.

72. Sara M. Evans and Barbara Nelson, *Wage Justice: Comparable Worth and the Paradox of Technocratic Reform* (Chicago: University of Chicago, 1989).

73. David Osborne and Peter Plastrik, "Rewriting Government's DNA," *The New Democrat* 9, no. 2 (1997): 8-12.

74. Benjamin R. Barber, *A Place for Us: How to Make Society Civil and Democracy Strong* (New York: Hill and Wang, 1998).

75. Thomas Bender, *Intellect and Public Life: Essays on the Social History of Academic Intellectuals in the United States* (Baltimore, MD: Johns Hopkins University Press, 1993).

76. Quoted in Craig Dykstra, *Growing in the Life of Faith* (Louisville, KY: Westminster John Knox Press), 55; Harry C. Boyte, "Reframing Democracy: Governance, Civic Agency, and Politics," *Public Administration Review* 68, no. 5 (2005): 536-546.

77. Steve Fraser, "The Labor Question," in *The Rise and Fall of the New Deal Order, 1930-1980*, eds. Steve Fraser and Gary Gerstle (Princeton, NJ: Princeton University Press 1989), 55-84; Thomas Spragens, *Getting the Left Right: The Transformation, Decline, and Reformation of American Liberalism* (Lawrence, KS: University of Kansas Press, 2009), details how popular agency, animating the New Deal popular movements, has been replaced in political theory by an emphasis on redistributive justice. Public histories like the iconic Roosevelt

Memorial in Washington illustrate the pattern, substituting pity for the poor for respect for work and working people.

78. Michael Sandel, *Democracy's Discontents: America in Search of a Public Philosophy* (Cambridge, MA: Harvard University Press, 1996), 225.

79. Boyte, *Everyday Politics*, chap. 2.

80. Mark Penn, *Microtrends: The Small Forces Behind Tomorrow's Big Changes* (New York: Hachette Book Group, 2007).

81. Judith N. Shklar, *American Citizenship: The Quest for Inclusion* (Cambridge, MA: Harvard University Press, 1991), 68.

82. John Dewey, *The Teacher and Society* (New York: D. Appleton-Century, 1937); Weil, *Oppression and Liberty*; Miroslav Volf, *Work in the Spirit: Toward a Theology of Work* (Oxford: Oxford University Press, 1991).

83. Linda M. G. Zerilli, *Feminism and the Abyss of Freedom* (Chicago: University of Chicago Press, 2005), 14.

84. Harry C. Boyte, *CommonWealth: A Return to Citizen Politics* (New York: Free Press, 1989); Edward Miller and John Hatcher, *Medieval England: Rural Society and Economic Change, 1086-1348* (London: Longman, 1978), 105, 106, 108-109.

85. Shklar, *American Citizenship*, 65; see also Daniel T. Rodgers, *The Work Ethic in Industrial America 1850-1920* (Chicago: University of Chicago Press, 1974).

86. Humphrey quoted in Sandel, *Democracy's Discontents*, 244. On Humphrey's views of the Preamble, see "Hubert H. Humphrey: The Art of the Possible," by Mick Caouette, Twin Cities Public Television, November 18, 2010.

87. Michael Denning, *The Cultural Front* (London: Verso, 1997); Lary May, *The Big Tomorrow: Hollywood and the Politics of the American Way* (Chicago: University of Chicago Press, 2000).

88. Scott Peters, *Higher Education and Democracy* (East Lansing, MI: Michigan State Press, 2010).

89. Margaret Canovan, "The People, the Masses, and the Mobilization of Power: The Paradox of Hannah Arendt's 'Populism,'" *Social Research* 69, no. 2 (2002): 403-422, at 418.

90. On organizing, Mark R. Warren, *Dry Bones Rattling: Community-Building to Revitalize American Democracy* (Princeton, NJ: Princeton University Press, 2001); Richard L. Wood, *Faith in Action: Religion, Race, and Democratic Organizing in America* (Chicago: University of Chicago Press, 2002).

91. Boyte, interview with Gerald Taylor, Chapel Hill, NC, April 26, 2002.

92. Boyte, *CommonWealth*, chap. 8.

93. Arendt, *Human Condition*, 200.

94. Harry C. Boyte, "A Commonwealth of Freedom: Response to Beltran," *Political Theory* 38, no. 6 (2010): 870-876.

95. Dietz, "Slow Boring," 89.

96. Edward T. D. Chambers and Michael A. Cowan, *Roots for Radicals: Organizing for Power, Action, and Justice* (New York: Continuum, 2003).

97. Taylor quoted in Boyte, *Civic Agency*, 22.

98. Rom Coles, "Of Tensions and Tricksters: Grassroots Democracy between Theory and Practice," *Perspectives on Politics* 4, no. 3 (Fall 2006): 547-561, at 550.

99. Piotr Perczynski, "Active Citizenship and Associative Democracy," in *Democratic Innovation: Deliberation, Representation, and Association*, ed. Michael Saward (London: Routledge, 2000), 162.

100. Ibid., 167, 162.

101. Saul Alinsky, "Is There Life after Birth?" June 7, 1967 (Chicago: I.A.F. reprint), 12-13.

102. Boyte, *Everyday Politics*, chap. 3.

103. Albert W. Dzur, "Four Theses on Participatory Democracy: Toward the Rational Disorganization of Government Institutions," *Constellations* (forthcoming), msp. 14-16.

104. Carmen Sirianni, *Investing in Democracy: Engaging Citizens in Collaborative Governance* (Washington: Brookings Institution Press, 2009).

105. John McDermott, *The Philosophy of John Dewey* (Chicago: University of Chicago Press, 1981), 334.

106. William Sullivan, *Work and Integrity: The Crisis and Promise of Professionalism in America* (San Francisco: Jossey-Bass, 1995), 28.

107. Albert W. Dzur, *Democratic Professionalism: Citizen Participation and the Reconstruction of Professional Ethics, Identity, and Practice* (State College, PA: Pennsylvania State University Press, 2008).

108. William J. Doherty, Tai J. Mendenhall, and Jerica M. Berge, "The Families and Democracy and Citizen Health Care Project," *Journal of Marital & Family Therapy* (October 2010) (accessed December 8, 2010) http://findarticles.com/p/articles/mi_qa3658/is_201010/ai_n56230125/?tag?content;col1.

109. John Saltmarsh and Matt Hartley, eds., *To Serve a Larger Purpose: Engagement for Democracy and the Transformation of Higher Education* (Philadelphia, PA: Temple University Press, forthcoming).

110. On changes at St. Catherine, Anne Colby, Thomas Ehrlich, Elizabeth Beaumont, Jason Stephens, *Educating Citizens: Preparing America's Undergraduates for Lives of Moral and Civic Responsibility* (San Francisco: Jossey-Bass/Carnegie Foundation for the Advancement of Teaching, 2003); on Public Achievement, Boyte, *Everyday Politics*, chap. 5.

111. On international civic agency trends, see Boyte, *Civic Agency*; in public health, Robert L. Milstein, *Hygeia's Constellation* (Atlanta: Centers for Disease Control and Prevention, 2007); in Africa, the East African Citizen Agency Initiative Twaweza, www.twaweza.org.

112. Boyte, *CommonWealth*, chapter two explores the debate stirred by Sombart over the 20th century; Tony Judt, "What Is Living and What Is Dead in Social Democracy?" *New York Review of Books* (December 17, 2009).

113. Harry C. Boyte, "Populism and John Dewey: Convergencies and Contradictions," *Dewey Lecture*, March 31, 2007, University of Michigan, http://ginsberg.umich.edu/downloads/Boyte_Dewey_Lecture2007.doc.

114. Boyte, *Civic Agency*.

115. Theda Skocpol and Lawrence Jacobs, "Introduction," in *Reaching for a New Deal: Ambitious Governance, Economic Meltdown and Polarized Politics in Obama's First Two Years*, eds. Theda Skocpol and Lawrence Jacobs (New York: Russell Sage Foundation, 2010), 1-72 (accessed online December 9, 2010).

116. George Packer, "The New Liberalism," *The New Yorker*, November 17, 2010 (accessed online, August 16, 2010).

117. Mark Lilla "The Tea Party Jacobins," *New York Review of Books* (May 27, 2010): 53.

118. On technocracy, William Schambra, "Obama and the Policy Approach," *National Affairs* 1 (Fall 2009), http://www.nationalaffairs.com/publications/detail/obama-and-the-policy-approach; David Brooks, "The Technocracy Boom," *New York Times*, July 19, 2010; on public opinion, E. J. Dionne and Robert Jones, "Emerging Religious Issues Promise to Shape 2012 Election," Public Religious Research Institute, November 17, 2010.

119. Arthur C. Brooks, "America's New Culture War: Free Enterprise versus Government Control," *Washington Post*, May 23, 2010.

ABOUT THE CONTRIBUTORS

DEREK W. M. BARKER is a political theorist and a program officer at the Kettering Foundation, a nonprofit research organization that studies efforts to strengthen democracy. He is the author of the book *Tragedy and Citizenship* and has published articles in *Polis, Kettering Review*, and *Journal of Higher Education Outreach and Engagement*.

HARRY C. BOYTE directs the Center for Democracy and Citizenship at Augsburg College and is a senior fellow at the Humphrey School of Public Affairs. He also directs the American Commonwealth Project, a higher education initiative to bring the democratic spirit of land-grant colleges to all of higher education. Boyte is author of 8 books and has articles in more than 100 publications, including *Political Theory*, the *New York Times*, and the *Wall Street Journal*.

JOHN S. DRYZEK is Australian Research Council Federation Fellow and a professor of political science at the Centre for Deliberative Democracy and Global Governance at Australian National University. His recent books include *Foundations and Frontiers of Deliberative Governance, Theories of the Democratic State* (with Patrick Dunleavy), and *The Oxford Handbook of Climate Change and Society* (coedited with Richard Norgaard and David Schlosberg).

ELENA FAGOTTO is a fellow at Harvard Kennedy School and a lecturer at LUISS School of Government in Rome. Her research analyzes public and private governance mechanisms with specific focus on the role of transparency and civic engagement. She has researched deliberative practices in the United States and internationally and has written articles and reports examining the impact of public deliberations.

ARCHON FUNG is the Ford Foundation Professor of Democracy and Citizenship at the Harvard Kennedy School. His research examines the impacts of civic participation, public deliberation, and transparency upon governance. He has authored 5 books, 3 edited collections, and more than 50 articles.

JANE MANSBRIDGE is the Adams Professor at the Kennedy School of Government, Harvard University. Her first books, *Beyond Adversary Democracy* and *Why We Lost the ERA*, focused respectively on the quality of deliberation in town meetings and alternative workplaces, and in social movements. Her work on deliberative democracy includes numerous articles, including, most recently, "A Systemic Approach to Deliberative Democracy," with seven coauthors (forthcoming in Parkinson and Mansbridge, editors, *Deliberative Systems*).

NOËLLE MCAFEE is an associate professor of philosophy at Emory University, the associate editor of the *Kettering Review*, and the cochair of the Public Philosophy Network. Her work is at the intersection of subjectivity and public life, drawing widely on various traditions in philosophy and from experiments in self-government around the world. Her most recent book is *Democracy and the Political Unconscious* (Columbia, 2008). She is currently writing a book on the democratic imaginary.

DAVID W. MCIVOR is a research associate at the Kettering Foundation. He received his PhD in political science from Duke University. In addition to his interests in deliberative democracy, he has research interests in collective memory and public rituals of commemoration. He has published recently in the journal *Polity*.

BERNARD YACK is the Lerman-Neubauer Professor of Democracy at Brandeis University. He is the author of *The Longing for Total Revolution*, *The Problems of a Political Animal*, and *The Fetishism of Modernities*, as well as the editor of *Liberalism without Illusions*, a memorial volume on the work of Judith Shklar. His latest book, *Nationalism and the Moral Psychology of Community*, will appear in 2012 with the University of Chicago Press.

IRIS MARION YOUNG (1949 – 2006) was professor of political science at the University of Chicago and the author of numerous books, including *Justice and the Politics of Difference* and *Inclusion and Democracy*.